Teaching Culture

Teaching Culture

Strategies for Intercultural Communication

H. Ned Seelye

National Textbook Company
a division of NTC *Publishing Group* • Lincolnwood, Illinois USA

1992 Printing

Published by National Textbook Company, a division of NTC Publishing Group.
© 1984 by NTC Publishing Group, 4255 West Touhy Avenue,
Lincolnwood (Chicago), Illinois 60646-1975 U.S.A.
Manufactured in the United States of America.
Library of Congress Catalog Card Number: 83-62964

2 3 4 5 6 7 8 9 ML 9 8 7 6

Foreword
to This Edition

Back in 1971 Ned Seelye masterminded for the American Council on the Teaching of Foreign Languages what must have been the first pre-conference workshop on the teaching of culture. About ten of us who were interested in the area of cross-cultural understanding were asked to serve as resource people at the workshop. I arrived on the scene a bundle of nerves—in awe of Seelye, in awe of Chicago, in awe of the sharp-beaked chambermaid who replenished my towel supply. Most of all, I doubted my own ability to respond intelligently in my role as workshop group leader. That night Seelye called a pre-workshop briefing for all resource people involved. I watched them come in to the meeting room—the great and the near-great in the teaching of culture. They exuded an aura of expertise. Their heads seemed to bulge with stores of wisdom. They fairly radiated confidence in matters cultural. I looked at that glittering cavalcade and my heart sank. Then Ned Seelye took me aside and indicated the group with a discreet nod of his head. "Genelle," he whispered, "about half of those folks know what it's really about when it comes to teaching culture. The other half I invited here to make sure they found out." Ned Seelye has been helping us find out how to teach culture ever since.

The 1974 edition of this book has fulfilled every expectation Emma Birkmaier held out for it in her original Foreword to the volume. It has opened the eyes of undergraduates to a critical area of their training in foreign language methodology; it has inspired research topics in the graduate seminar; it has salvaged the battered enthusiasm of dedicated inservice teachers. Now the new edition promises even more. Seelye has not only updated the original materials designed for foreign language teachers, he has added new chapters which make the book immediately useful to those who work in any capacity with people of other cultures.

In the first eight chapters, Seelye has trimmed out the less-essential and added new insights and illustrations. He has expanded Chapter 9 on Testing Culture to include the measurement of student attitudes as well as the testing of cognitive learning. Such tools as the social distance scale, the semantic differential scale, and the forced-choice questionnaire are amply illustrated.

The newly added Chapter 10 treats with sensitivity the problems of the bicultural—those individuals "who grow up with feet in two different cultures." Traditionally our bicultural citizens have been viewed with distrust by members of the mainstream culture. Seelye offers an intelligent discussion of the frequently expressed concern as to how much diversity a nation can tolerate without losing its national unity. He helps the reader understand the stresses which bicultural students face in their new school environments and explains the strategies that minority people use to adjust to multicultural settings. His discussion of cultural self-identity (how culture influences one's concept of self) supplies the insight we need to truly liberate ourselves from "the caprices of cultural conditioning."

Based on the supposition that no subject in the school system should be taught without a plural cultural perspective, Seelye, with his able collaborator, Jacqueline Howell Wasilewski, provide in Chapter 11 the rationale for such an approach and give specific examples of how to accomplish it. Teachers of social studies, math, language, literature, art, and physical education will find helpful suggestions. Perhaps most valuable from a scholarly standpoint is the discussion of theories of cognitive development and cognitive style as they relate to multicultural perceptions. Multicultural students must constantly evaluate their situation in order to respond with culturally acceptable behavior. The optimum environment for exploring choices is one which is characterized by flexibility and a high tolerance for ambiguity. Anyone who has spent any time at all in the schools of our land knows that this ideal learning environment exists all to rarely—even at the university level. We are much better at teaching subject/verb agreement than we are at helping our students develop minds that are "large, as the universe is large, so that there is room for paradoxes" (Maxine Hong Kingston). We find it easier to teach in an environment of conformity than in one where uniqueness, idiosyncracy, and originality are valued. The critical point is that not only is such an environment necessary for the multicultural student to develop fully his/her unique gifts, but it is equally important for the development of intercultural skills in monocultural students. Certainly if our world is to survive, the acquisition of intercultural skills is of critical importance to our students—an outcome so crucial that it must become an objective in every area of the curriculum.

This book supplies not only the rationale for the development of intercultural skills, but concrete suggestions for attaining them. It offers, too, an extaordinarily rich bibliography. Throughout the text, pertinent references are seeded as closely as clover along an Iowa highway.

I have been using the 1974 edition of this volume as a text in courses on "Teaching for Cross-Cultural Understanding" for almost ten years. As one student recently wrote in critiquing the materials used in the course, "Mr. Seelye's book helps us know more than facts of culture; it helps us *see* what to do and *feel* how to do it." This student happened to be from Taiwan. But knowing, seeing, and feeling are the critical components of learning and teaching across all cultures. Seelye's consistent empathy for the teacher and the learner shines through in this valuable new edition.

Genelle Morain
Professor of Language Education
The University of Georgia

Foreword to the First Edition

Ned Seelye, the author of this volume, is a distinguished spokesman for the learning of and teaching about foreign languages and cultures. He has been honored by learned societies and conferences in foreign language education for his yeoman work in the field. Outstanding anthropologists have taken cognizance of his work. He speaks to us as one who has helped students and teachers use foreign languages for the development of *humane* individuals and the achievement of *humanistic* goals.

In preparing this volume he has drawn upon his rich experience as a classroom teacher, as a keen observer and participant in many cultures, especially the Latin American, and as a director of many workshops devoted to the teaching of culture.

Some of the materials written by the participants in these workshops are used to illustrate and bring home to us the cultural hypotheses the author advances in this volume. Because these illustrative reports are written by groups of teachers who have had actual experience in working with students at various age and ability levels, the reader will find many encouraging examples of ways and means for making his or her program a truly cultural experience for his or her students.

The book is written primarily for the teacher. It will help teachers grow in their ability to comprehend what culture is all about, to help the student help himself by perfecting his ability to work out the processes and use the tools needed to penetrate a culture, and to assist the student in uncovering reasons for a culture and why its members behave as they do.

We find a plethora of interesting situations that illustrate the interaction of the cognitive, psychomotor skills, and affective aspects of learning. All three are important for cultural learning, but perhaps the most important is the affective attitude of the student that is built into him by what we do in our foreign language programs. Individuals do not change their behavior as a result of the attainment of their objectives, but *their subtle transformation is a result of the means they employ* to attain their objectives. For instance, the individual whose goal is to become wealthy and powerful but who uses illegal means to attain that goal is more likely to end up as a criminal rather than an influential member of his community.

Ned Seelye builds on the ideas of outstanding colleagues such as Howard Nostrand, Nelson Brooks, Robert Lado, William Marquardt, and others, to synthesize and put together a program for the purposeful teaching of cultures in foreign language programs. He starts with the elementary level, where the program is primarily focused on the concrete and observable, and ends with the higher levels of abstraction and value systems of a culture, which he deals with primarily at the upper levels in secondary schools, colleges, and universities.

Rather frequently one gets the disturbing impression that few educators, including foreign language teachers, know how the study of foreign language fits into the total experience of the student. Foreign language classes should, and in many cases do, meaningfully contribute to specific, realizable, and educationally sound objectives. So often we find foreign language curriculum guides stating that the primary objective of learning language, and rightly so, is to understand the way of life of a foreign culture and the individuals who live within its constraints. But the operative curriculum fails to a considerable degree in actualizing the objective in its in- and out-of-class practices.

Seelye makes a plea for the development of a creative organic conception of the nature and function of culture in everyday life and of ways and means for translating this conception into constructive action. Simply, clearly, and precisely, he outlines the complex of information, skills, and attitudes to which the teacher must pay attention. He uses the seven goals for cultural instruction, adapted from Howard Nostrand, to show the teacher how to write enabling and behavioral objectives, test them, and create learning activities for their implementation. As the author states, there is much evidence of insecurity and confusion with regard to what to teach in the cultural sense in a foreign language course. So much trivia and so many isolated facts are presented to the student in an irrelevant manner. This so-called trivia could be of considerable significance when restructured. By asking the right questions to help place them in the correct categories, these facts become effective instruments for achieving significant goals in the teaching of culture concepts.

Language and culture study, Ned Seelye says, can by brought together in several different ways—by having language teaching become interdisciplinary, by having the foreign language teacher immerse himself in a culture through a training program abroad, or by having the foreign language teacher develop instructional strategies that can be used in and out of class. The latter is his greatest concern in this volume. To be effective in the *affective* as well as the cognitive and skills domains, strategies and activities must include the new simulation techniques, sensitivity training, culture capsules, semiotic approaches, and audiovisual aids. These are exemplified and developed in the various chapters.

Activities capitalizing on the human as well as the cultural resources of communities and environments are desirable as a means of bridging the gap between life and school. In many ways cultural constructs and behavioral attitudes can be built and developed at home in our multiethnic communities. Activities that encourage interaction with ethnic groups and their members in students' own communities, as so well delineated in the later chapters of this book, are excellent starts toward developing good human relationships.

One of the interesting parts of the book is Chapter 6. The author uses William F. Marquardt's seven types of communications situations for observing the interplay between persons of different cultures in a piece of literature such as autobiography, biography, novel, story, play, poem, and essay to illustrate an analytical procedure that sensitizes students to detect misunderstandings that can arise between different cultures having different value systems. This is, to my way of thinking, *the* way to approach literature. It illuminates the human experience in various cultures and environments. It also conforms to the author's thesis that before the student has learned enough foreign language to study the productions of creative artists, he or she needs a knowledge of the patterns of everyday life to appreciate these.

The chapters on goals, behavioral objectives, how they are tested and evaluated, the kinds of questions that must be asked in the cultural area of foreign language teaching have perhaps never been put so succinctly. Here the author is distinctly the pioneer. To know a culture goes beyond the learning of isolated facts of geography, history, and culture as a cult form. Yet these are the only types of items usually tested even in the so-called sophisticated tests such as the MLA and ETS batteries developed in the foreign language field. Such knowledge is not the same as understanding and behaving competently when confronted with another way of life. Testing how students behave in another culture and with the people who live in it requires sophisticated techniques we are not accustomed to using in our field. Here we need to look toward the social and behavioral scientists for help.

Attempts at devising suitable testing techniques have been in progress but they will be more or less unsuccessful until the profession agrees on a taxonomy of behaviors, some of which are illustrated by examples in this volume. The two suggestions, a multidisciplinary endeavor and the development of a taxonomy, will enable the profession to develop the right testing items and evaluation procedures.

The bibliography at the end of the book is an important one for the foreign language specialist and teacher. Of special significance are those works mentioned in the various chapters. They should constitute a minimum key library for every prospective and inservice teacher in foreign language.

I consider this volume to be a top-level how-to-do-it book that is readable, practical, informative, and enjoyable. It has treated a most vexing area of teaching: student attitude. I am sure it will be underlined and dog-eared by professional teachers of cultural persuasion who want to produce students whose future actions will demonstrate how well they have learned, not only by their competency in subject matter, but also by their behavior when facing the dynamic cultural changes we will be experiencing in a future one-world society.

Not since the Stanford Language Arts Investigation in the late 1930s and early 1940s with its resultant two volumes, *Modern Languages for Modern Schools* and *Foreign Languages and Cultures in American Education*, has a powerful, insightful, practical study been made of the role that foreign languages and cultures can play in the development of human relationships. The present volume is such a study.

Emma Marie Birkmaier
Professor of Foreign Language
Research and Education
University of Minnesota

DEDICATION

Because the time to write this book was stolen from evenings and weekends at home, it is dedicated to my family. To those who suffered most—my three bilingual sons, David, Alan, and Michael Seelye-James—as a lame excuse for not playing kickball out back in the mud; to my wife, Clara James Aldana, for assuring me the necessary time and for not bugging me to take out the garbage. This book is also dedicated to the memory of my two grandfathers, Lyle Granger Seelye and William Griffiths, who would have smiled; to the memory of my father, Hugh Lyle Seelye, who would have gloated; and to my mother, Margaret Griffiths Seelye, who kept the faith and will show the book to my brother-in-law, Cataldo Catalano, and to my sister, Eleanor Seelye Catalano, who will ask me if I'm getting too big for my britches.

Contents

Introduction:
Initial Questions

Interpersonal communication requires skill. When communication is between people from different cultural backgrounds, special skills are required if the messages received are to resemble the messages sent. This introduction looks at why this is so and what should be done about it.

It was a cold Friday in another midwestern state, and I had spent the day helping teachers produce for their students brief units in which they mined newspapers and magazines for cultural nuggets.

"How," I asked, somewhat innocently, "do you see yourselves using these units in your classes next week?"

Two teachers who were seated at the back (why, I wonder, are the troublemakers always seated at the back of the class?) were particularly and candidly negative. They did not see how they could use the units at all. "We have a hard enough time covering what we are supposed to—the language structure. There's just no time left to teach culture, too."

I don't recall my response. Afterward, the state education supervisor drove me back to the airport.

"You remember those two teachers who said they didn't have time to teach culture? They are foreign language teachers in schools that are dropping foreign languages from the curriculum. In two years both will be out of a job."

"Then why," I asked, "do they cling so obstinately to a classroom organization that isn't working?" I pictured them using a textbook like a security blanket. "Why don't they take some chances and do something different?" He just shook his head in bewilderment.

Any teacher concerned with intercultural communication —teachers of social studies, ESL, English, bilingual education, cross-cultural training—typically experiences the same sort of misgivings when asked to expand the contents of his/her course. How do you restructure classroom time to accommodate additional activities? Teachers using the first edition of this book have found it to be filled with practical suggestions that fit rather well into existing courses dealing with understanding people of other cultures.

In this book I cite seven extralinguistic skills that must be developed if anyone is to understand the often perplexing behavior of people from other cultures. A recurring theme is that teaching must be purposeful if it is to lead to skill development.

In developing objectives for cross-cultural communication I attempt to show how to write objectives that help us understand language and other behavior as it is *really* produced by the target people. Objectives to achieve cross-cultural understanding identify basic *skills*, rather than *information*, the student needs for developing an intellectual and emotional appreciation of cultures other than his or her own. Facts are cheap. They are also meaningless until interpreted within a problem-solving context.

By a series of historical accidents knowledge is relayed and skills are developed through quaint and ethnocentric guilds called "disciplines" or "departments" in secondary and higher institutions. The kind of culture developed in this book is inconveniently obstinate. It does not recognize the genius behind the narrow little guilds. Sometimes it does not even seem to know the difference between the humanities and the social sciences. Culture as developed here requires, in short, an interdisciplinary approach. It implies the inadequacy of a unit on art, another on music, one on food, and still another on the War of Independence. Instead of approaching culture from the perspective of one genre or another, an interdisciplinary problem-solving approach is advocated. Our objectives are not to learn more art, music, history, and geography, but to learn to communicate more accurately and to understand more completely the effect of culture on humanity.

Because teachers are often concerned that their own knowledge of culture is inadequate they erroneously see their greatest need as one of locating content sources that will tell their students all about the target culture. This concern suggests a confusion in the proper role of the teacher. In the area of culture the teacher does not have to be a full information center. Information is available in the enormous number of publications relevant to target cultures. The teacher has to help students develop whatever skills are necessary to make sense out of a few facts.

When Should Culture Be Taught?

Culture should be taught when we have students to teach. In foreign language classes, for example, the national attrition rate of 90 percent at the end of the second year of language study indicates that culture must be taught during the first two years of foreign language study. Only a fraction of our efforts to teach cultural understanding should be directed to upper-level courses. Cultural concepts must be implemented by specific measures in the classroom. While many teachers see culture as merely providing the background to matters of linguistic concern—for example, using a trip to the market or a visit with a French family to introduce new vocabulary or structural patterns—Debyser (1967) points out that unless this is very well done one should not put great hope in the efficacy of this method.

Other teachers see language-related impediments to communication as something handled by the foreign language teacher down the hall. But the particular communication problems that are inherent in language—many of which are not at all obvious to someone who has not yet attempted to communicate in a foreign language—need to be faced by any teacher concerned with improving student skill in intercultural communication. One can anticipate certain types of misunderstandings that inevitably arise in a conversation between two people who are each thinking in a different language—regardless of whether they are speaking in English at the time or not.

The teaching of intercultural communication is often omitted for a number of reasons: lack of time, the belief that students will be exposed to it later, and the view of language as a communication skill divorced from social concerns, or as a social concern divorced from language issues. These reasons are unconvincing.

There's no time. Were we turning out students with a respectable degree of proficiency in intercultural communication, lack of time would be an important reason for us to limit cultural instruction to out-of-class activities. It is questionable within the present reality, however, whether more of the same dreary stuff is the answer to student achievement.

They will be exposed to it later. When? If intercultural communication objectives are not taught during the beginning or introductory courses, so few students will be enrolled that for all practical purposes the objective will not be taught. Students of the physical sciences, to take one example, will study language and culture *less* each year they are in school. Culture must be taught while most of the students are present in our courses.

Language and culture concern communicative skills that are divorced from each other. If a student (or teacher) is unaware of the cultural connotation of a word, he does not know the meaning of that word—irrespective of whether he is able to voice it or translate it. Sometimes this ignorance has far-reaching consequences. Often the student is led in classroom drill to the glib fluency expressed in simple questions such as "Where do you work?" and "Are you married?" which will offend the listener in many situations. Teaching a student to say a given phrase is not sufficient.

He must be taught the circumstances in which the phrase can be employed—and those instances where it should definitely be avoided. Prompted by curiosity, I once asked a second-year Spanish class to translate "How is your mother?" The best student answered—using one of the worst vituperative epithets available in the Spanish of most Latin American countries—"¿Cómo está tu madre?"

Illustrations of the interrelatedness of language and culture are not confined to this kind of heavy-footed blunder. How many students are taught any linguistic and extralinguistic cues to social class in Latin America or France or Germany? Take the innocuous sentence, "My little brother goes to school." With a little bit of context such as the social class of the family and place of residence, those who are culturally initiated can be intuitive about a good deal of culturally pertinent information: What kind of school? Public? Private? Religious or secular? Coed? Half-day? Full-day? Does s/he wear a uniform?

Many of the awkward mistakes of Americans abroad could be avoided if their classes had included the cultural connotations of linguistic units as part of the course content. If a student does not realize the nature of these cultural referents, how much skill in intercultural communication can he be said to have achieved?

Every language has devices—intonation patterns, function words, a sound system—that are indispensable elements of the language but lack meaning in and of themselves. Words in isolation do not convey meaning. Only within a larger context do individual words mean anything. The word "get," for example, has several hundred potential meanings; only in context is a particular meaning communicated. What provides this meaningful context? Often the nonlinguistic cultural referent enables us to communicate. For instance, a few years ago several teachers of Spanish visited me in Guatemala, where I had been teaching. The maid asked them if they would like something to drink and they requested *agua* (water). About 15 minutes later the maid returned with Coca Colas. In Guatemala, *agua* commonly refers to soft drinks. To get H_2O, *agua pura* should have been requested. But once the language barrier has been hurdled and a glass of water has been obtained, what does one do with it? Can it be drunk? It may not be the local thirst-quenching beverage.

An interesting example of misunderstanding prompted by ignorance of the cultural connotation of a linguistic unit was afforded in an advanced undergraduate class in Latin American literature. In preparation for the course a number of paperbacks were ordered from Mexico to be sold by the college bookstore. After the titles were announced in class, the students dutifully trekked to the bookstore, made the required purchases, then retired to their dormitories. Within an hour, three-fourths of the class had attempted to return the paperbacks to the bookstore because the books were "defective"—the pages had not been cut! Although these Spanish majors had been using the word *libro* for at least six years, they were not able to distinguish a defective book from a "normal" one.

This is not to say that because one cannot communicate effectively without a knowledge of the foreign culture we automatically teach culture when we teach language. Knowledge of the linguistic structure alone does not carry with it any special insight into the political, social, religious, or economic system. While a convenient place to begin learning about the target culture is in our foreign language classes, culture must be taught systematically *in addition to* purely linguistic concerns. And it must be taught *now*. Social studies courses offer another convenient starting place. But just as culture cannot be ignored in foreign language classes the role of language in human thought cannot be ignored in social studies classes that aspire to develop intercultural communication skills.

In What Language Should Culture Be Taught?

While one expects English language arts and social studies teachers to teach intercultural skills through the medium of English, what are foreign language teachers to do?

Whatever can be taught in the target language should be taught in the target language. Many of the activities suggested in this book can be accomplished in the target language even during the first two years of language study.

When this is not realistic, do it in English. The other logical option—do not carry out the activity—ignores the crucial importance of developing cultural skills. The well-meant conviction that cultural activities must be held in abeyance until they can be carried out in the target language has been too impoverishing. Cross-cultural communication and understanding are too important to be given short shrift any longer.

Activities done in English do not necessarily have to occupy class time. They can be completed outside of class, in many instances as project or homework assignments.

The success of a foreign language experience can be easily measured. How much fluency and how much interest and contact with the target culture does an individual maintain *five years after having studied our course?* The enlightened teaching of cultural concepts and skills can encourage a student in a lifelong study of the "foreign" people.

Culture is viewed too often as an elitist collection of facts about art, literature, music, history, and geography. Such an approach has two weaknesses. First, culture is not primarily a laundry list of facts, and second, it is not solely concerned with art, literature, music, history, and geography. Elitism—restricting the study in a given area to the academically gifted and disciplined, while divorcing the cultural content from those aspects of life that concern most people most of the time—is responsible for much of the boredom current in too many social studies and language programs today.

How This Book Is Organized

How broad a concept is culture? Chapter 1 is a systematic review of the controversy that has embroiled this question; the chapter concludes that the issue is spurious. Culture includes anything that people have learned to do. Chapter 2 is an examination of both the motivation behind behavior and the reasons why nationality affects behavior.

There are three initial steps to be taken in teaching cultural concepts. The first is that the teacher must identify the skills involved in cross-cultural communication and understanding that can be developed in our classes. Seven of these skills are outlined in Chapter 3. These skills become the goals of cultural instruction. A table at the end of the chapter illustrates how trivial, purposeless activities can be redeemed by relating them to a goal through the posing of significant questions. The goals are:

I. *The sense, or functionality, of culturally conditioned behavior.* The student should demonstrate an understanding that people generally act the way they do because they are using options the society allows for satisfying basic physical and psychological needs.

II. *Interaction of language and social variables.* The student should demonstrate an understanding that social variables such as age, sex, social class, and place of residence affect the way people speak and behave.

III. *Conventional behavior in common situations.* The student should indicate an understanding of the role convention plays in shaping behavior by demonstrating how people act in common mundane and crisis situations in the target culture.

IV. *Cultural connotations of words and phrases.* The student should indicate an awareness that culturally conditioned images are associated with even the most common target words and phrases.

V. *Evaluating statements about a culture.* The student should demonstrate the ability to make, evaluate, and refine generalities concerning the target culture.

VI. *Researching another culture.* The student should show that s/he has developed the skills needed to locate and organize information about the target culture from the library, the mass media, people, and personal observation.

VII. *Attitudes toward other societies.* The student should demonstrate intellectual curiosity about the target culture and empathy toward its people.

The second step, the process of writing end-of-course student performance objectives that are goal-related, is illustrated in Chapter 4. These performance objectives spell out what a student should be able to do at the end of a course. The skill or knowledge needed to accomplish course objectives will not be developed unless the teacher is able to provide the necessary experience either in class or as out-of-class assignments. Chapter 5 illustrates these goal-related learning activities, the third step in planning cultural instruction.

Chapters 6 to 9 give further examples of different types of learning activities. Chapter 6 is an examination of two techniques to develop sensitivity toward a second culture. Chapter 7 illustrates two techniques to focus on critical differences in the way people from two cultures respond to similar circumstances. A third technique demonstrates how separate cross-cultural episodes can be brought together in one classroom dramatization. Chapter 8 illustrates four approaches to aiding students to ask significant questions and locate pertinent content information.

Testing techniques are discussed in Chapter 9. Common weaknesses in culture tests are elaborated. Some of the special considerations that will help bicultural students (e.g., Chicanos, native Americans) increase their communication skills are the subject of Chapter 10. Global education, involving the whole curriculum, is discussed in Chaper 11. Some 800 sources of cultural information, including all of the references cited in the book's previous chapters, are listed in Chapter 12.

Acknowledgments

The first educator outside of my family who ignited my interest in the world beyond my doorstep was my third grade teacher in Selinsgrove, Pennsylvania, Miss Anna Troutman, now retired. Some of her units on foreign countries were so vivid that they remain with me four decades later, and her enthusiasm for learning continues to be an inspiration to me.

After a stormy tenure in high school that culminated in my dropping out at the end of my junior year, I hitchhiked to Mexico where, a few months later, I managed to get into college with the help of Father William B. Wasson, then a sociology professor at Mexico City College (now called the University of the Americas). Father Bill contributed to my intellectual stimulation, often by including me in many trips outside of the capital in the company of fascinating intellectuals, mostly Mexican. One of these, the late Fernando Horcasitas, had an especially profound influence on my academic development. It was he, in fact, who taught me my first course in Spanish and my first course in anthropology more than thirty years ago.

I count it a rare privilege to have studied with Miss Troutman, Father Wasson, and Fernando Horcasitas.

The friendship of three other colleagues, specialists in inter-cultural communication, has helped me think through the contents of this book: Howard Lee Nostrand, the late William F. Marquardt, and Ann Garcelon.

Appreciation is due to colleagues who offered suggestions for this revised edition: Frances B. Nostrand, Howard L. Nostrand, Genelle G. Morain, Dale L. Lange, Ernest Frechette, and Frederick L. Jenks.

Margaret D. Pusch, president of Intercultural Press, gracefully allowed me to include in this revised edition of *Teaching Culture* an updated and rewritten version of a chapter that originally appeared in a book she edited and published: *Multicultural Education: A Cross-cultural Training Approach* (Chicago: Intercultural Press, 1979). Both the original and the updated version of this chapter (Chapter 11 in *Teaching Culture*) were co-authored by Jacqueline Howell Wasilewski, to whom thanks is due also for permitting it to appear in the present book.

Finally, the patience and encouragement of Leonard I. Fiddle, Editor-in-Chief of National Textbook Company, has been a significant factor in the appearance of this revised edition as well as the first edition of *Teaching Culture*.

1

When We Talk about "Culture," What Are We Talking about?

Most of the argumentative discussions over the definition of culture have been colossal wastes of time. The objective of this chapter is to bury the issue so that teachers can spend their time operationally describing, rather than defining, the term. Anthropological and literary approaches to culture and the relation of language to thought are examined. Culture is seen to include everything people learn to do.

Teapot Tempest

Practically all of the discussions on culture by teachers during the 1950s and 1960s gyrated around the question of how culture should be defined. These argumentative, often hotly polemic discussions served to keep the question of culture before the reluctant audience of a profession preoccupied with grammar, literature, geography, and history.

One such characteristically unsuccessful attempt to coordinate the teaching of language and culture occurred at the 1960

Northeast Conference on the Teaching of Foreign Languages (Bishop, 1960). Livid professors, acting as though their basic value system were under attack from imperfectly socialized upstarts, defended with righteous indignation the appropriateness of a literary approach to cultural matters. (A dozen years later a second Northeast Conference on culture [Dodge, 1972] was characterized by greater acceptance of the legitimacy of culture in language classes, but there was little sign of progress in integrating it into the classroom.)

The controversy over the definition of culture amounted to a monumental waste. I know of no better way to ensure having nothing productive happen than for a department to begin its approach to culture by a theoretical concern for defining the term.

What Is Culture?

The first really contemporary effort to define culture was exerted by anthropologists. Culture, they reasoned, was what their science was all about. It was, therefore, imperative to define it precisely. How else, theoretical-minded anthropologists were prone to ask, could valid research be accomplished in the area? It seemed logically evident that to talk about culture one has to know what culture is. But each anthropologist had his or her own definition. Prompted by a desire to isolate the common denominator in the many diverse definitions of the term, three decades ago two well-known anthropologists, Kroeber and Kluckhohn, examined approximately 300 definitions in a study entitled *Culture: A Critical Review of Concepts and Definitions* (1954).

A precise common denominator was not found. Instead, if one is pressed to abstract the catholicity of the concept presented in the many definitions, culture emerges as a very broad concept embracing all aspects of human life. The anthropologist Leslie White (1968) concludes an article on this problem by quoting Alfred North Whitehead: "It is a well-founded historical generalization that the last thing to be discovered in any science is what the science is really about."

Teachers have been slow to accept culture as a broadly defined concept. For much of the profession culture has been defined almost exclusively in terms of the fine arts, geography, and history. This narrow definition of culture, unfortunately, does not fully prepare a student to understand the wide range of behavior exhibited by our species (Murdock, 1980).

An understanding of the way of life of a foreign people is important to survival in a world of conflicting value systems, where the boundaries that formerly isolated and protected people from alien ideas have been eroded by advances in the technology of communication or struck down by the angry clamor of the downtrodden in their search for a better life. How is one to liberate one's ideas from the stagnant recesses of ethnocentrism, from what Francis Bacon called the "fallacy of the tribe," if not through a study of other cultures? It is critical to acknowledge that to penetrate another culture, knowledge of the foreign language is imperative. Paul Simon (1980) pithily begins his book *The Tongue-Tied American* with the admonition that we should erect the following sign at each port of entry into the United States:

—Welcome to the United States—
We Cannot Speak Your Language

The late Nelson Brooks (1968), who has been so influential in causing teachers to recognize the importance of culture and its link with language, identified five different types of culture: biological growth, personal refinement, literature and the fine arts, patterns of living, and the sum total of a way of life. Brooks stressed the importance of never losing sight of the individual when we talk about culture as it is relevant to language classes. The same point is relevant to any course concerned with enhancing intercultural communication. The type of culture Brooks identified as most appropriate for beginning classes is "patterns for living," a concept defined as "...the individual's role in the unending kaleidoscope of life situations of every kind and the rules and models for attitude and conduct in them." These patterns enable the individual to relate to "the social order to which he is attached." Literature and the fine arts along with culture should be broadly sampled. As Brooks said, culture in the classroom "must not only answer the question: 'Where is the bookstore?' It must also answer the question: 'Where is the bathroom?'"

The Cultural Nature of Language

Dewey's (1897) famous essay "My Pedagogic Creed" appeared in an education journal eighty years ago. Dewey observed that "language is almost always treated in the books of pedagogy simply as the expression of thought. It is true that language is a logical instrument, but it is fundamentally and primarily a social instrument." If language is "primarily a social instrument," how can it be divorced from the society that uses it? Writing more than seventy years after Dewey, Chao (1968) in his study of language emphasizes that "action and speech are thoroughly mixed." Chao further observes that language is not even usually in the form of connected discourse such as sentences or paragraphs.

There is probably considerable correlation between linguistic change and social change. When for one reason or another members of one language community are forced to function either within or alongside another language, both their language and way of life inevitably change. Ilbek (1967) offers an interesting discussion of the effect of English on the native language of the French-speaking minorities of the United States. Ilbek gives examples of shifts of meaning caused by the presence of cognates in the language, direct borrowing of lexical items to designate new things, borrowing of patterns through translation, and borrowing of fixed forms directly or through translation. However, instead of using these data to arrive at insights into the nature of linguistic change or biculturation, the author disappointingly concludes that "as teachers of French we are pledged to fight this kind of interference and to keep our language pure . . . ."

Many teachers make this same mistake. While intrigued with the cultural implications of linguistic data, they get hung up on the form and fail to reach a cultural comprehension of the data beyond an assessment of its snob appeal. Despite three decades of descriptive linguistics, a lot of normative puritanism remains. Chao (1968) correctly characterizes language when he says that "there is no complete uniformity in any speech community; there is always mixture of dialects in the same locality; there is class difference; there is difference in the speech of different personalities even within the same dialect or the same class; above all, there is difference in style in the same individual." Chao adds that besides talking with people and hearing them talk with you, one should overhear them talk among themselves to learn to understand the nonstandard dialects. (Switching between two varieties of the same language is called "diglossia.")

Morever, since much of the world's population speaks more than one language, studies of bilingual situations in which a choice is made of which language to employ help us understand the cultural functions of language. Rubin's (1968) study of bilingual people in Paraguay describes the social context and consequences of switches between Spanish and Guaraní, an indigenous language. Spanish typically is used for formal occasions, in schools, in government, and in the transaction of most business. Guaraní, on the other hand, is spoken with friends, servants, when telling a joke, in intimate situations and in most casual situations (see also Farb, 1974, for a paraphrase of parts of Rubin's study).

In one of the best anthologies on cross-cultural communication published to date (Smith and Luce, 1979), each contributor gives many concrete examples of how language and culture interact. One such way is in public advertising and street signs; publications prepared for the foreign language classroom are available for Spanish (Bawcutt, 1977) and French (Paoletti and Steele, 1981).

Can Culture Be Taught through Literature?

Some professors dedicated to an analysis of literary style claim that literature affords the best tool to teach about life of the people. Here we need to be cautious, Nostrand (1966) advises, "in generalizing from literature. Many Russians of today have formed their idea of the American businessman and of Wall Street partly from American novels such as Babbitt which reflect a hostile attitude on the part of one subculture in the United States, the writers, toward another subculture, the businessman."

Lewald (1968), in an article that expertly reviews the problems associated with teaching about culture in language classes, comments on the use of fiction to illustrate a target culture by observing that it "has been defended on the grounds that all art is based on a conscious or unconscious contact with social reality and cultural patterns, present in the mind of the creative writer. Here the problem arises of determining which types of literature or art forms are most suitable to elicit cultural patterns or indicators. A case might be made for those forms that strongly reflect an outer reality." Lewald goes on to suggest that the contribution of psychological, surrealistic, or experimental writing would be questionable. If the interest is in contemporary culture rather than in a preindustrial historical period, the number of qualifying documents shrinks greatly.

One writer (Imhoof, 1968), cognizant of the cultural biases endemic in reading selections designed for use in our courses, sees the necessity for controlling the cultural variations that appear in the materials. However, in emphasizing the universal aspects of culture, one should avoid sidestepping the contrastive manifestations of the target culture. Literary works become important as they develop themes of universal interest, but to understand a culture's uniqueness study must also be directed to local nonuniversal cultural patterns.

Even in situations where the legitimate objective of a course is the study of fine literature, a knowledge of culture is not an irrelevant digression. One writer whose sympathies were definitely literary in nature came to the conclusion through teaching a course in English as a second language that in the study of literature the whole area of cultural comprehension is more likely than language to cause difficulty (Povey, 1967, p.44).

Another writer who reached the same conclusion sees harm in attempting to rely too heavily on cultural generalizations abstracted from literature. In describing the experience of some teachers involved in teaching adult Arab employees of an American company, Yousef (1968) recounts that

> ...it was clear to the teachers that literary values were not universal. These students of English as a foreign language would never be able to reach an understanding of the people and the culture of the United States by studying American literature. Instead, the study of American literature actually seemed to increase misunderstanding and confusion. It was apparent that the students would need pertinent cultural orientation before they could attempt any meaningful literature course.

Beaujour and Ehrmann (1965) maintain that in itself the study of culture is a humanistic discipline, which must recognize and develop its own tools. It cannot be dealt with as a series of disconnected footnotes to literature.

The quarrel is not with the value of literature or arts as a means to illustrate how the foreign people live, but rather with the restrictive inroad fiction offers as the major source of information. Since many teachers feel uncomfortable dealing with concepts and data of the social sciences, they tend to rely too heavily on literature to teach culture. Consequently, the common dual descriptor "literature and culture" has itself become suspect: it too often means a little culture and a lot of literature. However, "the study of culture and that of literature, which must be clearly separated, are neither irreconcilable nor antagonistic" (Beaujour and Ehrmann, 1967, p.154).

Marquardt (1967) suggested the value of certain carefully selected literary works as an aid to teaching cross-cultural communication. A doctoral dissertation by Christian (1967) combined his analysis of 25 Latin American contemporary novels and tape recorded interviews with 15 novelists with both social scientific and literary studies of Latin America in an effort to assess the reaction of different Latin American social classes to modern urban middle-class values. Christian's interpretation of both empirical and "mystical" data was especially sensitive. Literary approaches such as Marquardt's and Christian's do much to rekindle hope for an eventual rapproachement between those interested in Culture with a "big C" and those interested in viewing it more broadly with a "little c."

Literature can best be seen in the present context as illustrating the cultural patterns of a society once the patterns have been identified by the methods of the social sciences: social science as source, literature as example (see Chapter 2 for further development of this idea).

Folklore: An Ideal Compromise?

Morain (1968) and J. Dale Miller (1973) convincingly argue that folklore offers a logical bridge to service language teachers trained in literary analysis who are interested in getting closer to an anthropological understanding of culture but who are not equipped by disposition or background to deal with the empirical orientations of the social scientist.

Morain takes as her definition of folklore the comfortably loose description by Archer Taylor (1965):

> Folklore is the material that is handed on by tradition, either by word of mouth or by custom and practice. It may be folksongs, folktales, proverbs, or other materials preserved in words. It may be traditional tools and physical objects like fences or knots, hot cross buns, or Easter eggs; traditional ornamentation like the walls of Troy; or traditional symbols like the swastika. It may be traditional procedures like

throwing salt over one's shoulder or knocking on wood. It may be traditional beliefs like the notion that elder is good for ailments of the eye. All of these are folklore.

Morain argues that when it comes to mirroring the attitudes of large groups, folklore is superior to literary writing. The very durability of folktales, proverbs, slurs, and jests is an indication of the validity they have for a given people. A study of carefully selected folk materials could illuminate some of the important cultural themes that underlie a country's thought and action. While Morain's examples are taken from the French, Campa (1968) demonstrates how an analysis of folklore can illuminate the main themes of Hispanic culture. One-line proverbs, brief verses, narrative ballads, and riddles all afford lively illustrations of themes such as the "picaresqueness of the Spaniard," or his sense of "self-assurance."

Appearing in *Soviet Education*, an article by Khanbikov (1967) calls the folklore which is relevant for instructional purposes "folk pedagogy." He goes on to say that this folk pedagogy is of a democratic nature; it is the result of the creative contribution of many generations of working people to spiritual culture, its inalienable component. Many thousands of folk philosophers, psychologists and educators have worked on its creation. It is the expression of the ideals of the toiling majority, and it puts forward, in correspondence with the needs of the people, the most humane and democratic ideals in the education of the rising generation, rejecting everything that contradicts these ideals. This Marxist willingness to place faith in the culture of the masses contrasts interestingly with the reluctance of some "democratic" teachers to discuss in sympathetic terms the lifestyles of the French, Spanish, or German workers.

It is a great disappointment for many students, who have developed fluency in the language after four to twelve years of sequential study and have passed the advance placement test, to go on to advanced classes only to discover in college that if they are to continue taking courses in their second language, they have to study literature or "advanced grammar." Even the somewhat isolated Civilization and Culture course usually bases itself "solidly" on literature. If a student wants to satisfy any of the many interests he was led to expect from his high school teachers, he must often leave or avoid altogether the college foreign language department, for frequently it is easier to locate professors who are both fluent in the foreign language and interested in its culture in other college departments. Perhaps folklore is the door through which more culturally pertinent materials can be introduced into the rather arid genre-oriented college offerings.

Is Speaking the Language the Same as Thinking Like a Native?

One naive assumption occasionally made by teachers is that a mastery of the linguistic patterns of a foreign culture leads in itself to "thinking like a native." As Lewald (1968, p.302) properly points out, this belief is unwarranted. Unless the student is learning the language in the target culture, the cultural referents necessary to understanding a native speaker must be learned in addition. Jay (1968) argues the point in pertinently broad terms:

> It should be made crystal clear, however, that bilingualism itself does not insure ipso facto a respect for other cultural patterns. The traditional hostility between France and Germany has been until recently a bitter reality, even though the language of each was commonly taught and understood by the other. . . . Bilingualism is not in itself the answer to cultural understanding among people. An indispensable asset, it must be fortified by the strongest possible sensitivity education. With knowledge of the language must exist a similar knowledge of the social, religious, and economic attitudes of a people [pp. 85-86].

Some years ago Benjamin Lee Whorf (cf. Carroll, 1956), citing the earlier work of Sapir (1921; also in Mandelbaum, 1962), theorized that the world view of a speech community is reflected in the linguistic patterns they use. The implication was that the way "reality " is categorized in the underlying patterns of a language is an indication of how speakers of that language view the world; and, inversely, how they view the world depends on the language system they have. The proliferation of Eskimo words for snow, according to what was to become known as the Sapir-Whorf hypothesis, reflects the importance snow has in Eskimo culture. Similar instances are the Trobriand Islanders' multiplicity of terms for yams, the basis of their economy, and the truckloads of terms to designate automobiles current in contemporary United States culture.

Perceptions of colors, kinship relations, space and time, all differ from language to language and from culture to culture. The trick is to demonstrate an association between language and culture. (It may be recalled that Whorf advocated contrasting languages such as Navaho and English, or French and Chinese, and not languages within the Indo-European family.) Unfortunately, off-the-cuff pronouncements on the relation between language and culture are the rule in social studies and in language classes. The fact that the linguistic structure of some languages enables the speaker to become the object of the action (the glass broke on me) instead of the subject of the action (I broke the glass), to take an example, does not in itself demonstrate the speaker of the first example to view nature as an active agent and man as a passive one (e.g., Seelye, 1966b). To draw a cognitive conclusion from purely linguistic data is to wile away the hours in tautology. To draw a behavioral inference legitimately from an analysis of language structure a language pattern must be associated empirically with a behavioral pattern.

That the Sapir-Whorf hypothesis has been accepted as truth by so many communication teachers may be an interesting example of the tendency toward wish fulfillment. The theory is exciting; there is some corroborative evidence and, perhaps inevitably, a body of contradicting evidence also; the idea has been around long enough for most teachers to have forgotten its highly speculative nature; and if the theory were true it would imbue language and communication courses with newfound importance. Unfortunately, few writings by linguistic specialists are, at this stage in the science's struggle for respectability, comprehensible to most classroom teachers, and few classroom teachers have shown enough familiarity with the linguistic literature to be "linguistically respectable." Consequently, our acceptance of the Sapir-Whorf hypothesis must await either more empirical evidence or improved communication with linguists.

Farb (1974) summarizes the importance of these theories in this way: "The true value of Whorf's theories is not the one he worked so painstakingly to demonstrate—that language tyrannizes speakers by forcing them to think in certain ways. Rather, his work emphasized something of even greater importance: the close alliance between language and the total culture of the speech community" (pp.186-187).

Some of the books over the last three decades that treat this area include Hoijer (1954), Carroll (1956), Romney and D'Andrade (1964), Gumperz and Hymes (1964), Hammel (1965), Hymes (1964), Greenberg (1966), Lander (1966), Witucki (1966), Mathiot (1967), Manners and Kaplan (1968), Fishman (1968), Niyekawa-Howard (1968), and Pike (1971).

Cross-Cultural Communication

Besieged by an endless procession of cultural studies from anthropology, art, history, sociology, economics, political science, social psychology, music and literature, the teacher must ask himself what knowledge is relevant and what skills should be developed in students. Nostrand (1966b) proposed that teachers concentrate on two goals in teaching about a foreign way of life: cross-cultural communication and understanding.

The basic aim of a communication class is to have the student learn to communicate with people from the foreign culture. If people from the target culture do not speak English, the student must learn another language. Obviously, if fairly common emotions and thoughts cannot be understood apart from their cultural connotations, these connotations must be learned. Some examples of difficulties in cross-cultural communication that arise from ignorance of the target culture are recounted by several authors.

Barrutia (1967), in an article that discusses the relation of language development to cultural barriers, illustrates one type of cultural problem by contrasting near synonyms in English. The possible social consequences of a loose interchange of role-linked terms would be amusing to observe—in someone else. Barrutia supplies a verse to dramatize the sex connotation of many common words.

A woman has a figure, a man has a physique;
A father roars in rage, a mother shrieks in pique;
Broad-shouldered athletes throw what dainty damsels toss;
And female bosses supervise, male bosses boss.
Lads gulp, maids sip;
Jacks plunge, Jills dip;
Guys bark, dames snap;
Boys punch, girls slap;
Gobs swab, WAVES mop;
Braves buy, squaws shop;
A gentleman perspires, a lady merely glows;
A husband is suspicious; a wife, however, knows.

Debyser (1968) offers examples from the French to illustrate how the cultural connotations of common terms and phrases can be taught on the elementary level. To know the words denoting the various members of a family (mother, child, uncle) is not enough. To be able to use the words with impunity one must also know the specific social context within which each can be employed. The word *maman*, for instance, may be used by a person when he talks to his mother, but would rarely be used by him when talking about her to others.

Much misunderstanding in the communication professions concerning the degree of effort to get the students to act like natives is the result of confusing the ability to communicate accurately and the attitudes dictated by the foreign mores. There should be no controversy about the aim of accurate communication, and this includes understanding the culturally based mores of the target people but does not necessarily include professing or internalizing them.

Cross-Cultural Understanding

Nostrand's second basic purpose in teaching the foreign culture—understanding—can imply a restructuring of our attitudes and world view. Nostrand includes under the rubric of understanding, for example, such intangibles as "the psychological capacity to be magnanimous toward strange ways" (1966b, pp.5-8). In the final analysis, no matter how technically dexterous a student's training in the foreign language, if he avoids contact with native speakers of that language and if he lacks respect for their world view, of what value is his training? Where can it be put to use? What educational breadth has it inspired?

Unfortunately, some teachers themselves do not feel comfortable in the presence of native speakers of a foreign language. In part, this is because the teachers have not learned to follow speech at conversational speed, have not learned what to talk about and what to avoid, have not accustomed themselves to the amount of space separating them from the native or to the rules governing eye-to-eye contact, have not learned to share the target sense of humor or their songs, have not learned the cultural referents to the topics of discussion, and have succumbed to a regrettable ethnocentric tendency to underestimate the intelligence of a member of another culture.

The enlightened teaching of selected cultural elements can help prepare a student both to understand and enjoy a native speaker. There is no enjoyment in listening to what one cannot understand, and one cannot understand a native if his cultural referents, his view of the world, and his linguistic forms are novel.

The intercultural communication teacher can build bridges from one cognitive system to another.

Reaching a Consensus

The most widely accepted usage now regards culture as a broad concept that embraces all aspects of the life of man, from folktales to carved whales. Even in a few published articles concerned with teaching the older concept of culture as the limited but praiseworthy production of creative artists, the importance of a knowledge of patterns of everyday life as a prerequisite to appreciating the fine arts is recognized to an increasing degree. Some encouraging signs augur an eventual harmony between teachers whose major interest is literary and those who are primarily concerned with the other aspects of culture. In short, it is becoming increasingly apparent that the study of language cannot be divorced from the study of culture, and vice versa.

Intercultural communication teachers have not necessarily been able to define culture where others have not; we have finally been content to shrug our shoulders and admit that it doesn't really matter how it is defined as long as the definition is broad. The important thing is that intercultural communication involves many characteristics not often present in our classes.

Culture is seen to involve patterns of everyday life that enable individuals to relate to their place under the sun. When we peek in on people "relating," we see them mixing action and speech. They do ingenious things to foreign words to incorporate them into their own idiom. They talk in nonstandard dialects within the same speech area; they talk one way to strangers and another way among themselves. The words they use evoke cultural connotations of novel shapes and sizes. The speech of a person indicates one's sex, age, social class, and place of residence; and it evokes culturally peculiar images.

The parameters of a culture-based instruction are limited only by the imagination of the teacher. The subsequent chapters begin to describe, rather than define, the term operationally.

Suggested Activities

1. List 10 ways in which language and culture are linked.
2. Give a specific example of the mixture of speech and action in one of the languages you speak.
3. What are five extralinguistic cultural connotations of "child" in one of your languages?
4. Through an example, illustrate how an element of folklore may mirror the attitudes or cultural themes of a nation's thought and action.
5. Write a dialogue with three characters in which the speech demonstrates differences in the speaker's age, sex, social class, and place of residence.
6. Explain the difference between cross-cultural communication and cross-cultural understanding.
7. Identify in writing 25 ideas for cultural activities. Each idea should relate to a different category of Murdock's (1980) or Nostrand's emergent model.

2

Why Do People Act
the Way They Do?

People act the way they do to satisfy universal physical and psychological needs. This chapter examines several approaches (national character studies, basic postulates, and main themes) to understanding how societies evolve different ways to satisfy their basic needs. These "cosmic" approaches provide an interpretive framework for helping students explain the reason people of the studied culture act the way they do.

The Motive behind Human Behavior

We hear that "people are the same all over the world." Yet there are obvious differences. How can we reconcile this universality of man with the uniqueness of his many cultures?

People everywhere are impelled to satisfy certain basic needs such as for food and shelter, for love and affection, and for self-pride. Man has banded together to meet these needs. Predictably, different bands of people have developed different ways of doing so. An Eskimo might convey love and thoughtfulness to an elderly person by helping his friends and relatives hang him when he wishes to die; an American might manifest the same sentiment by attempting to prolong the life of an incurably sick elder in constant pain from cancer. The question students of intercultural communication can ask of any observed or reported behavior in the target culture is: What universal need is the individual trying to satisfy? (see Maslow, 1954; Aronoff, 1967).

One universal need is to eat. The World Relief Corporation sent forty tons of Canadian cheddar cheese to refugee camps in Thailand in 1975. The Thai response: "Thank you for the soap, but it doesn't wash clothes very well." A doctor at the site got them to eat a little cheese by letting them think it was medicine. Not only didn't they like the taste, they complained that when they perspired it made them smell like white people.

The attempts of some Southeast Asian refugees to feed themselves in the U.S. have met cultural resistance on the part of some segments of U.S. society. Reports that the refugees were trapping domestic animals in San Francisco city parks and eating them has outraged animal lovers in those parts. Animal lovers who, it might be noted, are not themselves vegetarians, have been vehemently unsympathetic to the practical suggestion by the city's Catholic charities that the refugees be allowed to get—and eat—unwanted pets from the humane society.

Similarly, a few months ago in Chicago there was an outcry of revulsion when "foreign speaking" individuals were asked what they were going to do with the pigeons they were trapping in Grant Park. Their response, in graphic pantomime, provoked an extended outcry in the city's newspaper columns.

Five hundred years before the birth of Christ, Confucius observed that "By nature men are nearly alike; by practice they get to be wide apart." We are by nature alike because we share the same basic needs. We all need to eat and to make friends, for instance. The different ways we go about doing this frequently puzzle and sometimes alienate people who are looking in from the outside.

To satisfy universal needs we have to employ behavioral patterns that will enable us to "bring home the bacon." For some

Southeast Asians, trapping dogs is an accepted behavioral option for getting food. In certain societies, dogs are eaten only on prescribed ritual occasions, while in others they taste good all year round. Here in Disneyland we slaughter domesticated bovines for daily food but shun the ingestion of domesticated canines on even the most sacred of ritual occasions.

It takes us years to become socialized in the do's and don'ts of need gratification, and it takes even longer to develop skill levels that allow us success in satisfying these needs. A lot of options, or patterns of behavior, are available in any society for the satisfaction of basic needs. In technologically complex societies such as our own, the role of "hunter of food" can be discharged through any one of 30,000 or more occupations.

The satisfaction of psychological needs, on the other hand, is less affected by technological complexity than it is by the amount of interpersonal uncertainty we feel toward the individuals with whom we must interact to satisfy a given need and by the extent to which need gratification supports one's sense of continuity of identity. In some situations, the salient identity is self; in other cases it is group.

Even the simplest of choices can plunge one into anxieties concerning self-identity. The importance of maintaining a sense of self-determination and historical continuity in the face of culture change is illustrated by the successful experience of one upper-Amazon tribe, the Shuar. These people, better known as the Jívaro of shrunken-head fame, have very recently changed from making their own clothes from fibers beat from trees to Levi's imported from abroad. This fiercely nationalistic group has effected a sartorial change without any sense of historical loss or cultural diminution because they consciously made a choice for themselves that was not imposed from without, even though the presence of choice in this instance was dependent on an event (i.e., the manufacture of jeans) outside their own culture.

Besides asking what basic human need does the observed behavior help people in that society to satisfy, there are important auxiliary questions to ask also: Is the observed behavior a frequently used behavioral option or is its occurrence rare in that society? What substitute behavioral patterns does the society allow for the satisfaction of that need? What complementary behavioral patterns are commonly associated with the observed behavior?

By itself, a behavior pattern is usually just a piece or fragment from one's repertoire of options designed for the gratification of any given universal need. When an observer of the human scene sees how a given behavior fits into the larger cultural context to enable the actor to satisfy a need everyone can identify with, the behavior makes sense and no longer seems quite as bizarre. It is at this point that understanding of another way of life begins to achieve significance.

How do we help students to develop skill in perceiving the functionality of "weird" behavior patterns encountered in "foreign" societies? Let me give two examples. The first example uses imagination as a catalyst to understanding; the second draws upon textual materials for its source of understanding.

1. Imagination as Source: *Dial-a-Soap [opera]*

Activity A: The objective of this classroom activity is to get students thinking about the analogous causes and different forms of human behavior. The students clip photos from some handy source such as a target-language magazine that portrays the target people in the midst of action. A student draws a clipping at random. Then s/he projects an imaginary scenario to "explain" why the person is doing the observed action, that is, what basic need has motivated the behavior. This activity is done without any pretense to even a semblance of authenticity. Rival scenarios are elicited from other students to "explain" the motivation behind the portrayed action. Again, the whole objective of this activity is to get the students to begin looking for the reasons behind human behavior; the classroom activity is not at this point concerned with ascertaining the "correct" explanation.

Activity B: The objective of this activity is to help students begin to gain insight into "The Fallacy of Projected Cognitive Similarity" (Alfred J. Kraemer's wording). This fallacy underlines the difficulty, if not the impossibility, of getting inside another person's mind. We all project the logic of our own reasoning to explain the actions of others. The result often makes the observed action appear childish, not because the logic of the target people is primitive but because of the inappropriateness of our own projected logic to explain causal patterns in another cultural system. Classroom activities are needed to provide cathartic companions to activities such as Activity A above, which, if left undisturbed, would lead students into a false sense of understanding.

In Activity B, students select one of the scenarios produced in Activity A for refinement of the cultural content. The assistance of one or more natives of the target culture is elicited to help make the scenario "more plausible" for its cultural setting. The student(s) report on the modifications that were suggested and the reasons behind them. Again, one should not expect this activity to produce an authentic rationale for the observed behavior, but it does reinforce the desirability of inquiry and serves to refine student skill in making culturally appropriate attributions.

2. Textual Materials as Source:
The Kapauku Papuans of West New Guinea

An excellent series of anthropological case studies were edited by George and Louise Spindler and published by Holt. One case study, written by Leopold Pospisil (1963), focuses on the Kapauku Papuans. Briefly, in this society wealth and prestige depend on the cost-effective harvesting of yams. Harvesting is done by wives. Obtaining and maintaining a wife is, as everybody knows, expensive. The trick is to make sure one's wives are neither too idle because there isn't enough land to tend, nor too busy to exploit the yam harvest because there are not enough wives to help. Adding wives at the right critical time, then, is essential for the accumulation of wealth (sea shells).

To demonstrate how the custom of plural wives among the Kapauku Papuans enables families to gratify both social and economic needs in a way that would not be possible in that society through monogamy, the student elects to do one of the following four activities:

Activity A: Present an oral or written report on "What limits the number of wives any one man in Kapauku society can have?"

Activity B: Act out a game or skit of his/her own making which shows how wealth and prestige are achieved in Kapauku society.

Activity C: Participate in a panel which discusses what changes might occur in other areas of Kapauku life if polygyny were outlawed.

Activity D: Take a brief quiz that tests how women relate to social, economic, and political life in Kapauku society.

The satisfaction of basic human needs is not necessarily the reason people *see* for doing what they do. The *conscious* rationale for action more often speaks of love, God, motherhood, and other lofty concerns. Inquiry into the reasons people give for their behavior provides the lexicology of euphemisms we need to communicate inoffensively with people from the target culture.

Each culture imposes needs upon its members to some extent through societal values that require a person to behave in a given way in given situations. Even the goals a person works toward are culturally influenced. Consequently, while physical and psychological needs are universal, the individual aspirations that give direction to these needs arise out of the basic values of a particular culture.

A productive approach to understanding another society involves ascertaining the way culture has influenced basic needs, both in terms of the relative importance assigned by that society to a particular need and the ways provided by the society to satisfy the need. While all cultural patterns relate to a need with which people from any society can identify, the patterns themselves may seem peculiar. A red-blooded American student can understand trying to win the respect of others, but he may not immediately identify with an Amazon Jívaro who shrinks heads as a means to this end. Not only do different societies satisfy universal needs through patterns that may be unique to that society, but the priority with which they rank a need may differ substantially from one society to another. An American might indicate the priority he places on the need for shelter by buying an opulent house in an affluent suburb and by equipping it with the latest electrical wonders, while a Buddhist from Laos might indicate a lower priority for the same need through satisfaction with a simple hut with a thatched roof and earthen floor. The Laotian Buddhist value of disassociation from all worldly passions and interests and the American value of conspicuous consumption born of "capitalism and the spirit of Protestantism" affect the way "adequate" housing is seen.

Each culture offers its people a number of options for satisfying any particular human need. Many of these options are widely shared across cultures; the cross-cultural occurrence of other options is rare. Except in highly conventional circumstances, one can rarely predict with precision exactly what a person will do. But one can, with great precision, indicate the range of options within which a person will act to gratify a particular need if he is to be considered "normal" by his neighbors. No matter how badly a United States politician may want to increase his wisdom, proclaim his bravery, or vent his anger he will not shrink heads.

Much of the individuality of a person's actions is the result of the *relatively* different set of options he has chosen to satisfy his needs. When regarded as an individual he is *relatively* unpredictable. But when viewed as a collection of individuals who share the same society (i.e., the same cultural ground rules), his behavior becomes *relatively* predictable. When faced with a particularly laudable or a particularly reprehensible act of an individual, we attempt to "explain" the act through the causal relationships that occur in the psychological recesses of a mind. When faced with a *societal* behavior, such as higher (or lower) frequency of divorce, war, mental breakdowns, suicide, crime, we look to an explanation, not within the recesses of an individual mind, but within the values of the society at large. The exceptionally broad potential range of human action is dramatically highlighted by Murdock's anthropological inventory of behavior (Murdock, 1980). Murdock outlines almost 100 general areas, with these further broken down into 900 subcategories.

National Character Studies

Just as many linguists maintain that an explicit knowledge of "rules of grammar" will assist students in learning to speak, so too do many social scientists hold that a knowledge of "codes of behavior" will help a student understand how people from different societies act.

If we do what we do because of our values and if values are widely shared within a culture but substantially disparate among cultures, knowledge of the few basic tenets of a culture should greatly aid one in predicting the behavior of that culture-bearer.

The late Margaret Mead, writing more than thirty years ago, observed that national character studies "attempt to delineate how the innate properties of human beings, the idiosyncratic elements in each human being, and the general and individual patterns of human maturation are integrated within a shared social tradition in such a way that certain regularities appear in the behavior of all members of the culture which can be described as a *culturally* regular character" (Mead, 1953). In a review article published four years later, Kaplan (1957) argued that while there is evidence of national variations of behavior, there is great variability within national groups and much overlap between the groups. Kaplan concludes by saying "the key to the diversity of behavior was seen to lie in the existence of any one of a small number of motivational tendencies which could be found in any society in the world."

Another review of national character studies by an anthropologist (Hsu, 1969, Chapter 5) acknowledges that most of these studies were done in the 1940s and 1950s, but says that "a temporary drop of enthusiasm for national character studies among anthropologists is no reason to presume their total demise." More recent still is an impressive social psychological study of the characteristic way members of similar subgroups in six different countries (Greece, India, Japan, Peru, Taiwan, United States) perceive their social environment (Triandis et al., 1972). Triandis sees enough cross-cultural variance of behavior ascertainable through statistical analyses to justify amply continued research into national character studies.

Osgood, May, and Miron (1975) applied tests of semantic differential (see Chapter 9, p. 168) across 27 countries in an attempt to identify cross-cultural universals of affective meaning for selected noncontextual terms (e.g., "good," "bad"). In looking for universals of affect, this ambitious study identifies interesting national variations. A study of the international differences in work-related values (Hofstede, 1980) examines elements such as power distance, uncertainty avoidance, individualism, and masculinity as they appear in 40 industrialized nations. On the individualism scale, for instance, Hofstede finds the U.S., Australia, and Great Britain to have the most individualistic workers, and Venezuela, Colombia, and Pakistan to have the least individualistic.

Harold R. Isaacs' (1975) provocative book on group identity makes the point that "no mind, no personality, no individual or group identity ever looks like a set of neat boxes." Isaacs goes on to say that he pictures group identity as "looking more like a cell of living matter with a sprawlingly irregular shape" (p. 44). Still, at least with regard to some dimensions, ethnic or national groups do have recognizable, if irregular, shapes.

The combined references cited in these writings provide an extensive bibliography of publications relevant to national character studies.

Cultural Values of Americans

Three books that describe American culture deserve special recommendation to teachers. *Meet the U.S.A.* by the historian Henry Steele Commager (1970) was written primarily for foreign visitors to the U.S.; *American Society: A Sociological Interpretation,* by Williams (1970), contains 100 pages on American values; and *American Cultural Patterns: A Cross-Cultural Perspective,* by Edward Stewart (1977), a psychologist who specializes in intercultural communication, is designed to provide an American with the kind of succinct description of his or her own culture that will help overcome the obstacles of adjusting to another culture.

An intriguing attempt to reduce the basic working philosophy of Americans to a series of postulates and their corollaries was written by Francis Hsu in his excellent little book *The Study of Literate Civilizations* (1969). Hsu is an anthropologist who has lived half his life in China and half in the United States. Before stating his nine postulates (and many corollaries) of life in the United States, Hsu describes pre-Communist China in terms of fourteen postulates. The raw material for identification of these postulates comes from personal experience, both literary and popular prose, social science studies, and studies of crime and other forms of societal breakdown.

Hsu's postulates of basic American values are the following:

1. An individual's most important concern is his self-interest: self-expression, self-improvement, self-gratification, and independence. This takes precedence over all group interests.

2. The privacy of the individual is the individual's inalienable right. Intrusion into it by others is permitted only by his invitation.

3. Because the government exists for the benefit of the individual and not vice versa, all forms of authority, including government, are suspect. But the government and its symbols should be respected. Patriotism is good.

4. An individual's success in life depends upon his acceptance among his peers.

5. An individual should believe in or acknowledge God and should belong to an organized church or other religious institution. Religion is good. Any religion is better than no religion.

6. Men and women are equal.

7. All human beings are equal.

8. Progress is good and inevitable. An individual must improve himself (minimize his efforts and maximize his returns); the government must be more efficient to tackle new problems; institutions such as churches must modernize to make themselves more attractive.

9. Being American is synonymous with being progressive, and America is the utmost symbol of progress.

Besides providing insight into U.S. culture patterns, Hsu's postulates illustrate a principle of observation that anthropologists slowly have come to accept. Namely, that no matter how well trained one is in objective social observation one can never leave the influence of one's own culture completely behind. How much of Hsu's selection of U.S. cultural items was provoked by the particular way the items contrasted to the Chinese norm that Hsu expected to find in the U.S.? For example, Hsu finds that privacy is very important to Americans (Postulate 2). Would a French observer, noticing office doors left open and residential windows facing the street like store windows, conclude that Americans do *not* value privacy? The more our concepts are challenged by people of different cultural frameworks, the more chance we have to understand them apart from the unconscious assumptions we make because of cultural conditioning. Hsu's postulates and corollaries for the United States are further elaborated in another book (Hsu, 1970).

One irreverent essay on the effect of TV on U.S. consumer choices, *Snap, Crackle, and Popular Taste: The Illusion of Free Choice in America* (Schrank, 1977), illustrates in example after example how Americans are conditioned to behave in predictable—if rather astonishing—ways. Much of this conditioning is accomplished by aiming a consumer product to fill a psychological need (e.g., the youthful "Pepsi generation" or the sensual "Oil of Olay"). Grocers keep their shelves full because researchers have discovered that partially empty supermarket shelves can cut sales by as much as 20 percent—shoppers have the feeling of being able to choose only from remnants or rejects of previous shoppers. Schrank reports that Campbell's recommends that grocers stack their soups more vertically than horizontally. Stacked-up soups sell 5 percent to 26 percent more!

As a spin-off product of a training course for U.S. government personnel stationed abroad, Alfred J. Kraemer (1973) identified 21 values of mainstream U.S. culture which influence behavior in Americans, behavior which is often rather "inscrutable" from the perspective of people from another culture. The identified values are:

1.   Individualism—the belief that each person is a distinct entity and ought to assert and achieve independence from others;

2.   Egalitarianism—the belief that all human beings are equal in their intrinsic worth;

3.   Action orientation;

4.   Perception of interpersonal encounters primarily in terms of their immediate utility, and downgrading of the social significance of such encounters;

5.   Universalism—the value attached to being guided in one's actions in a given situation primarily by an obligation to society (i.e., by general standards of conduct—laws, regulations, rules, established procedures, etc.);

6.   Definition of persons (including oneself) in terms of their work and achievements;

7. The belief that the collective wisdom of the group is superior to that of any individual;

8. The idea that the process of decision-making requires evaluation of the consequences of alternative courses of action, and selection of the one that, on balance, seems most advantageous;

9. The belief that competition is a good way of motivating people;

10. The idea that there is usually a best way of doing something, which should be determined and then followed;

11. The belief that knowledge gained through observation is superior to knowledge gained in other ways;

12. Unnecessary quantification—the tendency to quantify aspects of experience that require no quantification;

13. Placing a higher value on utilitarian aspects of experience than on aesthetic ones;

14. Problem orientation—the tendency to perceive "problems" in the world, and in one's existence in it, and to look for "solutions";

15. The belief that thoughts cannot directly influence events;

16. Reasoning in terms of probability;

17. Impatience—the tendency to be annoyed by the pace of activities, if it is slow by one's own standards;

18. The tendency to make comparative judgments;

19. The willingness to offer one's services for the benefit of "the common good";

20. The belief in the existence of a behavior pattern called "self-help";

21. The use of absurd suppositions to communicate ideas or to elicit ideas from other persons.

Kraemer selected the above as illustrative of the values commonly held by U.S. government personnel, values that provoke misunderstandings as the Americans interact with host nationals.

Cultural Themes

The leading advocate of an analytic approach to cross-cultural rules of behavior is Howard Lee Nostrand. Nostrand (1967) has sought the "main themes" of French culture in particular, and teachers of French will want to obtain his four-volume *Background Data for the Teaching of French.* As an aid in identifying main themes, he has adapted Murdock's *Outline of Cultural Materials* (1964; 1982) into a structured inventory which he calls the "Emergent Model" (Nostrand, 1978). *Emergent* because, while still an inventory, it is organized so as to favor its conversion to a model that will show the interaction of the parts. In it some thirty topics are grouped under six large headings.

Nostrand's Emergent Model

I. *The Culture.* Value system, habits of thought, assumptions about reality, verifiable knowledge, art forms, language, paralanguage, and kinesics

II. *The Society.* Organized under institutions: familial, religious, economic-occupational, political and judicial, educational, intellectual-aesthetic, recreational, the mass media, stratification and mobility, social properties *(Le Savoir-vivre)*, status by age group and sex, ethnic/religious and other minorities

III. *Conflicts.* Interpersonal and intergroup conflict, intrapersonal conflict

IV. *The Ecology and Technology.* Exploitation of physical resources, exploitation of plants and animals, demographic control, health care and accident prevention, settlement and territorial organization, travel and transportation

V.   *The Individual.* Integration at the organismic level, intrapersonal variability, interpersonal variation

VI.   *The Cross-Cultural Environment.* Attitudes toward other cultures and toward international and supranational organizations

Nostrand suggests that this organization of human behavior into six component relationships can best be taught by organizing the actions of a given lifestyle under its main theme—a theme being a value that is more fully defined in terms of its underlying assumptions and applications in human relations, personality structure, and interaction with the physical and subhuman environment. A theme, Nostrand explains, is "an emotionally charged concern, which motivates or strongly influences the culture bearer's conduct in a wide variety of situations" (Nostrand, 1974).

An essay by Nostrand (1973) elaborates on one manifestation of a main theme of French culture—intellectuality—within a historically evolutionary model. This manifestation is the French tendency "to seek understanding of any object of attention by looking for relationships within and surrounding the phenomenon one seeks to understand." Nostrand sees this characteristic in Frenchmen of various social classes. His essay superbly illustrates the thematic approach to understanding the behavior of a national group. For a discussion of Hispanic themes as illustrated in some Spanish plays of the 1960s, see Ruple (1965).

Applying Nostrand's Emergent Model to French and Hispanic cultures, Ladu et al. (1968) have developed a highly commendable booklet appropriately titled *Teaching for Cross-Cultural Understanding.* They describe and interpret many of the cultural aspects of French and Hispanic life under the four major categories of an earlier version of the Emergent Model.

An informative discussion of the thematic approach to cultural understanding, along with an analysis of the major themes of North India, was effected by the sociologist Opler (1968). Mathiot (1967) draws a distinction between those aspects of the cognitive system that are reflected in language and those reflected in nonlinguistic behavior. Consequently, she separates themes of the language from themes of the culture.

A detailed description of how songs may provide the basis for illustrating the main themes of a culture is presented by Damoiseau and Marc (1967). The authors pass over the two most frequent uses to which songs are subjected in language classes (as a literary text for linguistic analysis or as a vehicle for the study of the target culture as illustrated in song). Musical compositions, according to these authors, should be selected from writers who are involved with the daily life of the target society as seen through their thesis songs of social commentary. The main social problem treated in the song would be the first concern of the class. A linguistic analysis of the coexistence of both urban and more traditional vocabulary with a view to illustrating the direction of social change is suggested by the authors. They make the further suggestion that each thematic point could itself be carefully illustrated by a series of slides that show, for instance, the effect of urbanization on life in the target culture. Damoiseau and Marc also illustrate in considerable detail how lesson plans can be developed from this principle. The examples, as is the language of the article, are French.

In addition to the ability to detect the themes of values of a culture, Frances and Howard Nostrand (1970) identify eight other skills, or abilities, which the foreign language student can develop. The ability:

1. To describe a pattern or to ascribe it to a subculture of which it is typical
2. To recognize a pattern in an instance of behavior
3. To "explain" a pattern, whether in terms of its functional relation to other patterns or in casual terms
4. To predict a probable reaction to a given situation
5. To select an approved attitude
6. To evaluate the basis given for a descriptive generalization

7. To describe or demonstrate a method of analysis or of synthesis
8. To select descriptive knowledge significant for a common human purpose

Overview

The kaleidoscopic variety of human actions can be perceived as expressions of a few basic physical and psychological needs. The means for gratifying these needs are the behavioral options offered by one's culture. The behavioral options available in any one society are the product of its past history, its world view, its geographical setting, its technological advances, and its contemporary crises. These options are influenced by the central postulates and corollaries accepted by the society. Societal postulates are probably fiction in the same sense that rules of grammar are fiction. Both are attempts at explanation *after the fact*. It is daily usage in both language and nonlinguistic behavior that the "rules" have to accommodate. The interaction of these central assumptions, or their more detailed main themes, with the ecological and historical realities of a society is what gives each society its distinctive character. It is this mix which gives a society its flavor.

Nelson Brooks suggests that as teachers of intercultural communication our approach to a culture should "never lose sight of the individual" (Brooks, 1968). Our inquiry should focus on how societal values, institutions, language, and the land affect the thought and lifestyle of someone living in the culture we are studying. While an economist might study how a bumper crop of peanuts affects the price of soybeans, the intercultural communication student asks how price fluctuations in corn affect the way Juan Pedro García lives.

Motivation for behavior relating to food, for example, is obviously prompted by the most critical of basic physical needs. Yet the behavior associated with the collection, domestication, processing, marketing, and consumption of food can also be viewed as a response to psychological needs. Hsu's first postulate of United States culture is that an American's most important concern is self-interest. A corollary is that "an individual should seek the good life and pursue happiness." According to Hsu, in the United States the good life consists "primarily of the maximization of bodily comforts, food, and sexual enjoyment." Students of United States culture can be directed to explore the psychologically motivated behavior of Americans as they cultivate the good life through food. Students of other cultures can ascertain which foods have ritual significance (e.g., afternoon tea to express friendship; evening *crêpes suzette* and champagne to convey the hope of intimacy; raw termite queens to extend a red-carpet welcome). Both the nutritional and social aspects of food can become objects of student inquiry.

The broad perspective advocated in this chapter is that any behavior can be viewed as an outgrowth of physical and psychological needs. These needs are codified in the attitudes, adages, and advice on any given topic, such as food, that a student can elicit from natives and other sources of information about the target culture.

The perspective advanced by this chapter has two implications for teachers. First, it is intellectually satisfying to approach an understanding of complex phenomena (human actions) by process of deduction from a few major postulates or themes. This method affords the student at the onset of his inquiry the key (i.e., the explanatory postulate) to understanding any frequently recurring human action.

If, however, one approaches culture inductively, where the given is a perplexing action rather than an explanatory assumption, it is certainly helpful to have the vision that while the behavior of other people may look ridiculous, it is hardly absurd. Behavior occurs in largely patterned modes which can be characterized by a few basic assumptions. Whether these assumptions *cause* the behavior we see or whether they are accommodating rationalizations of behavior provoked by less lofty exigencies is probably a dilemma. The best likelihood is that they are interactive. That is, assumptions and actions influence each other. As Nostrand (1974) says, "There is no need for agreement on ultimate beliefs, but rather for agreement on working principles and modes of action" (p. 271).

Beyond this chapter, the intellectual style receiving most attention will be the inquiry, or inductive, approach. Attention will be focused on target behavior that can be empirically substantiated or on student skills that can be mastered in our classrooms. Nostrand (1974), a strong proponent of the thematic approach, says this about inductive techniques: "The Socratic technique has two great advantages over any other: that the learner values his hard-won knowledge and that meanwhile he gains experience in the skills of observation, creative imagination, and inferential reasoning."

Suggested Activities

1. List 10 universal physical and psychological needs (see Maslow, 1954).

2. List key questions you would ask to elicit how people of your target culture satisfy the need for food and shelter, for love and affection, for pride in oneself?

3. List five situations in which people of the target culture are expected to act in a conventional way.

4. How has culture influenced the basic need for food in your target culture? What are the range of options?

5. Choose one of Hsu's postulates and redefine or rework it to be appropriate for your culture area.

6. Identify the American values that both Hsu and Kraemer identify, and those where there appears to be a difference of interpretation.

3

Seven Goals of Cultural Instruction

Whenever a teacher wants to take students to a French res-
taurant or have them perform the Mexican Hat Dance or
learn the names of the principal rivers and harbors of
Germany, the teacher must know the cultural purpose of
these activities. This chapter provides a framework to facili-
tate the selection of cultural data that will increase student
skill in intercultural communication.

Cultural instruction must be purposeful if it is to lead anywhere.
The method of organization presented in this chapter makes
apparent the *reason* for doing any given cultural activity. While
courses should maintain enough flexibility to house the occasional
whimsy of aimless activities, aimlessness must not characterize
more than a minuscule proportion of the time spent on culture.
There should be a sound reason behind each and every cultural
activity.

Seven different goals of cultural instruction are described
here. To be purposeful, classroom activities should relate in a reasonable way to one of these goals. None of them justifies the learning of facts for their own sake.

The First Task: Identifying Goals

The Nostrands (1970) identify culturally relevant skills that can be developed in the classroom, and this is the logical place to begin identifying the basic cultural purposes, or goals, upon which teachers can base their instruction.

In writing cultural goals one generally begins with some large, innocuous-sounding statement replete with "understandings" and "appreciations"—a supergoal! Here is my supergoal:

All students will develop the cultural understandings, attitudes and performance skills needed to function appropriately within a society of the target language and to communicate with the culture bearer.

Supergoals must be delineated to be useful. The following seven goals are sufficiently detailed to enable a teacher to focus on the *reason* for using most cultural illustrations. Although they are not measurable in their present form, they are nonetheless stated in terms of student achievement rather than in terms of teacher process. These goals are a modification of the Nostrands' "kinds of understanding to be tested." I am proposing that they be employed as the basic goal-oriented frame for courses in intercultural communication. They can, of course, be reworded or otherwise modified or expanded to tailor them to the needs of any particular classroom.

Cultural Goal I:
The Sense, or Functionality, of Culturally Conditioned Behavior

The student should demonstrate an understanding that people act the way they do because they are using options the society allows for satisfying basic physical and psychological needs.

Today's newspaper featured a front-page photo of the State Department's leading international diplomat holding hands with an Arab diplomat of the same sex. Our international expert was using, appropriately, an Arab gesture to express friendship with an Arab. The intent of Goal I is to see the logic behind any example of cross-cultural behavior—however bizarre or perplexing the behavior initially may appear to ethnocentric eyes.

When an individual attempts to satisfy a basic need s/he usually has to employ many interacting cultural patterns that form a relatively cohesive structure. Some of these patterns are linguistic; others are not. For example, maintaining the respect of male peers in upper-class Guatemala City might involve skill in telling jokes and discussing literature, knowledge of English and of wines and liqueurs, having a resort home in which to entertain guests away from the city, and dressing conservatively.

There are excellent overviews which present many aspects of nonverbal behavior: Birdwhistell (1970), Morris (1977), Weitz (1979). Birdwhistell's work is the classic in the field. Morris' oversized book (8½" x 11") is replete with eye-catching photographs and illustrations and is written for the adult layperson. It treats 71 different manifestations of nonverbal behavior. One of its strengths is that Morris, an anthropologist, makes many cross-cultural comparisons. Weitz edits 26 chapters prepared by experts in the field. She divides the anthology into five sections: facial expression and visual interaction, body movement and gesture, paralanguage, proximity behaviors, and multichannel communication. A brief overview of kinesics prepared by a leading foreign language educator was prepared by Morain (1978). Two illustrated books deal with the gestures of Spain (Green, 1968) and Latin America (Saitz and Cervenka, 1972), respectively.

After the student has identified a basic need and translated it into the form of the target culture, questions can be directed toward perceiving the relationship among different patterns.

Cultural Goal II: Interaction of Language and Social Variables

The student should demonstrate an understanding that such social variables as age, sex, social class, and place of residence affect the way people speak and behave.

The admonition that "they do things differently there" does not seem to prepare us adequately for interaction with all segments of another culture. Nor is goodwill enough. Last year an adventuresome pilot, wanting to take "the trip of a lifetime," advertised in a newspaper for a "venturesome, intrepid, athletic, unencumbered, Spanish-speaking lady" to accompany him on a two-year country-by-country tour of Latin America in his brand new red-and-white Maule M-5 aircraft. Bill Loveless and his intrepid companion, Ms. Susan Walls, quit their jobs, sublet their homes, and sold everything they owned. To the envy of their friends, the two sailed out into last October's sunset. A little later, Ms. Walls, who had never been out of the U.S. before, met the local fauna at a run-down motel in Baja California. She was home in Seattle the next day. "I've never seen poverty like that," she was quoted as saying. "I'm not rich, but I'm accustomed to a low-middle-class environment and this just blew me away."

This leads us intrepidly to another fact of life: all societies are stratified, and each societal segment exercises some behavioral options that are not available, for better or worse, to other strata in the same country. When Ms. Walls made the startling discovery that boondock accommodations lack many of the amenities of the hotels she was used to, she was responding to two important determinants of behavior: social class and place of residence.

Since the behavioral options available in any given society for the satisfaction of needs are not equally available to everyone in that society, the way people speak and behave is affected by role stratification variables such as age, sex, social class, place of residence, and religion. This is always so, and this fact provides us with a key question to ask of behavior: *What stratum of society is involved in performing the observed behavior?*

No two people speak the same language. Voiceprints are as personal as fingerprints. Individual differences are an important part of the personality a person projects, as any amateur mimic knows. Of much greater interest to a student of the foreign culture, however, are the systematic variations in the speech of large numbers of people which are caused by differences in age, sex, social class, and place of residence. An eight year old talks differently from an 80 year old. The speech regarded as appropriate for women would raise eyebrows if spoken in a men's locker room, and acceptable male locker-room speech would not go unnoticed at an afternoon tea of the ladies' auxiliary. The speech of a dock worker is not often confused with that of a college professor, nor is the drawl of a Southerner (of any country) mistaken for that of a Northerner.

Students should learn to expect dialect differences. This expectation in itself goes a long way toward psychologically equipping a student to cope with the inevitable range of speech s/he will encounter outside of the classroom. This is not to say that we should teach students to speak different dialects. Exposing language learners to a wide variety of speech forms is a realistic way of having students learn the target allophones. Allophonic differences are usually ignored in language classes because, by definition, they do not change the meaning of a word. But this is not completely true.

First, recognizing whether a sound is an allophonic variation of a phoneme requires more than knowledge of the phonemic speech range of some "standard" dialect. To be able to "ignore" allophonic variations one has to learn what is allophonic and what is phonemic.

Second, allophonic variations often convey considerable social information, such as the social class and place of residence of the speaker. *Pygmalion*, or *My Fair Lady*, presents a clear dramatization of this linguistic fact. A very rich source for these "social markers" has been prepared by Scherer and Giles (1979). Drawing its examples from a wide range of languages, this anthology discusses speech markers of situations, age, sex, personality, social class, ethnicity, and social interaction.

Tape recordings provide a practical medium to bring these dialect differences to the students' attention. Students can be directed to identify which country the speaker comes from or whether the speaker is from an urban or rural area or whether the speaker is working class or upper class. It is best to use only the most obvious speech differences in these exercises.

In some situations such other variables as religion, occupation, political persuasion, time, or circumstance strongly affect behavior. These variables should also be considered within the scope of this goal.

Cultural Goal III: Conventional Behavior in Common Situations

The student should indicate an understanding of the role convention plays in shaping behavior by demonstrating how people act in common mundane and crisis situations in the target culture.

Custom resolves the awkwardness of responding spontaneously to the same situation over and over again by conventionalizing the response. When you meet someone new, in English you say "How do you do" or, in some settings, simply "Hi." Some cultures provide conventionalized linguistic responses where others do not. For example, the linguistic dilemma of what to write to an acquaintance upon the death of his mother is simplified in Spanish by the convention *"mi más sentido pésame,"* whereas the English, of my dialect at least, does not provide a conventionalized linguistic response. In the Spanish world *"mi más sentido pésame"* affords both parties satisfaction in a difficult encounter; in the English world the same function is performed by mailing commercial sympathy cards to the bereaved.

All conventional responses share several characteristics: (1) They are cued by common social situations; (2) Both verbal and kinesic responses are limited to a prescribed few; (3) While utterance of the expected response is mildly rewarding to the involved persons, absence of an expected response produces considerable anxiety. This is true of conventional responses to a mundane occurrence, such as wishing someone a happy birthday, as well as of responses to a crisis situation, such as consoling someone who has suffered a divorce or serious illness. The sociological foundation for conventional behavior is elaborated by Goffman (1971).

Elementary language texts always contain a number of low-key conventional responses, such as "good morning" or "thank you," which students learn to replicate when given the proper sociolinguistic setting. To exploit further the cultural aspect of conventional responses the teacher can manipulate social variables such as age, sex, social class, and country of origin.

Cultural Goal IV: Cultural Connotations of Words and Phrases

The student should indicate an awareness that culturally conditioned images are associated with even the most common target words and phrases.

To a desert Arab the thought of a beautiful woman might conjure up sensuous images of a 250-pound lovely, while to an American lexically equivalent words in English might connote a slim but disproportionately big-busted lass. One Italian neighbor of mine complains that in Italy men did not pay much attention to her because she was too skinny at 110 pounds, while in the United States the same fate has befallen her now that her weight has risen to 170 pounds. If only she could be "fat" in Italy and "skinny" in the United States, she would be "beautiful" everywhere. The cultural connotations of words can make the difference between an active social life and staying home.

How can an understanding of the relation between culture and semantics be developed? One way is for students to experience directly the cultural connotations of common words such as man, house, standing, walking, by observing these objects and activities as they occur in the target culture. This experience need not be limited to students studying abroad. The graphics of magazines, newspapers, and movies are well suited to convey these objects and activities in the target culture.

A simple classroom activity to assist students gain a perspective of cultural connotations begins by having them select a word that intrigues them. This word can come from any number of sources: a list provided by the teacher of the 100 most common words in the language or a word appearing in the glossary of the textbook or in a foreign newspaper. The task of the student is to compile authentic visual examples of his or her chosen word from newspaper and magazine clippings or from his/her own photography. One student of mine in a graduate course at the University of Hawaii illustrated through a collage of 30 magazine photos of *mujeres* (women) how social class, age, and Indian and Negro backgrounds affected the appearance of women in Latin America.

One of the many requisites to "thinking like a native," besides fluency in the target language, is the conditioned ability to visualize culturally appropriate images which language evokes. Whether it is the fat Arab coquette or the pleasantly cool mud home of the Masai, communion with a native of another language demands sharing meanings that go beyond listless dictionary definitions.

Cultural Goal V: Evaluating Statements about a Society

The student should demonstrate the ability to evaluate the relative strength of a generality concerning the target culture in terms of the amount of evidence substantiating the statement.

For the rest of his life the student will be hearing things about other cultures. He must learn to differentiate judgments that serve the ethnocentric bias of a national politic from judgments that have an adequate empirical base. There are many prerequisite skills for sorting through the pronouncements of our species. Among these are skill in balancing the evidence with the generality, in separating speculation from objective observation, and in discerning vested interest.

This goal is further elaborated in two subsequent chapters, "Asking the Right Questions" (Chapter 8) and "Testing Culture" (Chapter 9).

Cultural Goal VI: Researching Another Culture

The student should show that s/he has developed the skills needed to locate and organize information about the target culture from the library, the mass media, people, and personal observation.

Of utmost import are the classroom skills that stay with a student during all the years after he leaves our tutelage. Many students forget all the facts and lose their hard-earned linguistic fluency, but none loses the need for continuing his education. Despite historic precedents replete with isolationism and anti-intellectualism, we have been made painfully aware that even distant small countries importantly influence our daily options. Understanding other cultures is frequently a matter of life or death. In the best of times, knowledge of another culture is tantamount to moving out of a dark dank corner of the cave into more illumination.

The average college graduate has been the recipient of an education costing more than $25,000. Most of the content of this education soon becomes obsolete. This is not a criticism of the education, it is a tribute to our commitment to pushing back the frontiers of knowledge. Still, education is difficult to justify on the basis of the "facts" learned. Alfred North Whitehead in *The Aims of Education* (1928) utterly rejects this notion. The learning of facts, he writes, has not justified education since the establishment of libraries and the availability of paperbacks. If the actual content of education has little currency, what *is* of inestimable value is learning how to learn. Practically all learning of any value is learned outside of a formal classroom. Learning, however, can be greatly enhanced by an educational system that develops skill in *pursuing* knowledge.

Developing research skills is easily accomplished. There are only so many founts of knowledge amenable to rational inquiry—books, newspapers, magazines, other printed materials, films, recordings, pictures, other people, personal experience, and our own predilection for introspection. In its simplest form, an elementary school child can be taught to ask of any statement of "fact" about a foreign culture: "Who says so?"

Bibliographic and interview techniques are well developed and lend themselves to practice within a school setting. For help with the former, consult any librarian; for help with the latter, see Raymond L. Gorden (1980).

A stickier matter is the *organization* of information culled through standard retrieval techniques. Each academic discipline has many theoretical constructs that compete for attention. Some hold promise in getting an answer to certain questions, others in answering other questions. For the purposes of the student the simple framework offered by the seven goals described in this chapter and by the rationale of Chapter 2 provides enough organization to begin earnest cultural inquiry.

Cultural Goal VII: Attitudes toward Other Cultures

The student should demonstrate intellectual curiosity about the target culture and empathy toward its people.

Teachers tend to ascribe all the problems involved in the teaching of cultural understanding to attitudinal variables. "We must change the students' attitudes," they tell us. Much of what we do in the name of cultural understanding is seen as contributing to this affective change. To avoid the obvious danger of converting Goal VII into yet another impotent supergoal its scope must be defined somewhat narrowly. Only two components of attitude—curiosity and empathy—are included in the present statement of this goal. Both can be faked.

Fuzzy activities are sometimes launched to change attitude. I am uncertain of the effect a cross-cultural nude encounter session might have on a student's willingness to study social stratification in the target culture, for example. My own personal conviction, based on intuition and certain studies (Carroll, 1967; Gezi, 1965; Gardner and Taylor, 1968; Seelye and Brewer, 1970), leads me to believe that the single most influential activity a student can engage in to affect his attitude is to spend some time in the target country.

Another rational view is that positive and pleasurable achievement in the other six goals may provide motivation for attitudinal change.

Activities should be planned that place the student in the position of having to interact with the target culture bearer; some record can be kept of the nature and extent of this interaction, and academic credit may be given this behavior, but no attempt to assign grades to student attitudes should be made.

Goal-Relating "Trivial" Topics

"How do I work my favorite unit on food into the framework of these seven goals?" panic-stricken teachers ask. Indeed, how do *any* of the activities generally carried out in the name of culture fit into the goals described by this chapter? The answer lies in the way teachers relate their favorite units to a cultural goal. Table 3.1 shows how several common, often purposeless, activities can be made goal-related (see p. 59).

Suggested Activities

1. Choose an ordinary everyday occurrence within the target society which is rare in ours, and show how it helps satisfy a basic need. What other options does that society provide to enable its people to satisfy the same need?

2. Choose a word or phrase from another language and show how age, sex, social class, and place of residence affect its usage.

3. Choose a common situation with conventional behavioral patterns and discuss how social variables affect responses to it.

4. Do the project suggested on page 54.

5. Choose a trivial topic and relate it to each of the seven goals (as suggested by the chart at the end of the chapter).

Table 3.1. Goal Relating "Trivial" Topics

	TOPIC	
	Food	Cities, Rivers, Harbors
Goal I	What behavior patterns are associated indirectly with the production or consumption of food in the target culture (e.g., truck transportation, manufacture of utensils)?	What would one have to get done that would require a trip to Xique-Xique? How would one go about getting from X city to Y city?
Goal II	How does what target people eat depend on the country, or part of the country, in which they live? Do teenagers eat anything the rest of the population doesn't? How would a typical middle-class dinner differ from a working-class dinner?	What locales are agricultural? Industrial? Especially wealthy? Impoverished? How is the mode of intercity travel in X city affected by age and social class?
Goal III	What etiquette is usually observed at different meals? What are the common phrases one uses at mealtime or at the market?	To what extent does the way one greets someone in X city differ from the "textbook standard"? Do the rituals accompanying marriage and death differ from area A to area B?
Goal IV	What do different foods look like in the target culture? Do any of the foods figure in common jokes? What kind of meals does one associate with exceptionally opulent eating? With impoverished eating? With family meals? With snacks?	Do target people consider the people of X city to possess any special attributes? What images does a native think of when Y city is mentioned?
Goal V	Is any given statement (provided by the teacher) about food in the target culture sympathetic or ethnocentric? On how much evidence does it seem to be based? Are variables such as circumstance and social class taken into consideration?	What seems to be the most significant statement made from a text about X city/harbor/river? Can the statement be substantiated objectively?
Goal VI	How aptly can a student locate information concerning food in the target culture? To what extent are both print and human resources utilized? How does the student relate his report to significant issues?	Same questions as those opposite in the left-hand column, substituting the city/river/harbor for food.
Goal VII	How much interest does the student show in trying out new target foods? Does he develop a taste for something new?	What effort had the student exerted to make contact with someone from X? Has the student visited or does he plan to visit X?

4

After We Do Our Thing,
What Can the Student Do?

*To know whether students are moving toward achievement
of the seven cultural goals described in Chapter 3, measurable end-of-course objectives must be defined with precision.
This chapter illustrates the process of goal refinement by giving sample student performance objectives organized under
each of the seven cultural goals.*

Writing End-of-Course Objectives

Once the teacher has a purposeful rationale for introducing
various facets of culture into his or her classroom and after s/he
decides how many different cultural purposes or goals s/he will
include in the course, the next task is to identify a limited number
of specific competencies that encapsulate the intent of each of the
selected purposes. These competencies will be used as end-of-
course indicators of student achievement.

The first time around, end-of-course objectives should be
limited to two or three for each cultural purpose. Ask what one or
two things you would want a student to be able to do to show s/he

had developed the amount of skill or understanding you were looking for in each purpose. The instructional techniques available to help a teacher reach these purposes must be modified to suit the interests and maturity of his/her students (see Chapter 5). Because maturity levels generally correspond to the traditional designations of primary school, middle school, high school, college, and graduate school, some sort of cooperative division of labor with a view to minimizing costly duplication of effort and to maximizing an intelligent articulation from course level to course level is obviously desirable.

Previous Attempts to Define Cultural Competencies

Divisions can be made along several lines, depending upon one's understanding of the learning process. If Jerome Bruner's theory that any concept can be taught in an academically honest way at any age level is accepted, the methodological task becomes one of identifying examples and exercises to illustrate the concept at a level readily understandable by a given age group. If, on the other hand, one believes that effective teaching of a concept depends on assessing its difficulty and then presenting it to an age group that has reached the requisite level of maturity to comprehend it, the problem becomes one of arranging cultural concepts into a hierarchy of relative complexity. Certainly how a concept is presented to a student will depend on his maturity and educational background.

An eclectic scheme that suggests which cultural items might be presented at various sequential levels was developed by a 1968 committee of the Pacific Northwest Conference on Foreign Language Teaching (Nostrand, 1968). The committee, chaired by Nostrand, based its efforts on the previous work of Ladu (1967). An examination of some of the strengths and weaknesses of this report can provide insight into the ambitious nature of the committee's undertaking.

The committee's report calls for both behavioral and verbal responses to cultural stimuli at the first level. The student is expected at Level I (a level does not necessarily equal a year) to demonstrate physically how to behave in a number of situations including greetings, introductions, leave-taking, eating, and conduct "toward persons of one's own and of higher social status." S/he must also be able to describe in English two or more common leisure-time activities of adolescents in the foreign society and learn a poem and some songs.

Some minor adaptations to this proposal for Level I could easily be made to accommodate integration of preadolescent programs into the outline. Of course students who delay study of a foreign language until secondary school miss the enriching substance of childhood riddles, games, songs, and rhymes that contribute to the way the child of the target culture views his or her world. Students beginning language study at more advanced ages miss "adolescent culture" as well. Much of "adult culture" awaits the persevering curiosity of the developing student, not because a secondary student lacks the intellectual capacity for understanding the preoccupations of the middle-aged and older person, but because s/he is justifiably more interested in his/her own concerns.

The most detailed elaboration of the proposed standards for cultural levels is developed in the committee's outline for Level II. Two sets of standards are presented: a "minimal standard" and a "desirable standard." Because some schools will be able to teach more than others, no matter how uniformly drawn the definitions of levels, ambitious standards should be set for superior programs in addition to minimal standards for any accredited program. Somewhat disappointingly, however, neither minimal nor desirable activities at Level II require the student to do anything on a nonverbal level. The student is asked to "state orally" insights into literature, the family, education, cultural themes, and so forth. Although this verbal activity is to be accomplished in the target language, the proposed standards do not show enough awareness of the many language-connected ways in which speech reflects the culture, such as the cultural connotations necessary to understanding the spoken word, dialect variations, and ability to follow disconnected discourse. Nor do the proposals imaginatively explore the realm of nonverbal cultural skills. See Green (1971) for a discussion of this aspect.

The standards display some bias in expecting children to understand a relatively small segment of most countries, "a middle-class person in the foreign society." Many American children might prefer to identify with another class segment of the target culture. (An age bias also found in the outline seems pedagogically more justifiable.) Another class bias is evident in the statement that one should learn how to conduct oneself "toward persons of one's own and of higher social status." In a later article Nostrand (1974) recommends broadening a student's sympathies to include other social classes, ages, religious and ethnic groups.

While the most detailed sections of both Levels II and III use literature to illustrate the main cultural themes, at Level III the social structure belatedly receives more direct attention beyond the previous emphasis on the family and educational system. A discussion of how literature can be effectively used to illustrate cultural aspects of a society was published earlier by Nostrand (1963b). Level IV outlines more balanced expectations, but it is very briefly developed. See Steiner (1971) for a description of French Levels I to IV.

The Pacific Northwest Conference committee report (Nostrand, 1968) was done fifteen years ago. The considered direction the report took was promising, and one would have expected the intervening years to have seen further advances in defining end-of-year student behaviorals relating to cultural understanding by levels. Yet such is not the case. State departments of education have attempted to define cultural levels, but they have not produced meritorious work. There are several reasons for this.

The dynamics of these subsequent attempts to define levels generally have been characterized by selection of participants on the basis of language rather than cultural competence and by an action agenda that relegates discussion of culture to the end of an exhausting conference. Nostrand (ACTFL, 1982, p. 6) rectified this situation with new cultural competencies.

An attempt by the Alameda County School Department to describe "cultural concepts" for Level I development in Spanish (1969) and French (1971) deserves mention here. Some forty concepts for each language are textually annotated and cross-referenced to relevant units in three popular textbooks. While these booklets are excellent and I recommend them to French and Spanish teachers, they do not attempt to define end-of-course competencies; rather, they describe the content of many day-to-day learning activities.

Social studies teachers have an easier go of it. Good basal texts have clearly stated goals and objectives which can be illustrated by examples from virtually any culture area. Many of the activities suggested by this book can fit comfortably within a given text's organization. Other goals that are advanced here can be added to the scope of the text.

Goal-Oriented End-of-Course Peformance Objectives

Teachers are paid to change behavior. There would be little point in attending school if people who were "schooled" did not behave differently from those who were not. The assumption most commonly made, but not by any means uncontested, is that behavior changed by school is changed for the better. That is, school is seen as a catalyst for positive behavior that will benefit both the individual and society. The worth of the school can and should be measured by the nature of the lifestyle it inspires. A teacher or a taxpayer can legitimately ask at any point in the long obligatory sequence of education just what the student can do now that he could not do before he interacted with the teacher.

The current emphasis on measurable units of student accomplishment, usually called student performance or behavioral objectives, is based on two different kinds of logic. First, to change behavior effectively the teacher (the change agent) must be able to recognize the desired behavior when he sees it and have a plan for getting students to perform in the desired way. In other words, if you don't know where you're going it is hard to get there—or know you're there when you are! Second, the operation of our school system is entirely dependent on what the poet Allen Ginsberg has called "Moloch"—money. To help convince taxpayers, most of whom have been through your school systems, that students do learn something positive there, learning must be stated in a documentable fashion.

A performance objective should provide answers to four questions: (1) Why teach a given aspect of the culture? This is the purpose, or goal. (2) What should the student be able to do or say when he's learned the specific aspect? This is the terminal behavior that is the desired outcome of the learning. (3) What are the circumstances under which the student will be expected to do or say what he has learned? This clarifies the conditions or constraints associated with observance of the student's performance. (4) How well does the student have to perform under the stated conditions? This is the criterion of acceptable performace.

Simple, vague, ambiguous statements of intent gradually develop into full-fledged performance objectives. Good objectives are written in an ongoing process, continually stating the objectives with greater detail and precision. A performance objective is "strong" when five different teachers can agree that it has been accomplished by a student. It is "mature" when the performance objective is accepted by both students and teachers as a reasonable reflection of its avowed purpose.

To illustrate the kind of end-of-course performances I am describing, I list a number of them and organize them under appropriate goals. The most common activities for teaching culture are omitted in favor of activities that are not widely used.

In Chapter 3, I specifically recommend seven cultural purposes, or goals, as the basic ingredient for organizing classroom instruction. The following seven end-of-course performance objectives are meant to *illustrate* the process of goal refinement. They are not especially recommended in their present state of specificity to the teacher. For these end-of-course objectives to be relevant to any specific classroom, the age, interests, and fluency of the students and the nature of the course must be taken into account.

Goal I:
The Sense, or Functionality, of Culturally Conditioned Behavior

The student should demonstrate an understanding that people generally act the way they do because they are using options society allows for satisfying basic physical and psychological needs.

A common international social phenomenon is that rural people, especially in lesser developed countries, are leaving their towns to seek their fortunes in the city. The performance objective that follows invites students to look at one aspect of the lives of most rural people—religious celebration—and to relate it to need gratification. (This particular objective was written to tempt some students into reading an exceptionally well-presented ethnography—*San Pedro, Colombia: Small Town in a Developing Society* [Richardson, 1970].)

Performance objective 1: Religion in San Pedro

To demonstrate how religious ritual provides a model for rural Latin Americans that helps them face the exigencies of everyday life, engage in one of the following four activities (A, B, C, D).

A. TERMINAL BEHAVIOR: Present an oral or written report on "Why Holy Friday is considered by the people of San Pedro to be more important than Resurrection Sunday."

CONDITIONS: Oral reports should be about five minutes in duration and can be delivered in either English or Spanish. Written reports should be about 500 words, typed double-spaced, in either English or the target language. Both reports are to be presented to the whole class; written reports are to be duplicated and distributed.

CRITERION: The reports should make clear to most of the class the way suffering, resignation, and religious processions are related to everyday life. Mistakes in grammar, pronunciation, or spelling will not count against the student. To determine whether most of the class understood the relationships, a five-item, multiple-choice, teacher-made quiz will be given; 70 percent of the class are expected to score at least four correct answers.

B. TERMINAL BEHAVIOR: Act out or portray via drawings or clay figures of your own making, or via collages assembled from magazine or newspaper clippings, how religious processions might look in rural Latin America.

CONDITIONS: The presentation can be done in pantomime, in English, or in the target language, and can last anywhere from five to 20 minutes. In the case of artistic presentations, the portrayal will be exhibited in the classroom.

CRITERION: Same as in A.

C. TERMINAL BEHAVIOR: Be a member of a panel that discusses what changes might occur in other areas of life in rural Latin America if peoples' attitude toward religion were to fall into apathy.

CONDITIONS: The panel may use either the target language or English; discussion should last at least 15 minutes. Membership on the panel is limited to five persons. The presentation will take place at a meeting of the language club.

CRITERION: The panel should present the pros and cons of "fatalists" and "realists" as alternate descriptors of the people of San Pedro, and examine nonreligious manifestations of these philosophies. The panel should do this well enough so that 80 percent of the listeners can answer three out of four questions put to them by the teacher. Each member of the panel should speak a minimum of three minutes.

D. TERMINAL BEHAVIOR: Take a quiz that tests how suffering, resignation, and religious processions are related to everyday life in San Pedro.

CONDITIONS: Twenty minutes will be provided for the exam to be administered during class time.

CRITERION: Achieve a score of 15 or better on a 20-point multiple-choice quiz.

Goal II. Interaction of Language and Social Variables

The student should demonstrate an understanding that social variables such as age, sex, social class, and place of residence affect the way people speak and behave.

Performance objective 2: Hispanic dialects

To demonstrate some ways in which language and other behavior are affected by social variables, carry out two of the following five activities.

A. TERMINAL BEHAVIOR: Identify the places of origin of speakers from four different regions of Hispanic culture (Spain, Caribbean, Mexico, Argentina).

CONDITIONS: A one- to two-minute taped speech sample of five different speakers will be played twice during class time.

CRITERION: Three of the five speakers must be correctly indentified.

B. TERMINAL BEHAVIOR: Prepare a two- to four-minute oral presentation in Spanish, based on one written source and on interviews with at least two native speakers, about five words or expressions that are associated with one sex or age group.

CONDITIONS: For classroom presentation with at least two weeks advance notice.

CRITERION: Seventy percent of the class must be able to follow exposition clearly.

C. TERMINAL BEHAVIOR: Associate five sample dialogues, which will be given you in English and in writing, with the following social levels: urban working class, urban middle class, urban upper class, rural common people.

CONDITIONS: Each dialogue will be one page in length. Determination will be made within a 20-minute period during class time.

CRITERION: Four of the five dialogues must be correctly identified.

D. TERMINAL BEHAVIOR: Indicate on a blank map of the target culture the geographic range and variant linguistic forms of one word or expression of the student's choosing.

CONDITIONS: The student will have six weeks to prepare this map which will be turned in to the teacher.

CRITERION: The map must show how the linguistic form is employed in at least 25 different locations within Hispanic culture.

E. TERMINAL BEHAVIOR: Identify one or more qualities or beliefs (e.g., carrots for better vision, aphrodisiac effect of powdered ram's horn) associated with 10 different foods or drinks in one specific subculture of the target society (e.g., one's age, sex, social class, or regional group). Compare your findings to the responses from another subculture.

CONDITIONS: Four weeks will be allowed for completion of this task. The teacher will write the information in the target language and type it on a stencil to be distributed to each class member.

CRITERION: Each quality or belief must be conveyed in the target language as a direct quote from a specific source. The sources must be fully identified. The information should clearly contrast the data from the two compared subcultures.

Goal III. Conventional Behavior in Common Situations

The student should indicate understanding of the role convention plays in shaping behavior by demonstrating how people in the target culture act in common mundane and crisis situations.

Performance objective 3: The respectful Russian

To demonstrate how Russians show respect and affection through the conventional ways they address each other, complete two of the following three series of activities.[1]

A.   TERMINAL BEHAVIOR: The student will use the appropriate form of address, *Tbl* or *Bbl*, in the following social situations:

Two young people who are strangers converse.

Two friends converse.

A young person converses with an older person.

An older person converses with a young person.

Two adults who are strangers converse.

CONDITIONS: During a class period the teacher will assign to the students the roles of friend, stranger, or older person. The student will give three oral responses in simple phrases such as "How are you?" This conversation should take two to three minutes, with each participant responding to the other participant or participants.

CRITERION: The student has to choose the correct form, either *Tbl* or *Bbl*, in each of his three responses. Pronunciation has to be good enough so the teacher can identify which form the student used.

B.   TERMINAL BEHAVIOR: The student will use the appropriate form of address —Russian first names and surnames—in the following social situations:

Two Russian teenage friends address each other.

A young Russian addresses an older Russian.

An older Russian addresses a young person (1) when the young person is of high social status; (2) when the young person is of no special prestige.

Adult members of the same extended family address each other (1) when two close members of the family are alone; (2) when two close members of the family are in the company of other members of the family.

CONDITIONS: The teacher will assign to each student in class a complete complement of Russian names, such as Ivan Ivanovich Vania Dolgich, and will assign him one of the following roles: young person of high social status or of no special prestige, adult, relative. The student will then be assigned to one of the above six social situations. The student will ask the other participants three simple questions such as "Dostoyevsky, are you hungry?" The conversation should not take more than two or three minutes, with each participant responding at least once to the other participant(s).

CRITERION: The student must use the appropriate form of a person's name in each of his three responses.

C.   TERMINAL BEHAVIOR: Demonstrate the appropriate oral and kinesic response in five of the following six situations:

Someone compliments your new dress or suit.

You bump into someone.

Someone bumps into you and apologizes.

You congratulate an individual on the occasion of his birthday.

You are passing through the reception line at a friend's wedding and congratulate her.

You are introduced to someone of your own age and to a schoolteacher.

CONDITIONS: These activities will be performed in class in Russian, with the teacher or another student playing the role of the other person. Each activity should take less than one minute to complete.

CRITERION: At least one Russian gesture should accompany each activity. The oral response should be said well enough to be easily understood by a native and should be without grammatical error. The response must be situationally appropriate in each instance.

Goal IV. Cultural Connotations of Words and Phrases

The student should indicate an awareness that culturally conditioned images are associated with even the most common target words and phrases.

Performance objective 4: Nuances of a French word

To demonstrate an understanding that what one associates with an object or concept is to a considerable extent culturally determined, carry out the following two activities.

A.   TERMINAL BEHAVIOR: Identify photos of French cultures where the clues are clothing styles, physical types of people, and topology.

CONDITIONS: The teacher will display in the classroom 50 numbered photos from diverse sources; 25 portray authentically French scenes with people. The display will be shown for one week, after which the student will hand in to the teacher a list of the photo numbers that correspond to French culture anywhere in the world.

CRITERION: The student must score at least 18 correct responses.

B. TERMINAL BEHAVIOR: Identify the most likely images associated with five nouns and five verbs selected by the teacher from a first-semester vocabulary list.

CONDITIONS: The list will be given two days in advance of the required identification. The identification will take place during 30 minutes in class. During the examination the teacher will present 25 pictures or characterizations (walking, sitting, pantomime "talking") from which the student chooses those that relate to French culture.

CRITERION: The student must make correct identifications for at least seven of the 10 words.

Goal V. Evaluating Statements about a Culture

The student should demonstrate the ability to make, evaluate, and refine the generalities concerning the target culture.

Performance objective 5: German generalities

To show that you do not indiscriminately accept as factual everything you hear about German culture, carry out the following activity.

A. TERMINAL BEHAVIOR: Evaluate 10 generalities about German culture which will be given you in English and in writing in terms of *(a)* probably true, *(b)* probably false, *(c)* I don't know whether it is true or false. For the probably false generalities, state briefly evidence that would tend to contradict them. For those generalities in the "don't know" category, state briefly what additional information you would need to reach a decision. (You will be awarded the same number of points for correctly identifying the true and false statements as for those statements for which you indicate plausible additional information that is needed.)

CONDITIONS: The 10 generalities will be presented at examination time. Forty-five minutes will be given to respond.

CRITERION: A score of 80 percent or better must be earned.

Goal VI. Researching Another Culture

The student should show that s/he has developed the skills needed to locate and organize information about the target culture from the library, the mass media, people, and personal observation.

Performance objective 6: The research report

To indicate that you have developed an organizational procedure and a familiarity with relevent sources of information concerning the target culture, carry out the following series of activities.

A.   TERMINAL BEHAVIOR: Identify a question which intrigues you about the target culture and write it down. Then:

   1.   Locate the titles of at least five articles in periodicals and five books that may reasonably be thought to contain information on the topic you identified. At least one of the articles should be from a professional journal. Prepare a separate index card for each title, using a standard bibliographical model.

   2.   Skim the publications contained in your bibliography for pages relevant to your topic. Indicate the pages on the index cards.

   3.   Read the pages and transfer the most salient facts to the index cards.

   4.   Outline the subtopics and sequence of development you would use to develop the topic.

5.   List the major variables that affect your topic.

6.   Compose 20 questions that might be asked of a native speaker to provide additional information on your topic. Be sure to include several questions to establish the biases of your informant.

7.   Prepare a list of 10 additional sources of any kind that pertain to your topic. Prepare them on index cards the same way you did before.

8.   Present a brief report, either orally or in a paragraph not longer than 250 words, on the feasibility of pursuing the topic you originally identified.

CONDITIONS: Each of the above eight activities should be completed in a week or less. Each completed activity should be shown the teacher for evaluation and feedback.

CRITERION: A possible 10 points will be awarded to each of the first seven activities, and 30 points to the last. The student must score 70 or above.

Goal VII. Attitudes toward Other Societies

The student should demonstrate intellectual curiosity about the target culture and empathy toward its people.

Performance objective 7: Cultural curiosity

One hopes each student develops a very positive attitude toward people who live in the target culture. As an indication of a positive attitude, carry out the following activities.

A.   TERMINAL BEHAVIOR: Demonstrate intellectual curiosity by:

1.   Giving evidence of having read 300 or more pages about the target culture from any journal or book in the general bibliography the teacher gave you or from any other publication that meets the teacher's approval;

2.   Asking 10 or more questions of a classroom visitor from the target culture;

3.   Traveling, for any duration, in the target culture;

4.   Attending five or more films in the target language.

B.   TERMINAL BEHAVIOR: Demonstrate empathy toward target peoples by:

1.   Inviting a foreign exchange student home for dinner;

2.   Making contact with at least one person in your community who speaks the target language at home.

CONDITIONS: These activities are to be carried out on a volunteer basis at the student's convenience.

CRITERION: Teacher will grant extra credit upon presentation of evidence of having completed activity.

Refining the Objectives

Some of the performance objectives stated above must be further refined. Students have a legitimate concern over details such as what kind of test will be administered, how long it will last, how much time they will have to prepare for it, how well they have to do to pass it.

In the foregoing examples of end-of-course performance objectives, the same general format was observed in each. This was done to emphasize the component parts of a performance objective (goal statement, terminal behavior, conditions, and criterion), and to make it easier for the reader to follow.

There is, of course, no one way to write performance objectives. For example, what were listed as activities in the foregoing presentation could just as well have been called separate objectives since each contained the major components of a performance objective.

The process of refining objectives involves gradually removing the ambiguities until a student knows what to expect and until any teacher—not only the student's teacher—can grade the performance. Words like "understanding" and "appreciation" give us something to hide behind; more scrutable aims must be developed. Ultimately, the teacher would want to offer a wide

variety of ways in which the student could indicate his competency. Students can take a test, write a report, participate in a skit
or simulation, prepare a graphic or literary dramatization. The
circumstances surrounding a student's performance of an objective are determined by the familiar exigencies of time and the facilities available for observing and testing the performance, by the
maturity of the students, by whether performance can be measured directly, and so on. The writer of performance objectives
must anticipate the circumstances that will affect the performance
and clarify them in writing. Hindsight is a great aid in doing this.

Whenever there are two or more students present, they can
be counted on to perform at different levels of proficiency. The
teacher must decide what level of performance can realistically be
accepted as adequate. If the teacher expects mastery, the student
should be expected to perform the objective with 90 to 100 percent
accuracy. Failing mastery, the student would be expected either to
repeat the performance at another time or to carry out an equivalent activity. Student performance would not, under these conditions, be graded on a curve (norm referenced). The purpose of
many activities can be achieved, thankfully, with less than near-
perfect performance on the part of the student. Each individual
teacher must make such decisions concerning criteria.

There are several excellent aids in helping teachers draft performance objectives. The simplest and most helpful is the brief
paperback by Mager (1962). It can be read easily in 45 minutes. A
more detailed and technical guide is available in Popham (1970).
The most complete exposition aimed specifically at the foreign
language teacher is a book written by Valette and Disick (1972).
Superb self-instructional materials for language teachers have
been prepared by Jenks, Bostick, and Otto (1971). One article has
been published that specifically discusses performance objectives
for teaching culture (Seelye, 1970a). A package of 26 booklets of
about 22 pages each has been published to help teachers develop
performance objectives (Popham and Baker, 1973). Steiner (1975)
treats both affective and cognitive objectives.

Writing performance objectives is not easy. But without
them, how is a teacher able to evaluate the extent to which s/he is

succeeding in having students learn cultural skills? In the absence of performance objectives, program evaluation must ignore the most important product of the program and the only reason for its existence—what the student learns. Objectives that are not measurable are like desert signposts that advise "Nearing Oasis"—but don't say how near or how big or in what direction the oasis lies.

A number of classroom activities to help the student gain the knowledge and skills necessary for successful completion of end-of-course performance objectives are described in Chapter 5.

Suggested Activities

1. What do you consider to be a "minimal" culture standard for your course with the biggest enrollment? A "desired" standard?
2. Indicate three ways nonverbal communication can be introduced in your classroom in a natural way.
3. Choose one topic (women, clothing, food, social stratification, etc.) and write end-of-year performance objectives for it for each of the seven goals.
4. Adapt the end-of-course objectives that appear in this chapter under each goal to the exigencies of a course you will teach.

Note

1. Activities A and B were prepared by Judith J. Ratas in a workshop I directed on student performance objectives.

5

Giving
Classroom Activities
a Purposeful Punch

Whether students develop the knowledge and skills a teacher is looking for in a given course depends on how many and what kind of relevant learning activities the students experience. This chapter illustrates the process of developing learning activities that lead to a specific end. Sample activities for various languages are organized under each of the seven cultural goals.

The end-of-course performance objectives listed in the last chapter (or any other set of objectives) will not be accomplished unless the student can experience the necessary prerequisite activities. Some students need many experiences to develop a given skill, while other students need fewer. The teacher must provide a combination of classroom and out-of-class activities that will enable all students to meet the end-of-course objectives.

A teacher has only so much time and energy to expend in writing objectives. Most of it should go into composing end-of-course performance objectives, for it is at this point that the difference between the expectations of the teacher and those of his disciples become painfully evident. There must be no confusion regarding the knowledge and skills needed to succeed in the course.

Daily or weekly classroom activities present a different situation. In the give-and-take of daily classroom exchange there is ample opportunity to clarify and back up to regroup one's forces without much penalty. The learning exercises we use are chosen arbitrarily. Their selection depends on what instructional materials are available, on what appeals to our individual tastes, or on the teacher's ability to develop learning activities. Since we have all had different experiences and can call on varying amounts of time and energy, different teachers will use different means to accomplish the same cultural goals. This is as it should be.

This chapter will complete the picture begun in Chapter 3 of how cultural instruction can be organized effectively by teachers. Chapter 3 spelled out seven goals that constitute the basic understanding and skills to be learned. Chapter 4 illustrated the second step in organizing cultural instruction: developing end-of-course student performance objectives. These objectives are derived from each of the seven main goals. The third step in organizing cultural instruction is to provide the learning experiences necessary for developing the student performances identified in the previous step.

Ideas for the content of learning activities come from the purposes themselves, from student textbooks (if you read between the lines), and from articles on culture that appear in the journals. A gold mine for ideas is the annual *ACTFL Review of Foreign Language Education*. To date, four articles have appeared there that review ideas for cultural activities published in dozens of journals (Seelye, 1969b; Morain 1971; Nostrand, 1974; Jarvis, 1977; see also Allen and Valette, 1972). The illustrative learning activities presented in this chapter were developed by experienced teachers in either courses or workshops I have directed. As one would expect, the formats for these activities vary, as does the specificity of the activities' objectives. For teachers to become overly preoccupied with the imperfections in their statements of performance objectives at this daily level of activity is counterproductive.

The activities a teacher employs to teach cultural concepts in his/her next course should include those s/he already has found successful *and* purposeful, plus some new ones described in this book.

Learning Activities for Goal I

A learning activity may be quite simple. To acquire the knowledge needed to do the four Religion in San Pedro activities outlined in the last chapter (see Performance objective 1) relating to perceiving the functionality of culturally conditioned behavior, one of the following out-of-class activities may suffice.

A.   Seek to determine how religion fits into the tapestry of rural Latin American culture by interviewing someone from that background; or
B.   Read pages 72-78 in *San Pedro, Colombia: Small Town in a Developing Society*, by Miles Richardson (1970).

Learning Activities for Goal II

An entirely different approach to giving students the experience they need to accomplish an end-of-course objective (in this case Performance objective 2 which relates to the interaction of language and social variables) is exemplified in an activity for Spanish classes. It was prepared by Pilar Aurensanz, Hildegard Bals, and E. S. Rife, under the supervision of Madeline A. Cooke.

This activity consists of a series of dialogues that are either acted out or taped and illustrated by filmstrips. The object is to show how language and gesture in greetings are influenced by the age, sex, social class, place of residence, and relationship of the speakers.

Saludos

After observing the four dialogues contained in this unit, the student will carry out two of the following five activities:

A. The student will be asked to recall what happened.

B. Given dialogue statements, s/he will identify the relationship of the speakers.

C. Given similar circumstances and a dialogue statement, the student will be able to vary appropriately the expressions and gestures used in greeting a friend of the same sex, a friend of the opposite sex, and various relatives.

D. Students write and present a similar skit of one or more circumstances portrayed in these dialogues.

E. Students research other social situations and other geographical places which would alter these greetings and procedures.

Dialogue I. The Pérez family meets the uncle and grandmother in the park.

Personajes:	Papá	María Rosa
	Mamá	Abuelita (madre de papá)
	Juan	Tío

PAPÁ: *(besando a la abuelita en la mejilla)* Buenas tardes, mamá. ¿Qué tal están todos?

ABUELITA: Bien, hijo. ¿Y vosotros? ¿Cómo estáis?

PAPÁ: Juan está con catarro. *(dando un abrazo al tío)* ¿Cómo van los negocios?

TÍO: *(acercándose)* Así, así.

ABUELITA: *(besando a mamá)* Ya sé que Juan está con catarro. ¿Tienes mucho trabajo?

MAMÁ: María Rosa me ayuda mucho. Es muy buena ella.

ABUELITA: *(besando a María Rosa)* ¿Trabajas mucho? ¿Sacas buenas notas?

MARÍA ROSA: Sí, abuelita. Ud. lo sabe, ¿verdad?

ABUELITA: *(besando a Juan en la frente)* ¡Pobrecito! Vas al colegio, ¿verdad?

JUAN: ¡Claro!

TÍO: *(dándole la mano a mamá)* María Pilar, ¡qué guapa estás!

MAMÁ: *(sonriedo ampliamente)* Anda, anda, no seas mentiroso.

Dialogue II. Two teenage, middle-class, urban students

EDUARDO: ¡Hola, Daniel! *(smile and wave)*

DANIEL: ¿Qué hay de nuevo, Eduardo? *(smile and wave)*

EDUARDO: ¿Cómo te va?

DANIEL: Pasándola. ¿Adónde vas?

EDUARDO: Voy al cine. ¿Quieres venir?

Dialogue III. Two teenage, middle-class girls

CELIA: ¡Hola, Inés!

INÉS: ¡Hola, Celia! *(they embrace and touch both cheeks)*

CELIA: ¡Cuánto tiempo sin verte!

INÉS: Sí, de veras. ¿Qué me cuentas?

CELIA: Pues, es el cumpleaños de mi prima Margarita y voy a su casa para felicitarla.

INÉS: Ah, qué bueno. Felicítala de mi parte. *(they kiss again, touch cheeks, and embrace)*

CELIA: Entonces ¿hasta luego!

INÉS: Chao.

Dialogue IV. A teenage girl and a teenage boy

MARIO: *(walking toward the girl with an open hand)* Hola, ¿qué tal? *(shake hands)*

BELITA: *(greets him casually)* ¡Hola! Cómo te fue en el examen de matemáticas?

MARIO: No sé. Creo que bien. Regular, ¿y a ti?

BELITA: Bastante mal. No lo terminé.

MARIO: ¿No quieres tomar un helado?

BELITA: Bueno. Encantada. *(a un gesto de cabeza de Mario en dirección al heladero, Belita responde: "Vamos." Mario paga el valor de los dos helados al heladero.)*

Learning Activities for Goal III

Chapter 4 listed (under *Performance objective 3*) scenarios that can be enacted in class to train students in conventional responses to common situations. Each of these scenarios can be developed into skits, with students getting the necessary background information from native informants, books, or the teacher.

An example of how this might be done in the classroom was developed in a German unit by Adele Farger, David K. Aacladan, Dzidra Schllaku, Cecilia C. Baumann, and Richard O. Whitcomb, under the supervision of James Hammers. The activity limits itself to street encounters, which the students experience through slides, skits, and role playing.

Begrüssung

Dialogue I
A. View first slide plus tape recording of dialogue (street scene, two boys greeting each other with a handshake).
B. Two boys or girls from class are called upon to imitate the slide. Teacher gives points about handshake (i.e., firm grip, one shake).
C. Boys and girls demonstrate handshake again while the teacher models linguistic greeting. She stands behind the appropriate student supposedly speaking.

    HANS: Guten Tag, Klaus!
    KLAUS: Guten Tag, Hans! *(boys release hands)*

D. Students pair off with someone of the same sex, imitate the procedure for handshake, and imitate the dialogue lines after teacher model.
E. Teacher calls upon several pairs of students to demonstrate the ability to greet each other. If 90 percent of pairs respond accurately, proceed to dialogue II. If not, repeat D and E.

Dialogue II
A. View slide (boy meets girl on street) and hear tape recording.
B. A boy and girl imitate the slide. Teacher explains proper procedure (i.e., girl offers her hand first, boy bows slightly when shaking her hand).

C.   The boy-girl couple repeats steps while the teacher again models the dialogue lines.

JONATHAN: Tag, Heidi!

HEIDI: Tag, Klaus! Wie geht's? Was gibt's zu Hause?

D.   Students pair off with someone of opposite sex, imitate the handshaking pattern, and imitate simultaneously the dialogue lines.

E.   Teacher calls upon several pairs of students to demonstrate ability to greet one another. If 90 percent of couples respond accurately, go on to Dialogue III. If not, repeat steps D and E.

Dialogue III

A.   View slide and hear tape recording. (A student meets an adult friend of his father on the street.)

B.   Teacher takes the role of a friend of the student's father and calls upon a student to demonstrate the proper procedure. The adult offers his hand first, the boy bows slightly when shaking hands.

C.   Teacher and student repeat handshaking patterns while teacher models dialogue lines.

FRIEND: Guten Tag, Hans. Wie geht es dir?

HANS: Guten Tag, Herr Schulz. Es geht mir gut, danke. Und Ihnen?

FRIEND: Danke, auch gut.

D.   Students pair off, one of them assuming the role of the adult. They imitate the handshaking procedure and also the dialogue lines.

E.   Several of the students are called upon to greet the teacher. If 90 percent of them respond correctly, go on to test. If not, repeat steps D and E.

Test procedure

A.   Several students are called upon to:

   1.   Greet a student of same sex
   2.   Greet a student of opposite sex
   3.   Greet the teacher

Each greeting must include the appropriate handshaking pattern, a greeting, and an inquiry as to health.

B.   If more than 90 percent of the students respond to all three situations accurately, the unit is finished. If not, repeat steps D and E of the inaccurately portrayed situation. Repeat the test.

Learning Activities for Goal IV

The description of Goal IV in Chapter 3 suggested an out-of-class activity to illustrate cultural connotations that involved clipping photos from target newspapers and magazines to illustrate the "authentic" way a concept such as woman appears in that culture.

One exceptionally intriguing activity for probing cultural connotations was prepared by Gwen Shimono for students of Japanese culture. This activity can be experienced in two ways: through listening to the teacher's illustrated classroom presentation or by reading the illustrated presentation after class. There is much to gain by having a teacher personally present a lesson that inspires many fruitful tangents for subsequent exploration. After hearing Shimono present this lesson, I was convinced that it could well serve to introduce the student to everything Japanese. For example: Why do Japanese sit on the floor? How is this reflected in architecture? How are radishes prepared and eaten? What puns use the words *radish* or *actor* in them? What other forms of word plays do Japanese use?

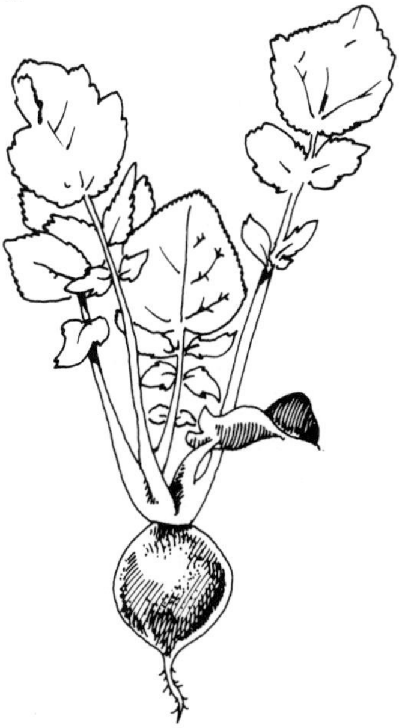

Figure 5.1   The European Variety

Futoi Daikon Monogatari (Saga of the Fat Radishes)

Daikon literally means "big root" and does not refer to radishes with small round red roots. The European variety has shorter leaves and a smaller root, and is mainly used to feed cattle in Japan. The larger ones, which originated from Southern China, are consumed daily by Japanese in many diverse ways. There is no land where *daikon* is grown in greater variety and in a larger quantity than in Japan. *Daikon* is so important in Japan that its price is quoted in reporting rising prices in general. There are about 34 varieties of *daikon* which range in size from the *Sakurajima daikon* which weighs as much as 23 kilograms to the *Moriguchi daikon* which reaches a length of up to two meters.

Daikon is a very important source of nourishment in the Japanese diet because it provides diastase, vitamin C, and lysine, which are not found in rice. It also helps digestion, and no matter how old it is, it never causes food poisoning, or *ataru* (attack or hit). Because of this, Japanese refer to poor actors as *daikon*-actors because neither the *daikon* nor the actors make a "hit" *(ataru)*.

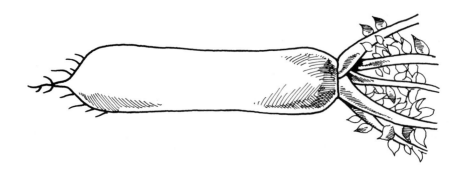

Figure 5.2   The Larger Daikon

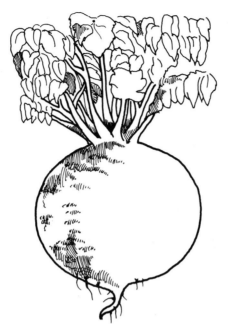

Figure 5.3   The Sakurajima Daikon

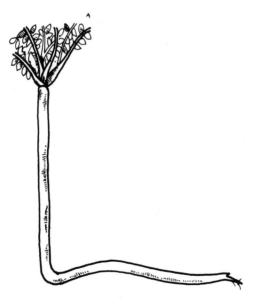

Figure 5.4   The Moriguchi Daikon

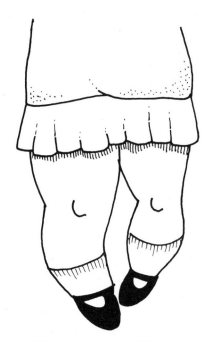

Figure 5.5   A Lady with Daikon-Ashi

Another idiomatic expression which uses the word *daikon* is *daikon-ashi* (heavy fat legs). *Daikon* connotes a long, thick radish which resembles a thick leg. There is no such term as "radish-legs" in English because the connotation of radish is entirely different.

Heavy legs are the result of sitting on *tatami* mats. When one sits on the floor Japanese-style, with one's legs tucked neatly under oneself, most of one's body weight is redistributed below the waist. So it is no wonder that many Japanese have *daikon-ashi*.

Cultural connotations of daikon

Compare the lady with *daikon-ashi* (see Figure 5.5) with the *daikon* commonly eaten in Japan (see Figure 5.2).

Japanese kimonos nicely cover this kind of legs, but most Japanese girls now wear dresses. To shed the excess flesh on their legs, many have given up sitting on the floor in favor of sitting on chairs. Naturally, Japanese men have such legs, too. However, not much is made of this fact because their legs are usually covered and women don't take interest in men's legs, with the exception, perhaps, of the legs of Mr. Takamiyama.

Takamiyama, the huge Hawaiian sumo wrestler who was a former football player, had the reputation of having "weak" legs. This, and the fact that he has to do certain exercises to build up strength in his legs—exercises which most other sumo players would not find necessary—has been much publicized. Being an American, he never sat on the floor Japanese-style before he went to Japan and took up sumo.

Say "Cheese"

Another approach to cultural connotations is illustrated by a French unit prepared by Carol Larson, Joyce Lopas, Dorann Klein, Carolyn Amelung, and Madeleine Kent.

Students will indicate the cultural meanings associated with the word "cheese" in the target culture by doing all of the following student activities:

A. Students will be able to give a popular saying that exemplifies the role of cheese in French culture.
B. Students will be able to cite an example from French literature in which cheese plays an important role (La Fontaine, *Le corbeau et le renard*).
C. Students will be able to point out examples in French advertisements and cartoons of the interrelationship of cheese and the culture.
D. Students will be able to list x number of examples of the relationship between cheese and the culture upon witnessing a short skit.
E. Students will be able to identify x number of cheeses by sight and taste.

Teacher Activities

A. Present popular saying. ("There is no complete meal without cheese.")

       1. Show students French menus to substantiate the saying.

       2. Have students memorize the saying.

B.   Present Fable (La Fontaine—*"The Crow and the Fox"*)

       1. Explain.

       2. Have students dramatize.

C.   Present French advertisements.

       1. Point out the frequency of cheese advertisements.

       2. Point out varieties of advertised cheeses.

       3. Point out prices of French cheeses (expensive, but even relatively poor families treat themselves to delicious food when they can).

       4. Aid the students in perceiving the appeal to cultural themes in the advertising of cheese (the family, *savoir vivre*, intellectualism).

D.   Present a French political cartoon. Discuss the importance of cheese as one of the three foods mentioned.

E.   Present a short skit.

       1. Prepare a short skit in which the importance of cheese is revealed.

       2. The personification of cheese. (Holes in Swiss cheese *[gruyere]* are called *les yeux.* The point of a wedge is called *le nez.*)

       3. A popular saying related to cheese "Ça se passe entre la poire et le fromage." *(Save important discussion for between the fruit and cheese course.)*

       4. Have some students practice and present the skit for the class, including information on how to eat cheese. (Cut with knife. Put onto bread with knife, or in formal situation, eat with fork.) Never eat with fingers.

F.   Provide for an assortment of French cheeses in the class.

       1. Purchase or have some students purchase cheeses.

       2. Introduce and allow the students to sample the various cheeses.

       3. Introduce a game in which students must recognize cheeses by sight and taste.

Learning Activities for Goal V

Statements about a culture can be taken from a number of sources, including the textbook, foreign visitors, and the classroom teacher himself for subsequent evaluation. The following 10 statements were fabricated for the occasion.

Is It True That...?

In class the student will be given 10 statements concerning Hispanic culture. After reading the statements, mark each statement either *(a)* probably true, *(b)* probably false, or *(c)* I don't know. For those statements you marked *a* or *b*, indicate briefly what evidence supports your judgment; for those you marked *c*, indicate what additional information you specifically need to make a judgment. The list will be given in class. You have the whole period to answer. You will not be graded on the basis of whether you answered *a*, *b*, or *c*, but on the strength of your supporting comments. Each statement is worth three points; you need 20 or more to pass.

1. Most Spanish-speaking people take *siestas* at noon.
2. Most religions are allowed in Spain, although Catholicism is dominant.
3. The Latin American's concept of space is such that among friends there is a fair amount of intimacy involved (e.g., embracing, patting on the shoulder, handshaking).
4. Flamenco is the music most typical of Spain.
5. Spanish is spoken everywhere in Latin America.
6. Shopping for groceries in Latin America is accomplished by going to a supermarket once weekly and getting all that is needed.
7. If one were to go to a bank in a Spanish-speaking country, he would have no trouble cashing a check since the banking system there is the same as that in the United States.

8. The tradition of girls being chaperoned when they go out at night is slowly dying out.
9. The *gaucho* of Argentina has been highly idealized through literature.
10. The appropriate response of a girl to a *piropo* would be to ignore it.

Learning Activities for Goal VI

The end-of-course performance objective listed in the last chapter to develop skill in researching another culture required the student to do eight exercises leading up to a report on a topic.

A classroom activity done with the assistance of a librarian has as its object getting students accustomed to searching for print sources. This activity takes the same statements contained in the activity just listed under Goal V but changes the performance objective to read:

The student is given a list consisting of ten statements concerning Hispanic culture. After reading the statements, s/he will list two or three sources s/he would consult either to verify what the statement says or to render the statement implausible. S/he must respond to all statements with two or three appropriate sources.

Learning Activities for Goal VII

This goal is one that encourages empathy with people in the target culture. To facilitate accomplishment of the optional activities listed under Performance objective 7 in the last chapter teachers can do the following:

A. Provide the students with a bibliography of interesting titles concerning the target culture.
B. Invite at least one native into the classroom each month.

C. Keep students informed as to the availability of movies in the target language.

D. Prepare a listing of local residents who belong to the target culture.

An Overview of Classroom Activities

To gain a quick overview of the breadth of one's cultural instruction, the teacher can categorize the cultural activities s/he plans under the appropriate goal.

The following format can be used to assess both the purpose of each learning activity and the breadth of instruction.

Cultural Goals							
I	II	III	IV	V	VI	VII	*Learning Activities*
X							Religion
	X						Saludos
		X					Begrüssung
			X				Daikon
							etc.

This process will often pinpoint a common testing problem—activities whose purpose appears to extend into many areas. While multiple-goal activities can be effective, before student achievement is measured it is necessary to avoid confusion as to which goal is being tested. The difficulty in allowing an activity to be aimed at a "supergoal," rather than at specific goals, is that after a student has done the activity (usually with uneven success), neither teacher nor student knows how adequately each goal is being reached.

Without adequate learning experiences a student has little hope of achieving the course goals. The above checklist makes it easy to spot goals for which few, if any, learning activities are planned. How can a teacher be assured that he has planned enough important activities for each goal? The answer is an "iffy" pragmatic one. *If* the end-of-course objectives are sound, the learning activities are adequate in number and quality *if* they teach what students need to know to accomplish the end-of-course objectives. At the beginning of a course the teacher makes an educated guess in this regard; the objectives or activities are then modified in the light of experience for the next time the course is taught.

The next three chapters highlight specific techniques a teacher may want to employ as s/he develops classroom activities to aid students in acquiring the skills they will need to accomplish the course's cultural goals.

Suggested Activity

Using the topic you chose in the previous chapter, devise a learning activity for each of your end-of-year performance objectives. (Some of these should be classroom activities and some should be for accomplishment outside of class.)

6

Building a Survival Kit for Culture Shock

*Two techniques to sensitize students to the miscom-
munication that always accompanies interaction with bearers
of another culture are described in this chapter. The first
technique involves out-of-class reading of "empathic" literature; the second involves a specially designed class skit called
a "mini-drama." Examples are included of mini-dramas for
French, German, and English as a second language.*

When Cultural Assumptions Clash

Conflict is present whenever two cultures come into contact. This
may be because of a clash of values—a cultural difference in the
perception of the appropriate way to satisfy basic physical and
psychological needs. The problem of cross-cultural shock is discussed in this chapter, and ways to sensitize students to anticipate
and detect misunderstandings that result from interaction with
culture bearers of another value system are suggested. *Sensitivity*
is the key word, for the approach of this chapter is through the
emotions. The subsequent two chapters follow a cognitive

approach to preparing one for communication with someone from another culture.

Only one person ever persuaded me he was successfully going to avoid the trauma associated with adjustment to another culture. He had a command of the target language, a well-paid professional position in the target culture, was personable, had an excess of good will, and possessed the boundless energy of the young. He would seek out natives with whom to converse, and when he was by himself he would practice out loud new idioms and difficult verb inflections. A little before completing two years of residence abroad (in this case in the U.S.), he was hospitalized due to a nervous breakdown caused by the stress of adjusting to another culture.

A prominent member of our profession tells of the frustration of a year's sabbatical in Germany. In his initial two months abroad he did not accomplish much that he had planned, and he blamed the target people. His hostility gradually increased until, one afternoon several months later, he came within a fraction of hitting a housewife who was blocking the sidewalk with a baby carriage. This so unnerved him that, out of fear of causing bodily injury, he kept himself locked up in his hotel room for the duration of the sabbatical, some six months. Most cases of culture shock are not this severe. More generally, guests in another culture suffer from cross-cultural fatigue rather than shock.

At a New Year's Eve celebration in an exclusive Guatemalan hotel, one American was overheard telling another, "You see all these people? They're all my wife's relatives. And every damn one of them has kissed me tonight. If another Guatemalan man hugs and kisses me I'll punch him right in the face!" The irritated American was disturbed by two things: the extended kinship patterns of the group and the *abrazo de año nuevo* as executed by the men (he did not complain of the female *abrazos*). Both customs—close family ties that extend to distant relatives and the *abrazo* given as a greeting or sign of affection devoid of sexual overtures—elicited hostility in the American who was bored by unintelligible language and depressed by nostalgia and alcohol. After a good day's rest and a cold shower, the *yanqui* probably achieved a peaceful coexistence with his wife's relatives.

But a hundred other strange customs await his every venture outside his circle of American friends—the bureaucratic *Qué vuelva usted mañana* ("Come back tomorrow"), the angry stares when he enthusiastically whistles at his favorite team's athletic triumph, the solicituous *Es suyo* followed by his *No, gracias*, which is in turn met by confusion. An American abroad suffers from the inevitable malaise of cross-cultural fatigue, fatigue occasioned by an exaggerated concern for hygiene, by having to work harder to do simple things such as use the telephone or catch a bus, by the constant irritation of dealing with people who "don't know how to get things done." All those who venture abroad for any lengthy stay contract it. Most recover within a few years, but recovery is gradual. It makes little difference whether it is an American terrified by the traffic patterns of Guatemala or a Guatemalan perspiring with claustrophobic anxiety in the subways of New York. Culture fatigue is not a respecter of persons.

That the people of one culture experience difficulty observing the same "reality" as natives of another culture has been demonstrated on many different levels. Linguistically, for example, the inability of many Chinese to distinguish between *rice* and *lice* or the problems Americans have differentiating the Spanish *bata* and *pata* or the inability of speakers of Spanish to distinguish the two English words *silly* and *Seelye*. In fact, this very observation that different languages *hear* different sounds (i.e., that they group certain sounds together) has led to the fruitful concept within descriptive linguistics of the phoneme.

One ingenious experiment positioned 10 pairs of slides for stereoscopic viewing. On one side were placed pictures of objects familiar to Mexicans—*un matador, una morena, un peon*—and on the other side were mounted pictures familiar to Americans—a baseball player, a blonde, a farmer. Each pair of pictures had the same general form, texture, light and shadows. Both Mexicans and Americans were shown the pictures and tested on their recall. The Mexicans tended to see only what was already familiar to them, and the Americans what was to them familiar (Bagby, 1957).

One acquaintance went blind shortly after birth but fortunately regained his sight at the age of 16. One of his major adjustments, he related, was then to learn *not to see* the inconsequential objects that came into his line of vision. For instance, while looking at a person across the room, everything within eyesight would demand equal visual attention. Our culture teaches us what to see and what to ignore. A newly arrived foreigner does not know what to *see*, let alone what to *say*.

When the wealthy, retired, vending-machine magnate leans back in his straw chair by the hotel swimming pool and lifts his martini to the rising mountains and exclaims, "This is a beautiful country; I like the people; they know how to take it easy; I understand this country," he is kidding himself. His illusion of empathy lacks the foundation of knowledge.

Kohls' (1979) readable booklet, *Survival Kit for Overseas Living*, lists a series of common descriptors of Americans: outgoing, friendly, informal, loud, boastful, hard-working, wasteful, confident they have all the answers, lacking in class consciousness, disrespectful of authority, ignorant of other countries, wealthy, generous, always in a hurry. Kohls then makes the point that to the extent an American fits the stereotypes s/he will be likely to experience problems abroad, since even our "virtues" may be considered liabilities by another society.

Everyone experiences difficulties as s/he attempts to function effectively in another culture. The best study to date of this phenomenon was done by a sociologist studying miscommunication that occurred while U.S. college students and Peace Corps volunteers resided in the homes of middle-class hosts in Bogotá, Colombia (Gorden, 1974a). Gorden made the startling discovery that miscommunication between the Americans and their hosts was *greater* when the Americans were fluent in Spanish. Americans who spoke hesitantly with a heavy accent were misunderstood less. The reason? The Colombians assumed that the fluent Americans who sounded as though they knew what they were talking about *did* know what they were talking about. Unfortunately, they rarely did for they had not been *socialized* into Hispanic life. They had acquired fluency in Spanish in a U.S. cultural setting. Their cultural referents were U.S., not Hispanic.

Why didn't the Americans who murdered the language get into more communication difficulties? Because when they spoke their halting Spanish they didn't sound as if they knew much. Consequently, the Colombian hosts assumed ignorance of everything, including many basic cultural assumptions. The Colombians worked harder to understand these innocents abroad.

Gorden focused on two types of communication problems. The first type of problem occurred because the Americans did not know the proper way to behave in the living room, the bedroom, the bathroom, etc. For example, the Americans were considered unkempt because they put their shoes in the wrong place in their bedrooms. Others were considered either too forward or too introverted depending on when they kept their bedroom door open or closed—and how open or closed they kept it.

The second type of problem Gorden focused on concerned inappropriate role relationships the Americans tried to maintain with the various members of the host household. For example, one American male, after "a terrific dinner party" in the host home, attempted to help the señora and the maid afterward by carrying a tray full of dishes into the kitchen. Gorden reports that the sight of a man in the kitchen trying to scrape the dishes was too disturbing to the Colombians' notions of social status and was more distracting than helpful.

Gorden concludes that the key to learning how to function effectively in another culture is to learn the discrete behavioral patterns that are employed there. His masterful book provides the answer to the question of just how this learning is to occur. It occurs when the right questions are asked in the right way. A reading of Gorden's book goes a long way to helping one develop this skill.

Ethnocentrism

The culprit behind cross-cultural fatigue is an ethnocentric outlook. According to Sumner's (1906) classic definition, ethnocentrism may best be described as a syndrome involving at least three basic factors: integration and loyalty among ingroup members, hostile relations between ingroup and outgroup members, and positive self-regard among ingroup members in contrast to derogatory stereotyping of outgroup characteristics. One important component of this syndrome is an acceptance of ingroup values and standards as universally applicable.

An exhaustive compendium of social science propositions dealing with ethnocentrism has been prepared by an anthropologist and a social psychologist (LeVine and Campbell, 1972). A junior high school social studies book that presents materials especially selected to reduce ethnocentrism and to provide insight into the nature of cross-cultural communication has been edited by Fersh (1974). Portraits of Americans abroad are available in several studies: Cleveland, Mangone, and Adams (1960); Lambert (1966); Seelye (1969a); Seelye and Brewer (1970); Gorden (1974a). For reports on overseas training programs, see DeCrow (1969), Decaroli (1972), Harrison and Hopkins (1966), and Althen (1970).

Within the context of the seven cultural goals, the two types of activities described here fall under Goal I, the functionality of culturally conditioned behavior. Both techniques attempt to elicit an emotional as well as an intellectual grasp of the problems of cross-cultural communication. The two techniques are the use of literary sources and classroom mini-dramas to create empathy.

Creating Empathy through Literature

A polyglot professor of English linguistics, the late William F. Marquardt, has described a method of sensitizing students to enable them to experience how it feels to be a member of another culture (Marquardt, 1969). Marquardt saw empathy, "the habit of trying in time of conflict to see things the other person's way," as the "most relevant magic in our day." He went on to say that empathy "is obviously a desired end-product of learning, but what is often overlooked is that it is also a starting point—particularly in the learning of communication skills."

Marquardt saw literature as ideally suited to develop empathy in the reader since creators of literature receive their basic motivation from a desire to explore the feelings of others and to communicate these feelings to their readership. Marquardt identified the following seven types of "communication situations" as the most useful for observing in literature the interplay between persons of different cultures.

Communication Situations

1. Works by mainstream culture Americans primarily for mainstream readers showing interaction between mainstream and minority culture members in the minority culture setting.
2. Works by mainstream Americans primarily for mainstream readers focused on minority culture and mainstream culture members interacting in the mainstream culture setting.
3. Works by minority culture members primarily for mainstream readers focused on minority and mainstream culture members interacting in a mainstream culture setting.
4. Works by minority culture members primarily for mainstream readers focused on minority and mainstream culture members interacting in the minority culture setting.
5. Works by mainstream culture members focused on presenting some specific feature of the minority culture primarily to mainstream culture readers.
6. Works by minority culture members presenting or interpreting some specific feature of the minority culture to mainstream and minority culture readers.

7. Works by minority culture members discussing some specific feature of the mainstream culture for mainstream and minority culture readers.

The main object of reading this type of literature is to increase awareness of the extent to which one's behavior is conditioned by one's culture. Marquardt provides a lengthy annotated list of titles falling within the range outlined above.

My own two favorites, neither of which is listed, are *Stranger in a Strange Land* by Robert Heinlein (1961) and *The White Dawn* by James Houston (1971). The former, which was personally recommended to me by Marquardt, is a gripping science fiction account of an earthling born and raised on Mars, then brought back as a young man to Earth, the "strange land." The latter novel tenderly relates the saga of three shipwrecked whalers who are befriended by Eskimos.

Additional titles can be obtained easily by asking librarians, other teachers, and, best of all, your students for suggestions. To make it easier to "scoop up promising items at every cast," Marquardt proposes a grid wherein the horizontal rows represent the seven communication situations, and the vertical columns represent literary *genres*.

Each grid contains one example. Many of the examples relate to the American black. There are two reasons for this: first, there is a voluminous list of good titles in this area; and second, Marquardt's article was especially aimed at creating empathy between United States mainstream and minority culture bearers. The literary works do not, however, have to relate specifically to the target culture to be effective. The principle of cross-cultural empathy is transferable.

FORM OR GENRE

	(a) Autobiog.	(b) Biography	(c) Novels	(d) Stories	(e) Plays	(f) Poems	(g) Essays
1	Griffin, Black Like Me (1961)	Kugelmass, Ralph J. Bunche: Fighter for Peace (1962)	Hentoff, Jazz Country (1965)	Dolch, Navajo Stories (1956)	Shulman, West Side Story (1961)	Rollins, ed. Christmas Gif (1963)	Durham & Jones, The Adventures of the Negro Cowboys (1965)
2	Buck, My Several Worlds (1954)	Shapiro, Jackie Robinson of the Brooklyn Dodgers (1957)	Archibald, Outfield Orphan (1961)	Faulkner "That Evening Sun"	O'Neill, All God's Chillun Got Wings (1932)	Culver, ed. Great American Negroes in Verse 1723-1965 (1966)	Henry, "White People's Time, Colored People's Time" (1966)
3	Davis, Yes, I Can (1965)	Bontemps, Famous Negro Athletes (1964)	Baldwin, Go Tell It on the Mountain (1953)	Hughes, ed. The Best Short Stories by Negro Writers	Baldwin, Blues for Mr. Charlie (1964)	Brooks, Bronzeville Boys and Girls (1956)	Baldwin, Nobody Knows My Name (1961)
4	Malcolm X, The Autobiography of Malcolm X (1965)	Bennett, What Manner of Man: A Biography of M. L. King	Hughes, Tambourines to Glory (1950)	Hughes, Simple Speaks His Mind (1950)	Couch, New Black Playwrights (1969)	Hughes, Selected Poems (1959)	J. Stands-in Timber & M. Liberty, Cheyenne Memories (1969)
5	Sexton, Spanish Harlem (1965)	Plate, Palette and Tomahawk: The Story of George Catlin (1962)	Steinbeck, The Pearl (1962)	Porter, Collected Stories (1965)	Duberman, In White America (1964)	Rasmussen, Beyond the High Hills: A Book of Eskimo Poetry (1961)	Goldin, Straight Hair, Curly Hair (1966)
6	Thomas, Down These Mean Streets (1967)	Bontemps, Chariot in the Sky (1951)	Killens, And Then We Heard the Thunder (1963)	Harris, ed. Once Upon a Totem (1963)	Charles, Jannis (1966)	Walker, For My People (1942)	Hughes, The First Book of Jazz (1954)
7	Baldwin, The Fire Next Time (1963)	Terkel, Giants of Jazz (1957)	Owens, Walking on Borrowed Time (1950)	Wright, Uncle Tom's Children (1940)	Richardson & Miller, eds. Negro History in Thirteen Plays (1935)	J.W. & J.R. Johnson, The Books of American Negro Spirituals (1940)	Samora, La Raza: Forgotten Americans (1966)

COMMUNICATION SITUATION

Reprinted with permission of the Florida FL Reporter and William F. Marquardt from the special anthology issue, Linguistic-Cultural Differences and American Education, 7, No. 1 (Spring/Summer 1969): 134-35. Alfred C. Aarons, Barbara Y. Gordon, and William A. Stewart, editors.

Since this technique revolves around students' reading interesting literary works in a language they can easily enjoy—English—the ideal accommodation would be for the foreign language teacher to cooperate with the English teacher. Two concerns need to be worked out: the incentives to be offered by one or both to encourage students to do the reading and the follow-up strategy to employ so that the students will have an opportunity to share their insights and to "sell" the reading selection to other students.

A complementary technique that goes one step further and establishes personal contact with a culture bearer of another society is described by Marquardt in a brief paper (1972). This article is contained in a two-volume collection of papers on intercultural communication which offers many insights of value to teachers of intercultural communication (Hoopes, 1971 and 1972).

Cultural Mini-Dramas

A sociologist from Antioch College, Raymond L. Gorden, has developed a prototype for sensitizing students to cross-cultural miscommunication through a "mini-drama." A version of Gorden's mini-drama, edited for junior high students, can be found in Fersh (1974). The use of skits and brief simulations is not new. They had been used previously at Wayne State, for example, by Behmer and Jencks (Behmer, 1972a). What Gorden brings to this tradition is a carefully developed format that carries the capability of evoking an emotional response in addition to providing cultural information.

The mini-drama consists of from three to five brief episodes, each of which contains one or more examples of miscommunication. Additional information is made available with each episode, but the precise cause of the misunderstanding does not become apparent until the last scene. Each episode is followed by a discussion led by the teacher.

Gorden uses the mini-drama format to expose the student to a "process of self-confrontation." This process consists of three parts. The student is led to experience the vagueness of much cross-cultural communication due to the different cultural connotations of words. Then, by identifying with the American youths in the drama, the student experiences the realization that "this could happen to me, too." Finally, by making the same incorrect assumptions as the Americans in the drama, the student has the chance to demonstrate to himself his own tendency to jump to false conclusions because of his own culturally determined "silent" assumptions.

To enhance emotional effects of the "self-confrontation," any threatening interaction between the mini-drama, the student, and the teacher must be avoided. The best way of doing this is for the teacher to establish a nonjudgmental atmosphere during the discussion periods that follow each episode.

Gorden admonishes the users of mini-dramas to "avoid any remark when introducing the mini-drama or in the discussion which would give any hint that the problem is basically one of communication. Let them discover this themselves!" To aid this personal expression of views, Gorden outlines two additional techniques for the teacher to use while asking questions during the discussion periods. Broad, open-ended questions should be used by the teacher, especially at the beginning of each discussion. The kind of question to avoid is the narrow-scope question which can be answered by yes or no. Gorden gives the following five examples of both kinds of questions:

Broad-scope

1. What are your impressions of this scene?
2. What is happening in this scene?
3. What do you think about this scene?
4. What are the feelings of the people interacting in this situation?
5. Why does the Colombian customer do what he does?

Narrow-scope

1. Is there conflict in this scene?
2. Is there any miscommunication in this scene?
3. Does this sound like the kind of thing that could really happen?
4. Do the Americans have a positive or negative feeling toward the Colombian in this situation?
5. Does the Colombian customer feel he has been wronged by the American?

Another reason to avoid narrowing the scope of inquiry is that the teacher might raise questions that have not yet occurred to the student—for the same reasons that they did not occur to the Americans in the mini-drama.

The second technique is meant to supplement the open-ended questions just described. It involves using "neutral probes" to encourage the student to give more information, while at the same time it avoids leading him to any specific area. Comments such as "Uh huh," "I see," "Very interesting," "Go on," "What else did you notice?" fall into this "neutral probe" area. Gorden also recommends that the discussion leader briefly summarize at the end of each discussion the reactions of the group.

Shortly after Gorden's "Cross-Cultural Encounter in a Latin American Bank" became available through the ERIC system (Gorden, 1970), I tried it on a graduate class of teachers—all of whom had resided abroad. The results were dramatic. At the end of the first scene the class strongly identified with the "wronged" American Peace Corps members. But by the end of the last scene the light had dawned, and the Colombians emerged clearly as the wronged parties. This changed perception drew mixed reactions. Several teachers who had served in the Peace Corps vehemently attacked the authenticity of the mini-drama. Peace Corps members, they contended, were too smart to make mistakes in cross-cultural communication. By identifying with the Americans of the drama and by misinterpreting the same cultural cues, the teachers had almost to a person experienced the embarrassment of a cultural *faux pas*. The emotional sensitivity came from knowing that they were all vulnerable to lack of empathy. They shared the same barriers to communication. They also learned that knowing the vocabulary is not enough to avoid miscommunication.

The emotional sensation of self-confrontation that many experience through mini-dramas cannot be repeated often. Beyond the first or second, the objective of further mini-dramas becomes largely cognitive. The affective potential of this approach depends on the novelty of the initial experience or so.

In presenting mini-dramas in class, each episode's dialogue can be given to the student actors a few minutes before that particular episode is enacted. Thus, they, too, can experience self-confrontation.

A foreign language educator, Barbara Snyder, developed 53 mini-dramas for classroom use, all of which are written in the target language, Spanish (Snyder, 1975). Other similar mini-dramas for foreign language classes have been prepared for French (Levno, 1977) and German (Shirer, 1981).

Three Mini-Dramas

Examples of the dialogue portion of a mini-drama for French, English as a second language, and German are presented below. The teacher may want to try an appropriate one in his/her classes. Teachers interested in writing their own mini-dramas should model theirs on the one by Gorden (1968b; Fersh, 1974).

Les Achats: Un Mini-Drame

This French mini-drama was prepared for high school by Emily Dewhirst, Jill Lohmann, Sam Russenburg, and Sister Christine Feagan.

Characters: Narrator, Cindy, Debbie, a fruit vendor, and a policeman.

Act I

NARRATOR: Two young American students, Cindy and Debbie, are in Cannes for their summer vacation. They pass an expensive dress shop.

CINDY: Debbie, isn't that a beautiful dress? Look, the price is 200 francs. I'd love to buy it!

DEBBIE: The store won't be open for another half hour. Let's take a walk and come back later.

NARRATOR: The girls pass an open air market where farmers are selling their fruits and vegetables.

CINDY: It's so hot! I'm thirsty! Look at that table of fruit over there...the one where the fat woman is sitting.

DEBBIE: She has some beautiful peaches. Let's go over and take a look at them.

CINDY: You're right, those are nice peaches. *(She starts to pick out the peaches she wants to buy.)* Let's take this one and the one over there...

VENDOR: *(sarcastically)* Eh bien, mesdemoiselles, you're planning to buy the whole tableful?

DEBBIE: *(whispers to Cindy)* Is she ever rude! I wonder what her problem is! Probably had a fight with her husband this morning.

(Class discussion)

Act II

DEBBIE: *(handing peaches to the vendor)* We'll take these three peaches, please. *(The fruit vendor takes the peaches and wraps them in a piece of newspaper.)*

CINDY: *(whispers to her friend)* She's too cheap to even put them in a bag for us! *(Cindy takes the peaches from the woman and bites into a peach as Debbie asks...)*

DEBBIE: How much do we owe you, Madame?

VENDOR: Two hundred francs, Mademoiselle.

CINDY: *(choking on the peach)* I hope she's kidding! I've heard of people being cheated in France, but this is ridiculous! The *dress* was only 200 francs!

VENDOR: Two hundred francs, Mademoiselle!

(Class discussion)

Act III

VENDOR: Give me my 200 francs!

CINDY: You're crazy, Madame! We're not giving you 200 francs for three peaches! That's ridiculous!

VENDOR: That's not too much for good peaches! *(talks to bystanders who are watching the dispute)* It's easy to see that these girls are Americans! They don't know what work is...spraying trees, picking fruit, packing it...everything is done by machine in their country! *(to the girls)* Give me my 200 francs!

DEBBIE: Not on your life. That's highway robbery!

VENDOR: Monsieur l'Agent, come over here, please. These Americans owe me 200 francs for some peaches, and they refuse to pay.

POLICEMAN: Girls, what seems to be the problem? You have the peaches, so why not pay the lady?

DEBBIE: But 200 francs! How could they cost that much? You can buy a dress for that price!

POLICEMAN: Oh, I see what is troubling you, mesdemoiselles, but let me assure you that the price is just.

(Stop here for brief class discussion, then continue.)

It is a question of new francs and old francs. This woman wants you to pay her 200 old francs which is the equivalent of two new francs. Some years ago the government changed our franc. One hundred old francs became one new franc. However, many of the older people still count in old francs.

CINDY: I see. But tell me, why was the woman so upset when we picked out our fruit before we paid for it?

(Stop here for brief class discussion, then continue.)

POLICEMAN: Mademoiselle, in France one does not touch the fruit in a display. The vendor selects the fruit for you. Much time is spent arranging a display of fruit. It is a shame to spoil it by pulling out a piece here and there.

ESL Mini-Drama: School

This mini-drama was prepared by Julia Estrada, Raymond Ellison, Chloe White, Gardenia Hung, and Margaret Duran.

Scene I

NARRATOR: Typical city school. José, a recent arrival from Mexico, and his American classmates are returning from recess and are lining up at the fountain.

JOSÉ: I want drink.

BRUCE: Ow! My chin!

JOSÉ: ¡Ay, perdón!

BRUCE: Why did you push me? *(begins to cry)*

TEACHER: What's going on here?

BRUCE: He pushed me when I was drinking and I hit my chin.

TEACHER: José, did you push Bruce?

NARRATOR: José looks at the floor and says nothing.

(Class discussion)

Scene II

NARRATOR: Teacher puts aide in charge of class and talks with José. Bruce is in the hall.

TEACHER: All right, boys. What exactly happened?

BRUCE: Well, we were lining up; we were thirsty after tag; it was my turn to drink at the fountain. Then José pushed me and I wasn't even finished.

TEACHER: José, now you tell what happened. Was it like that?

NARRATOR: José doesn't answer but begins to cry softly.

TEACHER: Maybe we'd better talk to the principal. I've had this problem with you before.

(Class discussion)

Scene III

NARRATOR: In the principal's office the boys are left in the outer office while the teacher discusses her problem.

PRINCIPAL: Good Morning, Mrs. Smith. What is it?

TEACHER: Well, Mr. Brown, it's José Ramírez again. It seems he pushed a boy, bruising his chin at the water fountain. The main problem, though, is that I never can get him to answer a question. He does understand what I'm saying, I know he does; he just won't answer me. I'm getting tired of talking to a brick wall. The child lacks respect.

PRINCIPAL: Let me talk to the boy. We'll get to the bottom of this or call on his parents through the community representative.

(Class discussion)

Scene IV

NARRATOR: In the home of the Ramírez family, the community representative is talking the matter over with the parents.

COMMUNITY REPRESENTATIVE: ...so you see, Mr. Ramírez, José's teacher is concerned about his rudeness toward her and the principal.

SR. RAMÍREZ: *No puedo creerlo.* My son has never shown lack of respect toward his elders. What could they say to him to make him talk back?

COMMUNITY REPRESENTATIVE: But, Sr. Ramírez, that's precisely the problem. José never says anything, he won't even look the teacher squarely in the face.

SR. RAMÍREZ: But of course not! What impudence!
    (Class discussion)

Scene V

NARRATOR: The principal's office where the community representative is
    discussing his visit with the principal.
PRINCIPAL: Come in, Mr. Martínez.
COMMUNITY REPRESENTATIVE: Well, Mr. Brown, the Ramírez family was quite
    upset about the school's treatment of José.
PRINCIPAL: Pardon me?
COMMUNITY REPRESENTATIVE: The parents are proud of the upbringing they've
    given their children. The problem seems to be that when the child is
    being castigated he is not to refute the teacher's comments but lower
    his head in respectful submission. I explained to the parents that in the
    United States the child is taught to look at the person speaking to him.
    Averting the eyes is taken as a sign of culpability.
PRINCIPAL: I never realized that facet of the Mexican character. This will be
    taken up at our next inservice meeting.

The Noon Meal: A German Mini-Drama

This mini-drama was prepared by M. Cohen, Judy Moses, Anke
Culver, and A. Bogucka.

Characters: Frank and Betty Harrison, Jack, their son, two German businessmen,
    a waiter, restaurant guests

Scene I

It is about 1:00 P.M. on a pleasant spring afternoon in Göttingen. Frank and
Betty, a middle-aged couple from Chicago, have come to Göttingen to visit their
son Jack who is spending the year studying chemistry in Göttingen on a Fulbright
grant. They spot a restaurant, *Zum Goldenen Adler,* go in, and wait to be seated.
FRANK: I'm starved.
BETTY: I wonder how long we'll have to wait to be seated. Do you see the
    hostess anywhere?
FRANK: No, but there are a few empty tables. We shouldn't have to wait long.
    (long pause)

BETTY: *(greatly irritated)* Just look at that, will you? Those people are just going right past us and sitting down.

FRANK: Well, why don't we just do the same? There's a table for four. Let's grab it before someone else does.

(Class discussion)

Scene II

Frank and Betty are seated at the table when the waiter gives them two menus on his way to serve another table. The waiter returns.

WAITER: What would you like?

BETTY: (pointing to the item *Wienerschnitzel* on the menu) I'd like that.

FRANK: I'll have the *Sauerbraten*. We'll both have beer to drink.

The waiter leaves. In the meantime the restaurant has filled up and two well-dressed German businessmen come to the table.

1ST GERMAN MAN: *(with heavy accent)* Is the place still free?

The Harrisons do not understand what he has said but they smile.
The men sit down and continue their animated conversation.

BETTY: *(with a questioning look)* Frank, do you know these people?

FRANK: No, I've never laid eyes on them.

BETTY: It's strange. I swear these are the same two men who were standing with us in line at the airport.

The waiter brings the meal and Betty and Frank eat in an uncomfortable silence.

(Class discussion)

Scene III

Later on that day the Harrisons discuss the incident with their son as they stroll through the park.

BETTY: It's peculiar, Jack, but I think we are being followed. The same two men who were behind us at the customs sat down at our table in the restaurant.

FRANK: The only thing they said to us was *"Mahlzeit,"* and if I remember
     correctly the little high school German I had, I think it is a dirty word.
JACK: Oh, come on, both of you. This is ridiculous.
                    (Class discussion)

BETTY: What do you mean ridiculous?
JACK: First of all, it was a coincidence that you ran into those two men
     again. Secondly, in Germany it is perfectly all right for any person to
     sit down at a table with unoccupied seats, even though there are other
     people already sitting at that table.

Doing Business Abroad

Businessmen and women from industrial societies often find
themselves—like Marco Polo before them—in exotic environs, and
they too have to survive.

To the rescue come many books obtainable through the
Intercultural Press Inc. (current [1985] mailing address: P.O. Box
768, Yarmouth, Maine 04096). These include *Training for the
Cross-Cultural Mind* (Casse, 1980), *Training for the Multicultural
Manager* (Casse, 1982), *International Negotiation: A Cross-
Cultural Perspective* (Fisher, 1980), *Managing Cultural Differences*
(Harris and Moran, 1979), and *Managing Cultural Synergy*
(Moran and Harris, 1982). A recent book published by John Wiley
and Sons belongs on the bookshelf: *Marketing by Agreement: A
Cross-Cultural Approach to Business Negotiations* (McCall and
Warrington, 1984).

The techniques described in this chapter can be used advanta-
geously in beginning classes. The next chapter lists two more techniques (culture assimilators and culture capsules) that can be
employed during the first-semester course, and a third technique
(culture clusters) which may be more appropriate for second-or
third-semester students.

Suggested Activities

1. Identify 10 recently published books suitable for creating empathy. They need not relate specifically to the target culture.
2. Develop a mini-drama based on your own experience in another culture.

7

Culture Assimilators, Culture Capsules, Culture Clusters

This chapter illustrates three techniques for teaching cultural concepts. Through culture assimilators (six examples are given), students have interesting programmed readings which they do outside class. Culture capsules (four examples are given) are presented in class in a five-minute talk illustrated by visuals. Culture clusters (one example is given) build upon two or three related culture capsules to simulate in class an event from everyday target life.

The three techniques described in this chapter have proven popular with teachers in culture workshops across the country. The first two techniques, culture assimilators and culture capsules, deal with "mini-exposés" of a small unit of target behavior that is confusing to an American. The third technique, culture clusters, sketches broader relationships among several cultural fragments.

Culture Assimilators

Several social psychologists have developed a programmed, out-of-class technique to facilitate adjustment to another culture (Fiedler, Mitchell, and Triandis, 1971). This technique, called the culture assimilator, provides the student with as many as 75 to 100 episodes of target cultural behavior. Each episode describes a "critical incident" of cross-cultural interaction that is usually a common occurrence in which an American and a host national interact, a situation the American finds puzzling, conflictful, or which he is likely to misinterpret, and a situation that can be interpreted in a fairly unequivocal manner, given sufficient knowledge about the culture.

After reading the episode, the student chooses the correct response from four plausible explanations of the behavior described in the episode. The student is provided with feedback which, if the student has erred in his choice, redirects the student and asks him to make another selection. The whole process takes about three minutes for each episode.

Culture assimilators have three advantages over the more common procedure of presenting information via books. Assimilators are more fun to read; they actively involve the student with a cross-cultural problem; and they have been shown to be more effective in controlled experiments.

The content of the assimilators can be varied to suit the instructor's purpose. For example, within the organizational framework argued in this book, about 20 episodes that pertain to each of the seven cultural goals could constitute an assimilator. The validity of the episode and the correct response are ascertained by pretesting with host nationals.

Culture assimilators have been constructed for the Arab countries, Iran, Thailand, Central America, Greece and for black-white interaction in urban U.S. The following two illustrative episodes are taken from the Honduras Culture Assimilator (Symonds, O'Brien, Vidmar, and Hornik, 1967). Each response to each episode appears, in the original, on a different page.

Culture Assimilator Episode 1: Honduras

George was involved in a serious conversation with the schoolteacher. He was trying to find out why the educational standards were so low and why the teachers did not unite in an endeavor to better their working conditions and improve the educational standards. He told the teacher that back home in Chicago the teachers had gone on strike and refused to teach until their working conditions were improved. He also stated that since the teacher is a professional, the teacher must promote new and better methods of teaching and not wait for the school board or the government to initiate changes. The teacher merely smiled wanly, shrugged, and changed the subject.

Why do think the teacher did not seem to be interested in what George had to say?

A. Teachers, like all Hondurans, are lazy. So long as they get paid, they do not really care about educational standards.
B. Unions are illegal in Honduras.
C. Teachers in the villages are appointed by the government and have very little to say about what or how they teach.
D. The teacher himself was poorly educated and did not feel competent to discuss the matter.

You chose A

It is unlikely that a person would voluntarily become a teacher if he did not have some interest in helping to educate people. You have made two assumptions here that are not warranted by what you have read in this and past episodes. The assumptions are that Hondurans are lazy and that Hondurans have a strong affinity for money at the expense of other values. Do not make assumptions like this unless you have good reasons for doing so.

Reread the episode and make another choice.

You chose B

This answer might explain the teacher's behavior, if it were the case. Have we given you any indications that unions are illegal? Do not make assumptions like this when you are going through the assimilator. Try to apply information you have already learned.

   Reread the episode and make another choice.

You chose C

Even if you were not aware that teachers are appointed by the government, you should have been able to apply the information you learned in the last episode, about the situation of the mayor, to this episode and the situation of the teacher. Their situations are somewhat similar. Teachers are required to conform rigidly to the curriculum laid down by the Honduran Board of Education, a department of the government. Not only that, but their position as teacher is dependent upon the government. Quite often when there is a change in government a teacher is out of a job and is replaced by another teacher. Under conditions of such instability the teacher is not in a position to exert much pressure upon the Central Government.

You chose D

There may be some truth in this, but on what evidence are you basing your choice of this alternative? Use information you have already learned and try to apply it from one situation to another.

   Reread the episode and make another choice.

Culture Assimilator Episode 2: Honduras

George and his friend had made plans to visit some of the surrounding *aldeas* (very small villages, or hamlets). They intended to travel quite a considerable distance, so they decided to rent some burros. They went to the mayor of their village who promised to have two burros ready for them the following morning. The boys were up early and ready to leave by 8:00. When the burros had not arrived by 8:30, they went in search of the mayor. He told them the man with the burros was up in the hills and would be back about 10:00. The boys waited and finally the man arrived at 11:00. He told them that he had some burros, but that he would not be able to get them that day since someone else had them. He said that if they wanted to leave the next day, he would have them for them by 8:00 the next morning. The boys were annoyed and told the man that since they were paying for the use of the burros, they expected that he would have them ready for them. The man just shrugged. The boys realized there was nothing else for them to do so they agreed to wait till tomorrow. After searching for the man the next morning, they finally found him at 9:30. He told them he had forgotten about the burros but would have them for them in a few minutes. At 11:00 he finally showed up with only one burro, stating that the other one was still away and the boys would have to take turns riding and walking.

Which alternative best describes the reason for the behavior in the episode?

  A. Hondurans are inconsiderate.
  B. Neither the mayor nor the other man really believed the North Americans would pay for the burros, so they were not putting themselves out.
  C. Hondurans have many different values from North Americans. One of them is very little concern for the passage of time.
  D. The man with the burros and the mayor both felt that the North Americans should not visit the *aldea*. They felt the boys should spend all their time in the village, so they were making it difficult for them to make the trip.

You chose A

By now you should have realized that this just is not so. Hondurans are very hospitable and easy to get along with. They would not consciously be inconsiderate to a visitor.

Think this over more carefully. Reread the episode and make another choice.

You chose B

This choice is not consistent with what you have already learned about the hospitality and friendliness of the Honduran.

Reread the episode and make another choice.

You chose C

This is the alternative that you should have been able to choose by a process of elimination, if nothing else. The other alternatives are either inconsistent with the idea of Honduran hospitality or emphasize only individual personality differences of one or two people.

An incident such as the one described in this passage could occur, and does, many times in Honduras. By North American standards, Hondurans are unreliable. However, you cannot use North American standards when you are interacting with people of another culture.

The Honduran conception of time is somewhat different from that of the North American. The villager is not at all concerned with what we would call procrastination. He does things if and when it pleases him and cannot easily be pushed. It is not so much that he is stubborn or inconsiderate; it is just that he cannot understand why anyone else should be in a hurry when he is not. This is, by and large, a general aspect of village life. It is slow and easy. What does not get done today can just as easily wait till tomorrow, or next week. You will encounter this and have to contend with it in all your dealings with Hondurans.

You chose D

It might be possible that this explanation could account for an isolated incident, but the assimilator is not concerned with isolated incidents. An attitude such as that expressed by the mayor and the other man is not really consistent with what you already know about the hospitality of the Hondurans. While there might be one or two Hondurans who feel this way it would certainly not be a general attitude.

Reread the episode and make another choice.

A practical forum for writing assimilator episodes is a workshop where each participant suggests some. The most promising of these episodes should then be validated on natives of the target culture. Four unvalidated episodes appear here—one for German, one for Spanish, and two for French. These episodes were prepared by experienced teachers (many of them experts in the target culture) in courses or workshops I directed. Several were written under the direct supervision of Harry Triandis.

Culture Assimilator Episode 3: On a Train in Germany

This episode was prepared by Ildiko Bodoni.

> Susan was traveling from Hamburg to Frankfurt. The train ride was rather long, so she decided to buy a ticket for a *Liegewagen*. It was only slightly more expensive that the regular ticket and she would be able to get a good night's sleep. When she entered the compartment, she was surprised to see four men and a lady already seated there. Since she could see no beds, she assumed that later on they would go to another compartment, with the men separate from the women. Imagine her astonishment when the porter came, folded down the seats so that they formed six bunk beds and gave everyone a pillow and a blanket! She sat upright on her bunk bed, not sleeping all night, afraid of the men.

Why was Susan upset?

A.   The German ticket agent had cheated her and sold her the wrong ticket.

B.   She thought that she should have moved to the correct compartment and was angry at herself for not doing so.

C. She had confused the concept of a *Liegewagen* with that of a *Schlafwagen*.

D. Germans have very loose morals and she might have been the object of "improper" behavior.

Your answer was A

This answer is incorrect because Susan had received the correct ticket for the amount of money paid and for what she had requested.

Go back and reread the article carefully.

Your answer was B

This answer is incorrect; all the compartments in that car were alike, and her ticket had specified this compartment.

Go back and reread the article carefully.

Your answer was C

This is the correct answer because Susan had confused a *Liegewagen* with a *Schlafwagen*. In a *Liegewagen* one does not have a private compartment with a made-up bed, and strangers ignore each other. Susan was thinking of a *Schlafwagen*, which is similar to the American Pullman car, when she had bought the ticket.

Your answer was D

This answer is incorrect, because it is a false generalization.

Go back and reread the article carefully.

Culture Assimilator Episode 4: Colombia

This episode was prepared by Diane Pretzer.

Bob and Mary Jones, recent arrivals in Bogotá, have been invited to the home of a Colombian coworker for a dinner party. Their host mentioned 9 P.M. Bob was surprised at the late hour of starting, but he and Mary made it a point to arrive right on time so as not to delay dinner.

Arriving at the door, they rang the bell. After a long pause, they rang again. Finally a servant appeared and ushered them into the living room, which was dark until that moment when the lamps were lighted. Rather puzzled looks passed between them as they sat silently for a while, and they finally began to talk, almost in whispers. "Do you suppose we got the wrong house or the wrong night?" Anxiously they watched the door. At 9:45 their host appeared, greeted them cordially, and said he and his wife would be with them shortly. At 10:30, host and hostess appeared, followed by servants with drinks, and soon, other guests arrived. Still puzzled, the Joneses relaxed, but were certainly glad when dinner was finally served at 11:30.

What best explains the delay?

A. Bob and Mary did have the wrong night, but their host and hostess were graciously and valiantly trying to make the best of it. They hurriedly dressed, got some neighbors to come in, and gave a pretty good impromptu party.

B. Bob and Mary hadn't discovered yet that, regardless of time mentioned, no host would expect his guests to arrive until at least one or one and one-half hours later.

C. Bob was mistaken when he thought they were told the party was at 9:00. His friend had said there would be nine guests.

D. Bob and Mary forgot to change their watches when they arrived in Bogotá.

You chose A

This is not the right choice. Latins may be known for hospitality, but not *that* much!

You chose B

This is the appropriate choice. Few nonnatives would know it until they had such an experience, or were especially cautioned by those in the know. The party would proceed at a very leisurely pace, and it might be after midnight when dinner is served. The party might last till 3 A.M., even on a weeknight.

You chose C

If Bob's Spanish was adequate for work in Bogotá, he isn't too likely to mix up *"a las nueve"* and *"habrá nueve invitados."* This is not a good choice.

You chose D

Since they probably have been there at least a few days, this choice is extremely unlikely.

Culture Assimilator Episode 5: France

This episode was prepared by Genelle Morain.

> As a young American tourist in Tours, France, you have been invited to dinner at the home of a French business associate of your father. You know that under such circumstances it is considered polite to bring a bouquet of flowers to the hostess. Accordingly, you arrive at the door of the apartment with a handsome bouquet of white chrysanthemums. As your hostess greets you, you offer the bouquet to her. You notice a look of surprise and distaste cross her countenance before she masters herself and accepts your offering graciously.
>
> All evening you are haunted by the feeling that you have done something wrong. You would like to apologize —but you are at a loss to know what for.

What could explain your hostess' reaction?

A.   A bouquet of chrysanthemums is considered an apology for a serious blunder in French culture.

    B.   A bouquet of chrysanthemums is considered a proposal of marriage in French culture.

    C.   Chrysanthemums are considered the flower of death in French culture.

    D.   The hostess was allergic to chrysanthemums.

You chose A

Although this symbolic use of flowers would be valid in some cultures, the French do not consider the chrysanthemum as a flower of apology.

You chose B

This would seem to be a logical possibility but in French culture the symbolism of the chrysanthemum is allied to an aspect of life other than romance. The French consider the rose the flower of love.

You chose C

Your choice is the correct one. The chrysanthemum is considered *"la fleur de mort"* because it is traditionally used in conjunction with funerals and interments in France.

You chose D

To the allergy-conscious American, this would seem a logical assumption. The French, however, are not so obsessed with allergies, preferring to blame most physical troubles on the liver.

Culture Assimilator Episode 6: France

This episode was prepared by Jane Wright.

> Mary Jones, an American coed majoring in French, was spending her junior year abroad in Paris. She was extremely eager to improve her language skills and to gain deeper

insights into the workings of the French culture. Shortly after Mary's arrival in Paris, she made the acquaintance of Jeanne Dupont, a French girl in one of her classes. Jeanne, her parents, and her brother live in an apartment building about four blocks from Mary's dormitory. The two girls sat together in class and often went to a nearby café after class with a couple of other students for coffee.

Mary has been hopeful that Jeanne would invite her to her home some evening, perhaps for dinner, so that she could meet Jeanne's family, learn more about the French family structure, and see a "real French home." Mary considers Jeanne a friend and can't understand why she hasn't been invited to her home for a casual evening. Finally, Mary decided to drop a subtle hint. In a group one day, she commented that it was difficult to understand much of French culture while living in a dormitory and never really getting on the "inside." Jeanne displayed no reaction to Mary's "hint" and still did not extend such an invitation to her. Mary wondered why.

Which of the following "explanations" most accurately describes why Jeanne has not invited Mary into her home?

A.   Mary's hint was rather "brazen," and the French are disdainful of such forward behavior.

B.   French people tend to invite only very good friends into their home. Jeanne and Mary simply do not know each other well enough to be "friends," as Jeanne sees it.

C.   Jeanne probably does not like Mary very much. Mary should take the hint and not pursue the relationship.

D.   Most French people have negative feelings toward Americans visiting in France. Mary must understand that fact and realize that she will probably never be permitted by Jeanne's parents to visit in their home.

You chose A

It is understandable that you have chosen this explanation because neither Americans nor the French value forward and brazen behavior. However, in this case, Mary was subtle and tactful in dropping her "hint." There must be a different reason for not being invited into Jeanne's home. Think about characteristics typical of the French culture and try again.

You chose B

Correct. It is true that French people tend to invite only very good friends into their homes. Such a tendency does contrast with the American custom of opening homes to casual friends as well as to very close friends. For the French family, the "home" is one's very personal and private domain—not to be invaded by just anyone. Rather, only *very close friends* are invited to *share* an evening with the family. Mary must understand how the French value the home and the concept of friendship. She must be patient and continue to nurture her relationship with Jeanne. If their friendship continues to mature, perhaps she will someday be invited into Jeanne's home.

You chose C

To us Americans it would, indeed, seem plausible that Jeanne simply does not like Mary. However, if we try to step outside of our own culture for a moment and examine the situation more objectively, we see no other indications that Jeanne dislikes Mary. Rather, they seem friendly. Our only indication of any "problem," according to Mary, is that she has not been invited to Jeanne's home. Go back and try again.

You chose D

It is true that we hear many negative things about the "ugly Americans" in France. But to believe that most Frenchmen dislike most Americans on the basis of exposure to a few bungling tourists *alone* would indeed be a misconception. Certainly if Mary is considerate of her French friends and is a friendly person, she will be accepted.

Culture Capsules

Culture capsules are generally prepared outside of class by a student but presented during class time in five or 10 minutes at the end of a period.

The concept was developed by a foreign language teacher, the late Darrel Taylor, in collaboration with an anthropologist, John Sorenson. A succinct description of the technique appeared in *The Modern Language Journal* (Taylor and Sorenson, 1961). Briefly, a culture capsule consists of a paragraph or so of explanation of one minimal difference between an American and a target custom, along with several illustrative photos or relevant realia. Taylor and Sorenson offer the example of a Mexican bullfight to illustrate a cross-cultural difference.

The minimal cultural difference to be highlighted in the capsule can be selected in much the same way as the episodes in culture assimilators are selected. So that culture capsules are not merely disassociated fragments of the life of a society, the capsules' content can be chosen to represent the various relationships outlined in Nostrand's Emergent Model (see Chapter 2).

Like culture assimilators, the subject matter of culture capsules can be quite varied. There are several differences between the two techniques. In assimilators the student has to identify culturally appropriate explanations for the described situation; in culture capsules the explanation of the cross-cultural difference is presented to the student in both the textual description and in the accompanying multi-media razzle-dazzle. Teacher-made assimilators represent essentially out-of-class activities, whereas capsules can be prepared by students for oral delivery during class.

Many well-defined culture capsules have been developed into a series of classroom activities by J. Dale Miller. Under his direction, 100-page units have been developed which examine U.S.-Hispanic and U.S.-South American cultures (Miller, Drayton, and Lyon, 1979), U.S.-French (Miller and Loiseau, 1974), and U.S.-Mexican (Miller and Bishop, 1979). V. Lynn Tyler, a specialist in intercultural communication, has prepared four-page "culturgrams" (i.e., culture capsules) for 75 countries. These are periodically updated; all 75 were revised in 1980–81. (Tyler can be contacted through the BYU Center for International and Area Studies, 130 FOB, Box 61, Provo, UT 84602.)

Culture Capsule: French Bread

This example was prepared by Blossom Adler for the junior high level.

> We speak of a thing being as good as gold, but the French people speak of a thing as being good as bread. The French love and value bread as an important element of life. The French eat bread at every meal. It comes in various shapes and sizes.
>
> The urban French housewife does not bake her own bread. She goes to the bakery daily to buy fresh bread. If bread is left over from the evening meal it will not be wasted. It will be used in cooking or will be toasted for breakfast to be eaten with butter and/or jam. Bread and butter is called *une tartine.* Except in Normandy and Brittany, butter is served only at breakfast or with certain foods (e.g., radishes, Roquefort cheese, on dark bread *[pain bis]* with oysters).
>
> In rural areas, families often make their own delicious dark bread, *pain de campagne* (country bread), which keeps well. Traditionally, a person of honor in the household, perhaps the grandfather, makes a cross on the loaf with a large knife, then cuts slices for all, holding the loaf against his chest and drawing the knife toward himself. Nowadays, this custom is rare, especially in urban areas. Taking a slice of bread, each person places it on the tablecloth above the fork. To eat it s/he will break off a bite-sized piece and hold it in his/her left hand as s/he eats. The person will use the bread as a

"pusher." When it is full of sauce or meat gravy, he will pop it into his mouth and break off another piece. He will use his bread as a pusher for sauces, salads, and between courses to "clear the palate."

French bread is made without shortening or preservatives. Therefore, it dries quickly, and a fresh supply must be purchased for each meal.

Questions

1. How often do the French eat bread?
2. How do they indicate the importance of bread?
3. Why is bread often purchased just before the meal?
4. What happens to any leftover bread?
5. What is a *tartine?*
6. Is butter always served with the bread?
7. How is the bread traditionally sliced in rural France?
8. How does each person eat his slice?
9. Is it polite to use bread as a "pusher" in France?
10. Have you tasted French bread? Do you like it?

Material and instructions to be included with capsule

TITLE OF CAPSULE: Bread

VISUAL EQUIPMENT: Slide projector

RECOMMENDED USE: Junior high students studying a unit on food (e.g., Unit 6, ALM, 2nd Edition)

MATERIALS: Enough French bread for each student to have a slice; enough chunky chocolate bars, broken into pieces, for each student to have a piece; one napkin for each student.

REUSABLE MATERIALS: Slides: Street view of a *boulangerie*, inside view of a *boulangerie*, people carrying bread, several *baguettes*, boy or girl eating their snack of *pain au chocolat* (a roll with chocolate bar baked inside), family table scene.

Chart showing various shapes of bread and their names (taken from Volume 2 of J. Child's *Mastering the Art of French Cooking).*

When each student is served with a napkin, bread, and chocolate, the teacher tells him/her that s/he is about to experience not
only French bread but what French boys and girls eat at snack
time *(le goûter)*.

VOCABULARY TO BE STRESSED: *le pain, la boulangerie, la tartine, le goûter, la
baguette.*

A hundred French culture capsules have been prepared by J.
Dale Miller, along with a helpful teachers' guide (Miller, 1972).

Culture Clusters

Culture clusters consist of about three illustrated culture capsules
which develop related topics, plus one 30-minute classroom simulation which integrates the information contained in the capsules.
In the culminating simulation, or skit, practically all of a classroom can be actively involved in dramatizing one or another of
the roles. This active integrating skit is accomplished by having
the teacher act as narrator to guide the students (through stage
directions) to the appropriate actions and speech.

The concept of culture clusters was developed at the University of Georgia by two teachers, Betsy Meade and Genelle Morain.
The technique is succinctly described in English and well illustrated in French with an example of a French country wedding
(Meade and Morain, 1973).

The easiest way to develop culture clusters is to begin by
thinking of a slice of target life that leads itself to a half-hour skit,
then work backward by identifying three or four component segments that can be explained through culture capsules. Assignments for preparation of the capsules can be delegated to students.

Besides the excellent illustration of this exciting technique
contained in the article by Meade and Morain, another example is
given below. It was prepared by Marsha Rybski for a French class.

Culture Cluster: Un Repas Familial

CULTURAL GOAL: *The student will demonstrate awareness of French behavior in a conventional situation in the target culture: a family meal in a French home.*

Performance objective 1:

TERMINAL BEHAVIOR: The student will place the following items of table service correctly on the table in the position in which they would be placed by a French housewife: tablecloth, plate, glass, silverware/knife rest, napkin, loaf of bread.

CONDITIONS: The student will place the items on the table in the presence of the teacher. He may have as much time as is necessary to place all the items on the table.

CRITERION: The student must correctly place five of the items from the above list.[1] The silverware items will, as shown on the list, be considered as one.

Performance objective 2:

TERMINAL BEHAVIOR: The student will demonstrate proper French table manners in eating the following foods: soup, bread, an apple, meat.

CONDITIONS: The teacher will provide the student with a slice of bread and an apple. (These are difficult to pantomime.) The student will pantomime appropriate manner for eating soup and meat. The student will be seated at a table and provided with a French place setting.

CRITERION: The student will correctly demonstrate French etiquette while eating three of the four items mentioned above.

CULTURE CAPSULE I: How to set the table

CULTURE CAPSULE II: How to act at the table

CULTURE CAPSULE III: The family together at the table

SIMULATION: A family dinner (meal)

DISCUSSION: (Time—fifteen minutes for each cluster, over three days, thirty minutes for simulation and discussion, final day)

Culture Capsule I: How to set the table

OBJECTIVES

1. The student will be able to set a table in the French manner.
2. Identify and pronounce correctly in French the words for the various parts of the table service.

PROCEDURE

1. Teacher holds up objects, one at a time, that belong on table; pronounces their label in French; and asks the students to repeat. As each item is labeled, a flashcard for that item is displayed on a flannel board in the front of the class.

   Visual 1: Table service items and table
   Visual 2: Vocabulary cards and flannel board

   Cards

la cuiller	*le porte-couteau*
le couteau	*le plat*
la fourchette	*le verre*
la cuiller à soupe	*l'assiette creuse (à soupe)*
la serviette	*mettre le couvert*
la nappe	

2. Teacher then gives capsule information, placing items correctly on the table as each is described.

   Alternate: Student may place items on the table as teacher gives following narrative:

In a French home, the table is set for a meal in this way: A tablecloth, *la nappe*, is nearly always used. The plate, *l'assiette*, is put at each place, and the glass, *le verre*, is placed to the right and above the plate. The knife, *le couteau*, and the large soup spoon, *la cuiller à soupe* go to the right of the plate. The spoon, *la cuiller*, is usually placed above the dinner plate, facing bowl down on the tablecloth, rather than at the right beside the knife as is the American custom. The forks, *les fourchettes*, are placed on the left. You may notice however, that the spoons and forks are turned over and placed on the table. When soup is being served, *l'assiette creuse* is put on the plate. The French bread is placed directly on the tablecloth. Bread and butter plates are not used at each place. A napkin made of cloth, *la serviette*, is put at each plate, usually on the plate. In its position at the right of the plate, the knife is rested on a knife holder, *le porte-couteau*.

3.   Evaluation: Teacher holds up items again, eliciting answers to where the object is placed.

Culture Capsule II: How to act at the table

Teacher may review vocabulary items from previous day with flashcards.

OBJECTIVE: The student will be able to pantomime dining in a French home using the appropriate table manners.

PROCEDURE
Visual 1: Set table and chairs
Visual 2: Loaf of bread and bottle of "wine"

1.   The teacher gives capsule information while acting out the described behaviors.
     Alternate: Student may act out behaviors described in the following narrative:

Table manners in France are somewhat different from ours. First, you place the napkin on your lap; the men might tuck them into their belt. The wine is then served. (While most French adults drink wine at lunch and/or dinner, a bottle of mineral water and a carafe of tap water are always served as well. Many adolescents prefer soft drinks and fruit juices. In some families, especially those in rural areas, children drink wine mixed with half water.) As you may have guessed, when soup is eaten, the large *cuiller à soupe* is used. However, the French spoon the soup toward themselves and eat from the end of the spoon, not the side. While eating, it is proper to keep your free hand on the table, not in your lap. Also, the bread is quite handily used to scoop up vegetables or sauces and clean up the plate at the end of the meal. To cut food, the knife is used in the right hand and the fork in the left. Food is then put directly into the mouth with the left hand and the fork. The knife is held in the right hand while chewing or returned to the *porte-couteau* while not being used. This protects the tablecloth from getting dirty. When whole fruits (such as apples or pears) are served, they are not eaten with the hands. The fork is again used in the left hand to hold the fruit and the knife is used to cut and peel the fruit. The pieces of fruit are then eaten with the fork in the left hand. It is important that the plate be empty at the end of the meal since this shows you have enjoyed the meal. At the end of the meal, in some French families, children thank their mother for the food she prepared.

2. Evaluations:
    A. Teacher asks for volunteers to come up to table to demonstrate correct manners for eating bread, cutting and eating meats and vegetables, eating soup. *Visual 3:* (student furnished) apple or pear, knife and fork
    B. Each student demonstrates ability to eat a piece of fruit in the French manner.

Culture Capsule III: The family at the table

OBJECTIVE: The student will be able to state three reasons why the family meal is so important to the French.

PROCEDURE
Visual 1: Slide—family seated at table
Visual 2: Picture of French woman at work in kitchen

The teacher explains the following attitudes and customs:

The French family meal is considered an important time of togetherness. Problems and ideas are discussed as a family while everyone enjoys the meal. Since this is an important part of the day for each member of the family, each makes a point of allowing time for this meal, which may last two hours or more. During this time the family may talk together about the day's events, vacation plans, events in the news, and so on. Most French families have this large meal at noon. However, in cases where the father or children do not come home during the middle of the day, the family dines together in the evening. Food is a very important part of the French way of life. The average French family spends about a quarter of the budget on food, economizing to save for occasional treats. The family meal is especially important to the mother since she has spent much of her day shopping for and preparing the food with care.

EVALUATIONS
1. Teacher asks students for three reasons why the family meal is important to the French.
2. Discussion, led by the teacher, may deal with differences between American and French attitudes toward eating together as a family.
Simulation: A family meal

OBJECTIVES
1. Demonstrate ability of students to set the table in the correct French manner.
2. Demonstrate proper French table manners.

3. Demonstrate understanding of the rapport within family and importance of the meal by enacting roles of the family members.
4. Contribute to class discussion of French attitudes such as importance of food, importance of family, role of mother as cook, respect for traditional formalities, and the importance of "receiving" guests with proper *consideration*. (Except in the case of intimate friends, guests are usually entertained at cafés and restaurants.)

PROCEDURE[2]
Realia: Desks arranged as tables. Table service items, "wine," fruit, bread.
1. Teacher divides students into groups of four and assigns roles as family members.
2. Students arrange themselves at tables as "families."
3. Teacher names items to be placed on table in French as students place them correctly on their family table.
4. Students playing roles of mother and father begin serving on instruction from the teacher.
5. Students simulate a family meal together, simulating behaviors learned in culture capsules.

DISCUSSION
1. Teacher leads discussion on attitudes illustrated in simulation (see Goal 4).
2. Teacher asks students to discuss differences and similarities in the behavior they just exhibited and the behavior they exhibit at their table at home.

EVALUATIONS
1. Postsimulation discussion.
2. Students may be asked to name items from table service in French.
3. Students may be asked to draw diagram of a properly set table in France.

4. Role-playing:
   a. Students might perform a short dramatization showing the French reaction to Americans eating in a French café.
   b. Students might dramatize the visit of a French exchange student to an American home for dinner.
5. Students may be asked to discuss their personal reactions to the attitudes expressed in the simulation.

Suggested Activities

1. Write a culture assimilator for the topic you chose in Chapter 4.
2. Prepare a culture capsule relating to your chosen topic.
3. Prepare a culture cluster composed of three culture capsules including the culture capsule you have prepared.

Notes

1. They are in relatively the same positions on the table as in an American home.
2. The teacher may wish to provide a narrative by which the students can tell what food they are eating to demonstrate correct manners. In this case the teacher has chosen to circulate around the room, observing behaviors, including discussion, as they would more naturally occur since everyone at the table would not necessarily be eating the same food at the same time.

8

Asking the
Right Questions

Several approaches to helping students ask significant questions are explored in this chapter. First, a technique is suggested for patently bizarre and trivial questions. Second, a technique is illustrated which uses newspapers and magazines as a base for the generation and refinement of student hypotheses. Third, a simple but effective way to develop student skill in information retrieval is described. Fourth, methods of interviewing native informants are discussed.

A major charge of education consists in motivating students to ask productive questions and then teaching students skills that will enable them to find answers to their questions. Yet it is common practice to give students answers before they have formulated the questions. Little wonder that a frequently heard classroom adage is "it goes in one ear and out the other!" Perhaps the most significant answer given in the twentieth century, Einstein's famous $E = MC^2$, is utterly meaningless to those of us who have not formulated the necessary questions in advance of hearing the "answer."

The Exotic as Springboard

What immediately hits the student of a foreign culture is that things are done differently there. These exotic differences are two-edged swords. They provoke interest but they reinforce the ethnocentricity of the learner. ("Those Frenchmen are really crazy—the men kiss each other!" "Latin Americans are really lazy—they're always taking siestas." "Italians are so emotional—always waving their hands around.") Culturally contrastive patterns can best be exploited for their motivating interest by using them as points of entry into the target culture. Once inside, the student should be helped to discover that even seemingly bizarre behavior usually makes perfect sense once it is seen within the context of the rest of the culture. Once its relationship to other patterns and to universal needs is seen, it makes sense.

The two principles that people everywhere satisfy the same basic needs (although the relative importance of these basic needs and the patterns available to satisfy them differ from culture to culture) and that many different patterns interact in concert for basic needs to be satisfied, along with Brooks' reminder to focus on the individual, help us ask significant questions about relationships in the target culture. But, alas, human curiosity is not limited to "significant" questions. Curiosity, however perverse, is such a strong and useful motivator that it is not to be trifled with.

How can the teacher capitalize on a student's offbeat interest in something such as whether most belly buttons in Italy are inverted or protrude? To assist the student's perception of significant relationships in this patently absurd instance, he can be asked to list things that might affect the appearance of navels and, conversely, things that navels might plausibly affect. The list might include things such as whether it is a matter of genetic determination and, if so, whether the gene pool for inverted navels in Italy differs in frequency from that of other culture areas; whether techniques used by doctors or midwives during birth affects the phenomenon; whether infant care in Italy, such as swaddling, has an effect; whether one form or another is considered more aesthetic; and if so, whether this affects fashion in any way.

While any one of these topics may be interesting, plotting the interrelation of several topics affords practice in making guesses within a cultural context which is broader than the "we do it this way but they do it that way" of much contrastive analysis. The object is to get the student *into* the target culture in a way that makes it easier for him to see how behavior systematically and logically fits together. The teacher is not, of course, expected to know, or even care, what the answers are to most questions posed by students. The modern teacher is more interested in the process of inquiry than in having students memorize disembodied facts.

Another example of turning trivia into something more promising involves a student with no known academic or intellectual accomplishments or interests except two: girls and stealing cars. He might be cajoled into making a scrapbook of clippings of girls from the target culture and photos of cars culled from a stack of Mexican magazines. If the teacher is female, the student will undoubtedly try to test her sophistication with some of the pinups he has collected, so she might want to forget about part of the initial assignment and emphasize the inanimate. Pictures of cars can be catalogued according to make, model, year, number of occupants, whether male or female is driving, type of highway, and so on. The student's summary of this information (e.g., number of cars collected, number of females driving) can be presented to the class to see what kind of "conclusions" (hypotheses) might be ventured concerning the economic structure, transportation facilities, and position of women in the country based on the data. The class can be asked to suggest other kinds of information that might check the "conclusions" (e.g., number of licensed women, number of cars imported annually from Europe). Some of the South American magazines would be more interesting to old car buffs. Some Peruvian taxis, for example, are virtual antiques. The main pedagogical point in these exercises is to (1) get the student interested in the target culture; (2) direct this interest, step by step, into pertinent areas of concern; and (3) develop student skill in discovering things about peoples and places.

The teacher's role in a problem-oriented approach such as this is to assist the student in defining the problem that interests the student. The more precisely a problem is defined, the less trouble a student will have in researching it, and the more fruitful will be the outcome. (It is not desirable to have the student stymied by an extensive background search. As would be the case with the car pictures, sometimes it is advisable to jump in and begin manipulating the "documents" and fill in background as the need arises.) The teacher, with the cooperation of the school librarian, can also guide the student in his or her bibliographic work. Rather than be told to read a book on the general topic chosen, students should be taught to skim and to read carefully only limited sections that are really relevant to their specific area of interest. Otherwise, the student will fast become bogged down in the fantastic explosion of knowledge that threatens to engulf all scholars, especially those in science and the social sciences. If the student report is to be written, the teacher can offer invaluable assistance and encouragement in the first draft. If the report is presented orally, sympathetic questions can help a student evaluate his or her own work.

Brooks (1964, pp. 82-96) asks many promising questions about some 64 different topics such as: "In what ways are age, provenance, social status, academic achievement, degree of formality, interpersonal relations, aesthetic concern, personality, reflected in . . . speech?" "What common words or expressions in English have direct equivalents that are not tolerated in the new culture, and vice versa?" "What objects are often found decorating the bureau and walls of a young person's bedroom?" "What careers have strong appeal for the young?" The particular aspect of the target culture that initially motivates a given student is of little importance as long as some of the questions inspired by the interest lead to a discovery that cultural patterns interact and that they are used by people to satisfy universal needs.

An especially strong source to aid teachers pose fruitful questions of any culture area has been prepared by Volunteers in Asia (Darrow and Palmquist, 1977). The hundreds of articulated questions are grouped under topics such as Roles of women and men, Religion and beliefs, Food, Music and art, Education. Another source for relevant cultural questions is available in Saville-Troike (1978). She asks, for example, how insults are expressed, who may talk to whom, what significance dress has for group identity.

Generating Cultural Hypotheses

Facts are the fodder we use to propel our thoughts; thus they become victims in the planned obsolescence of a growing mind. Schools often unwittingly reinforce greater respect for teacher authority than for the value of student intellectual discovery. Yet a practical opportunity to demonstrate respect for individual intellectual inquiry exists in the teaching of culture. The profession's lack of training in cultural concepts need not be a crippling disadvantage in activities where the focus is on developing in students the ability to hazard productive guesses about the target culture. This approach to guessing, or hypothesis refinement, helps us avoid what Alfred North Whitehead (1928) has called the Fallacy of Dogmatic Finality.

We did not get to the moon by holding sacred the scientific facts of the 1950s. We never move away from the cozy dark corner of the cave, where self-serving myths soothe our troubles, unless we are open to new facts as well as old facts in fresh combinations. The folk wisdom of many cultures tells us that experience is the best teacher. To learn from experience is to change our way of doing and understanding.

One realization that should be exploited is that generalities can be made from even the bits of authentic cultural information contained in foreign language newspapers, even by students with little if any fluency in the target language.

Simple facts can be used as building blocks to develop skill in extracting meaning from these news fragments. This is the same technique an archeologist uses when he examines pottery shards. What is important is not the acquisition of a broader base of arbitrary and pointless facts, but the ability to gather facts from a variety of sources—and then to do something with the facts! It is the human mind that organizes and assigns importance to facts. Many great insights are formed by people who are puttering around with data in an attempt to tease out something which makes sense.

"Mini-media" units can begin with a simple question or two to help focus attention on the "document," the newspaper clipping. The next several questions zero in on aspects of the everyday life of some target people. The student is then asked to generalize beyond the specific information contained in the clippings. He should not feel under much pressure to generate a "correct" hypothesis, or educated guess. No hypothesis starts by being correct. Some are more useful than others. One often does not discover which are useful until a lot of time has been spent on a problem and one realizes that understanding of the problem is still where it was at the beginning. Such is the reward of scientists.

A second concept these mini-media units develop is that hypotheses (or guesses or insights or generalities or whatever) must *always* be refined. If X is true, under what circumstances is it true? For the purpose of mini-media units, it is much more important to begin identifying what additional knowledge is necessary to check the soundness of your generality than it is to get the information needed to refine it. The easiest way to begin refining a hypothesis about human behavior is to ask how the generality is affected by age, sex, social class, and place of residence.

The cultural generalization that results from the guess or hypothesis should be based on empirical evidence. The ad illustrations in foreign language newspapers and magazines are an ideal source of authentic empirical evidence. Mini-media units have been developed for Hispanic (Seelye and Day, 1982; Day, 1977), French (Schulz, 1982; Jorstad, 1976), Italian (Rallo, 1976), and

German (Culver, 1976) cultures to sensitize students to the potential of these "documents" in developing cultural insights. The example on pages 146-47 of a brief exercise to develop student skill in making and refining hypotheses is taken from the first of a series of these mini-media units, and it deals with Hispanic culture (Seelye and Day, 1982). The unit is entitled *"¿George?"*

Another, somewhat longer, unit from the same source uses physicians ads as the cultural "documents" to be scrutinized (pp. 148-49).

This ad ran in an Argentine newspaper. The word *George*, which appears three times in the ad, is an English proper noun and has no other meaning in Spanish.

Check the best response.

1. What kind of business establishment is *George?*

_____(a) a general notions store for men and women

_____(b) a men's store

_____(c) a women's store

_____(d) a children's store

_____(e) not enough information to determine

2. The ad implies that the reader should buy gifts for _____.

_____(a) children

_____(b) parents

_____(c) mothers

_____(d) fathers

_____(e) not enough information to determine

3. Why do you think the advertiser chose to use children in the picture?

4. Why do you think English was mixed with Spanish in this ad?

• DIRECTORIO PROFESIONAL •

Unit 13: Is there a doctor in the ad?

The training required of a medical doctor in Spain or Latin America is about the same as that required in the U.S. Mexico, for example has some of the world's most distinguished specialists in heart disorders. The authors of this booklet, or their families, have received medical treatment, some of which required surgery, in five different countries of Latin America. For us, the competency of Latin American physicians is well established. One of the best of these was a neighborhood doctor who made house calls for fifty cents in an urban slum area where one of the authors was living. Latin America may be one of the few places in the hemisphere where doctors still make house calls.

As you can see from the ads shown in this unit, medical doctors (as well as other professionals) advertise. Based on these ads, all of which appeared on one newspaper page, answer the following questions.

Check the best response, or answer in the space provided.

1. How many women doctors appear in the ads?

____(a) one   ____(b) two

____(c) four

2. Which doctors are advertising treatment for disorders?

3. Which ads are advertising treatment for children?

4. Which ads are advertising treatment for allergies?

5. How many doctors have one or more "last" names that seem to be of non-Spanish origin (i.e., German, North American, etc.)?

____(a) less than 5   ____(b) 6-9

____(c) 10-13

6. What does the initial stand for in a name such as Dr. Lorenzo Machado M.?

____(a) indicates his medical speciality

____(b) indicates his mother's surname

____(c) none of the above

____(d) not enough information to determine

7. What is an *otorrinolaringólogo?*

____(a) an ear specialist

____(b) a throat specialist

____(c) a foot specialist

____(d) none of the above

8. List at least one characteristic of the language of the ads.

9. What is the significance of the name Matute in Dra. Gladis López de Matute?

____(a) It's her mother's surname.

____(b) It's her father's surname.

____(c) It's her husband's surname.

____(d) none of the above

10. What does V.° B.° stand for?

____(a) Visto Bueno

____(b) Vias Bacteriologicos

____(c) Venas Buenas

11. List as many hypotheses about life in Latin America as you can (for some future refinement, perhaps), based on your analysis of the documents in this unit.

The following stab at writing an end-of-year performance objective which might apply to many mini-media units helps let students know what is expected of them.

Goal V: Evaluating statements about another culture

TERMINAL BEHAVIOR: To demonstrate skill in generating and refining cultural hypotheses the student will:

1. Observe a cultural pattern from a picture, cartoon, drawing, or news fragment;
2. Make one generalization about the culture drawn from examination of the picture, etc.;
3. Indicate five sources of information to which one might refer in order to further refine the generalization.

CONDITIONS: The illustrations in 1 will be given in class. You will be allowed to choose one from among five; all will be taken from target newspapers or magazines which have been available in class for at least one month. You will be given 30 minutes to complete the three terminal behaviors.

CRITERION: At least four of the five chosen sources must be valid choices.

Finding Information

Key Ideas

Chapter 12 in this book identifies many specific sources containing cultural data. The present section is addressed to the question of how to develop students' skill in identifying sources to answer their questions.

One approach (Seelye, 1968b) took 23 "key ideas" of a culture area, Latin America, and had students prepare an annotated bibliography of relevant sources from 40 books that were available to the classroom. The key ideas in this case had been identified previously by a group of historians and social scientists (Gill, Conroy, and Cornbleth, 1967) and were organized under six headings:

I.   The physical environment

II.   Historical backgrounds

III.   Contemporary society and the family

IV.   Contemporary culture values, ideals, and creative expression

V.   Contemporary economics

VI.   Contemporary politics, government, and international relations.

The following example of how one of the key ideas was indexed illustrates the process. The titles referred to are annotated in Seelye (1968b, 1972b).

> *Key Idea III.* C. Relations among the many ethnic groups vary from nation to nation, although in general there tends to be less overt racial discrimination and hostility than in the United States.
> Adams (1960); Alexander (1962:29-56, the people); Arciniegas (1967:215-33, Negroes and whites in Haiti); Hanke (1967b, new Latin American nationalism); Heath (1965:342-60, social stratification in Latin America; 475-556, world-views); Keen (1967:456-89, society in transition); Loprete (1965:206-26, social life); Mörner (1967); Schurz (1964:51-87, the people); Wagley (1968:155-74, concept of social race); Wagley (1958:93-118, Negroes in Martinique).

This type of exercise combines development of basic bibliographic skills with the spin-off effect of teaching key ideas. An excellent source for learning how to learn in cross-cultural situations is available in Wight and Hammons (1970b).

Topical Performance Objectives

An effective approach to teaching cross-cultural research skills in elementary school social studies classes has been prepared by Ernest L. Rock (1973). Rock is an exceptionally creative person who took his doctorate in foreign language education. Even though these instructional materials are aimed at the later elementary school social studies student, many teachers report success with them on the junior high and tenth grade levels.

The materials include 100 performace objectives ("I can name at least three ways by which a ＿＿＿＿＿ person entertains himself in his home") contained in a series of booklets (e.g., *What's to Eat, What the People Wear, It Happens Every Day*). Students are not given information on the topics; rather, they are guided through a series of "prerequisite activities" to finding the information themselves. A number of creative activities are suggested for each topic to interest students in using their newfound information.

The following examples illustrate how Rock's technique was adapted by foreign language teachers. Three examples are for French classes, one for Spanish. The first example was prepared by Blossom Adler; the second example was written by Emily Dewhirst; the third was jointly prepared by Connie Layton and Sister Clare Eileen Craddock; the last one for Spanish was prepared by Jerome Carvajal.

The French Telephone

Performance objectives

1. I will be able to describe at least one feature of a French telephone that differs from ours.
2. I will be able to use the telephone in the French manner of composing the number using good French pronunciation.
3. I will begin a conversation with a friend using the French pattern of *politesse*, with good pronunciation.

Prerequisite activities

1. In the library, consult the *Encyclopaedia Britannica* and the *World Book.* Look up "France, communication."
2. Look into the stack of back copies of *Bonjour* on the table at the back of the French classroom. Look for pictures of phones and skits about the use of phones. Practice reading the words and phrases aloud. Ask your teacher for help with pronunciation.
3. Look into the stacks of other French magazines on the reserve shelf in the school library. Look for pictures of people using phones or of phones alone. Study them to see if the French phones are different from ours.
4. Ask your teacher or audiovisual department to help you locate filmstrips, slides, etc., on "The Telephone in France."

Creative activity

1. From pictures available, enlarged (line) drawings may be done by willing/artistic members of the class.
2. Constructively creative students may add an *écouter* to a toy telephone so that there are two "French" phones to use for role playing.
3. Each student will perform in front of the class in pairs, using the phone, composing the number orally as he reaches his number (after dialing), and with French *politesse*, begin a conversation with a friend.

Breton

Performance objective

The student will list four Breton customs and write a paragraph in French on each with no more than five errors. Each paragraph is to explain the significance of the custom.

The student will name and tell how four Breton customs (including language and costume) represent values that differ from those held by French people in general.

Prerequisite activities

1. In the library, consult the card catalogue, encyclopedias, and the *Reader's Guide to Periodical Literature.*
2. Consult the books on French civilization and culture in the foreign language learning center.
3. Check the list of filmstrips, slides, and other visual materials in the language center.
4. Consult the card box for French people in the area who have knowledge of Bretagne and are willing to be interviewed.
5. Look up recent articles on Bretagne in the *National Geographic.*
6. Write to the French National Tourist Office for information on Bretagne.
7. Write or phone airline companies or travel bureaus for information and brochures.
8. Check the record collection of French music (learning center).
9. Listen to the tapes of people from Bretagne (see instructor).

Creative activities

1. Decorate a bulletin board illustrating Bretagne and its customs.
2. Draw a traditional Breton costume, describe it to the class in French, and explain when it is still worn.
3. Compile a scrapbook of information, pictures, and sketches concerning one of the following topics: a Breton church, a *pardon.*
4. Correspond with a French student in Bretagne. Exchange at least three letters.

5. Build a model of a Breton cemetery, explaining to the class in French the significance of the different parts.
6. Look through copies of *Réalités, Paris Match, National Geographic,* etc., for pictures to illustrate a five-minute talk in French contrasting *l'Arcoat* and *l'Armor.*
7. In a five-minute talk in French, explain the history of the Breton language and the furor in present-day France over the use of the language today.
8. In a written paper of not less 500 words or in a five-minute speech in French, give examples of five famous Breton sailors and their exploits.
9. Draw a *menhir* and a *dolmen* and explain what they are to the class in a five-minute talk in French.

The French University

Performance objectives

1. I will be able to discuss at least four social activities of a French university student.
2. I will be able to discuss at least five academic activities of a French university student.

Prerequisite activities

1. Consult French magazines and periodicals in the library or in the French language room.
2. Interview French exchange students.
3. Contact a member of a French student organization.
4. Write to a French university for copies of schedules and curricula.
5. Contact the French embassy for posters, flyers, etc., relating to French student life.
6. Write to the *Services Culturels Français,* 972 Fifth Ave., New York 10021, for their series of brochures on French education.
7. Consult the *International Index to Periodicals* for articles on French education.

8. Consult reference works (e.g., civilization books) containing information on French education.

Creative activities

1. Write a paper contrasting requirements for a university degree in France and in the United States.
2. Present a skit of a classroom situation in French university life.
3. Make a notebook of newspaper articles on French academic life.
4. Prepare a discussion on student organizations at French universities.

La Comida

Objective

I can identify appropriate Mexican foods eaten at the four meals: *desayuno, comida, merienda (refacción),* and *cena.*

Prerequisite activities

1.   Study the menus from several Mexican restaurants.
2.   Study the food ads in Mexican newspapers.
3.   Refer to Lesson 36, pages 189-91 in textbook *Primera Vista.*
4.   Refer to Lesson 28 in textbook *Bienvenidos.*
5.   Refer to menu, pages 352-54 in *Usted y Yo.*
6.   Ask native speakers to describe what they eat.
7.   Go to a Mexican restaurant.
8.   See the filmstrip *Skimpy come un buen desayuno.*
9.   Refer to the Time-Life series *Mexican Cookbook.*
10. Talk with the home economics teacher.
11. Write letters to the Del Monte Company, asking for menus and recipes.

Creative activities

1. Cut out pictures of food and people in restaurants from Mexican newspapers and magazines and make a notebook.
2. Draw your own conclusion from the data you have collected and incorporate them into writing your own menu for one of the four meals.
3. Make a bulletin board.
4. Illustrate a menu for a Mexican restaurant using art media of your choice.
5. Learn how to make one of the foods and offer it to the class.
6. Take the information you have gathered about Mexican food and hypothesize that the same food is eaten in all Hispanic cultures. How would you refine (test) this hypothesis to see to what extent it is true?

Interviewing Informants

The following exchange was overheard between a Korean elementary school student and a Chicago ESL teacher:

TEACHER: "How old are you?"

STUDENT: "I was ten but now I'm eight."

How to make sense of this? (And, it turns out, it makes perfect sense.) The obvious answer is to seek additional information from someone who has lived extensively in Korea. Fortunately, the teacher had a Korean colleague in the same school. The answer was simple: Koreans consider themselves to be one year old at birth and two years old as soon as the New Year arrives. A person born the day before the lunar calendar New Year's Day would be two years old his/her second day of life. The "... but now I'm eight" refers to age adjustment made by the U.S. cultural system to the child's age.

Intercultural communication teachers have an insatiable need for all kinds of culture-specific information if the behavior of the people they study is to be understood. There are several ways teachers can put students into contact with the best source of information—natives of the target culture.

Locating native informants within the local community can become a class project. Once a directory is compiled, the teacher can enhance student interaction with bearers of the target culture by inviting them into class for visits, by encouraging students to talk to them out of class, and by establishing a strategy for communication via the telephone or mails. As with any other type of instructional device, purposeful activities that students pursue for credit should be planned. Students should be assigned to interview native informants.

By high school age, the natural curiosity of primary school children often has degenerated into a self-conscious reticence which makes interviews with strangers difficult. Embarrassing silences and martyred attempts at yes or no questions characterize many classroom "confrontations" with natives. With a little bit of planning, much of this awkwardness can be avoided.

Spending an hour every two or three weeks with a classroom visitor from the target culture does not rob time from an in-depth analysis of the imperfect subjunctive so much as it dramatizes what intercultural learning is all about—direct personal communication with another culture. Regular planned interviews with natives should become an integral part of language instruction. (William F. Marquardt used to conduct whole ESL courses this way, with a different informant each day. Students subsequently wrote letters to each informant, making comments on the substance of what the informant said during the class interview.)

Culture shock is a two-way street, as many visitors to American classrooms can painfully attest. Planning for an interview begins with concern for putting the guest at ease and establishing quick rapport. This is not so difficult to achieve. Everyone responds to people who are genuinely interested in them, especially when the interest is not marred by a display of ignorance so dismal as to be insulting. It does not generally go over very big to ask a visitor from Costa Rica about life in South America, or to ask a Brazilian to speak Spanish.

Preparation begins with the students locating the most detailed map available of the guest's country and studying it to get a feel for the land and place names. Next, a brief survey of the vital statistics of the country should be read by all students. This need not exceed two pages in length; encyclopedias or almanacs are adequate sources. The background gleaned from the map and survey equips the student interviewer with the minimum necessary knowledge to begin the next step: preparing the initial interview questions.

Each student can prepare three questions on relatively neutral areas of the target culture that cannot be answered by yes or no. Questions that reflect a little background research concerning climate, food, music, and sports can be asked in the initial stages of the interview to break the ice. In addition to writing out these questions beforehand, each student should practice his or her questions orally. (I am assuming the interview will be effected in the target language.)

Each student should next prepare three more questions (both in writing and orally) concerning the things people like and dislike and the way people (but not necessarily the person interviewed) relate to each other. Would a typical person from Aix want a large or small family? Where do teenagers go for recreation? Do wives like to hold jobs outside of the home? What are some differences between city and country people? How are children disciplined? By whom? For which meals does the whole family get together? What responsibilities does each member of a family generally have? What are the most popular religions? How much social contact does a family generally have with the church leader?

Some questions should be avoided. Areas that have some social stigma associated with them obviously fall into this category. Potentially offensive questions include: How many years of schooling do you have? Do you have your own house/car/TV? What are your ethnic origins? To what social or economic class do you belong? When in doubt about how to word a question, try asking the guest "What question should I ask to find out...?"

Each student should then prepare three more questions (this brings the total to nine) that directly relate to whichever of the seven cultural goals is being currently studied in class. This task should be carried out in cooperation with the rest of the class to avoid asking the same question twice.

Each interaction with a stranger is an adventure into uncharted territory, and one cannot predict the turn of events. The informant should be invited to ask questions of the interviewers, too. Nevertheless, the teacher should try to have students structure the session. A performance objective given in advance of the session will aid them. These objectives will change according to the experience and sophistication of the students and their guest. A detailed how-to text on interviewing techniques has been prepared by a sociologist with extensive experience in cross-cultural interviews (Gorden, 1980). An extensive review of the area of face-to-face cross-cultural interactions has been prepared by a social psychologist (Brislin, 1981).

A simple objective might require a student to write in English a minimum of four facts that s/he learned from the interview. A little more involved objective would require the student to write the answers in the target language to those of the nine oral questions that s/he prepared in advance and subsequently asked in the interview.

An example of a more detailed performance objective relating to interviews follows. It was prepared by Marsha Rybski.

Performance Objective for Native-Informant Interview

Cultural goal

The student will demonstrate his awareness of cultural meanings associated with everyday target words (Goal IV).

Performance objective

TERMINAL BEHAVIOR: The student will demonstrate his ability to describe the word *le déjeuner* beyond the translated meaning of lunch.

CONDITIONS: The student will write on a piece of paper a report on *le déjeuner* describing the following points: what is eaten, how long the meal lasts, what time of the day it is eaten, where it is eaten, who fixes the meal, how the student knows it is an important daily event. The student will write his report in 30 minutes in class the day after the informant's visit. The report will be written in English or in French.

CRITERION: The student must describe in his report at least five of the points mentioned above. The description may be as simple as answering the who, what, or where in the question.

To Question Is to Discover

Interviews are structured, not to drive out the spontaneous, but to have something to fall back on to keep the conversation rolling, and to facilitate the gathering of specific information.

Our most becoming stance as students of culture is one of inquiry. This chapter has suggested several techniques to assist a student in asking questions about the target culture. The point of the chapter can be realized only in classrooms in which the process of inquiry is rewarded at least as much as the capture of ephemeral facts.

Zanger (*Exploracion Intercultural: Una guía para el estudiante.* Rowley, MA: Newbury House Pub., 1984) has written a superb manual to guide second-year (or beyond) students of Spanish into interaction with Hispanic peoples. Each chapter focuses on a topic such as greetings, gestures, politeness, family structure, roles of males and females. The chapter begins with an insightful reading on the topic, followed by questions that probe how the student feels about different issues raised by the reading.

The heart of the chapter contains relevant questions for the student to ask of Spanish-speaking people in his/her community. (Most communities in the U.S. count Spanish-speaking people among its residents. In Chicago, for example, one out of every six inhabitants lives in a Spanish-speaking home.) The results of these interviews can be processed in class. Zanger provides questions to help the student to analyze individual and group differences in the responses, and the patterns which are associated with one social variable (e.g., age, sex) more than another. At this writing, Zanger has a second book in press (same publisher) that is aimed at ESL students. These students interview English-speaking people on various cultural topics. (One also could use this book for English-speaking students of intercultural communication who want a structured approach to interviewing people from any other cultural group.)

In early 1985 an innovative journal, *World Cultures* (P.O. Box 12524, La Jolla, CA 92037-0650), began "publishing" directly on microcomputer diskettes (IBM PC and other formats) rather than on paper. This electronic quarterly provides data bases and accompanying codes on "any aspect of human groups" worldwide. Murdock's *Ethnographic Atlas* is one of the data bases included. Students can begin by asking of the data base, "How common is some cultural practice that interests me?" They can then progress to hypothesizing what variables are most associated with the cultural practices that interest them. These hypotheses can be easily checked with the aid of any simple correlations program that will run on the school's or on the students' microcomputers.

Suggested Activities

1. From a trivial topic write five testable cultural hypotheses. (If you chose women, a starter might be: Women between the ages of 18 and 36 never wear their hair down to their shoulders.)
2. Prepare your own mini-media unit based on your chosen topic. (If you chose men, you could use photos showing their reactions to death, to children, to sports, etc.)

3. Prepare a learning activity based on your chosen topic to teach cross-cultural research skills. (Use as many facets of media as are available to you.)

4. Carry your topic through to an interview with a native from the target culture. Prepare 10 questions that would elicit information on it.

5. Prepare a performance objective for your intended interview.

6. Compile a human resources directory of community residents who were raised in the target culture.

7. Some anthropologists estimate that as much as 90 percent of any given culture is the result of cultural borrowing and the acceptance of technological innovations invented by people from different cultures. Prepare a list of 50 such traits currently observable in a country of your choosing.

9

Testing Culture, or How Do You Know They Learned Something?

Four examples are presented of ways to measure shifts in attitudes toward the target culture by student groups. Most culture tests measure superficial knowledge, rather than intercultural skill development. This chapter emphasizes that concern for both reliability (i.e., tests that are capable of yielding consistent results on repeated trials with the same students) and validity (i.e., tests that test what they are supposed to test) is effort well spent. Test writers are alerted to threats that commonly undermine the validity of individual test items. Much of the chapter, after the initial discussion on attitude testing, deals with multiple-choice test formats. Six other testing formats also are briefly outlined.

Attitudes toward the Target Culture

Do students alter their opinions of the target culture after studying about its language and society for a semester (or year)? If attitudes toward the target culture do become more positive as classroom exposure increases, does this positive regard transfer to other cultures as well? Do students of French, in other words, begin to feel more charitable toward Hispanic as well as French culture?

The easiest way to get an objective overview of attitude shift in students is to give them a pretest at the beginning of the course, and a posttest at the end. Before I suggest four specific ways to do this, I want to emphasize that none of the ways is good enough to use for drawing conclusions about how any individual student has changed his/her attitudes. The tests may be helpful, on the other hand, in giving the teacher a general idea of the direction of any change in the attitudes of the class as a whole. Attitude tests of the type intercultural communication teachers might administer should be completed anonymously by the students.

There are many reasons why the usefulness of tests may be limited to measuring general *group* characteristics rather than what an *individual* knows or feels about a chosen topic. Most of these reasons relate to one or two concerns: validity and reliability. For a test to be valid it has to test what you want it to, and not, inadvertently, something else. To be valid, a test *also* must be reliable. Perfect reliability would be achieved by a test if each time it were given the same students would make the same scores (assuming that nothing happened in the intervals between testing to alter their knowledge or feelings on the topic tested). But everyone has his/her good days and his/her dog days so student performance at different times is never quite the same.

There are a lot of sources for variability in test scores. Besides interference from distractions, headaches, and heart throbs, the wording of some test items is interpreted differently by people of varying roles, ages, social classes, and so forth. There is one item in a widely used I.Q. test for children that pictures a man relaxing (he is smoking a pipe) in a rocking chair on the lawn in front of his home during a heavy rainfall. The children are asked what is wrong in the picture. In Mormon Utah, many children answer that what is wrong is that the man is smoking. Within their religious framework, getting wet is certainly a lesser evil than smoking.

It is easy to build ambiguous item choices during test construction. Once I was in charge of coordinating the testing of a dozen sections of a college Spanish course. When it came time to draft the final semester examination, I asked each teacher to choose a different chapter and write 10 multiple-choice items for that chapter, each item with four choices—one of which was to be correct. I then gave the draft version of the test to a half-dozen educated native speakers of Spanish from several different countries and asked them to check all the right answers. For about 80 percent of the items more than one answer was chosen as correct, and for 20 percent of the items all four responses were checked as correct! Although these teachers were fluent in Spanish and well trained (all had graduate degrees), they all introduced "secret" contexts into the test. If all you had learned of Spanish was what Chapter Ten had told you, then you would do reasonably well on the test, but if you had learned a lot of Spanish from sources outside of Chapter Ten then you would be in deep trouble. (The teachers, by the way, were very unhappy to have this state of affairs brought to their attention. They insisted that *their* right answer was the *only* right answer.)

Because of all of this unwanted static that creeps into our tests, it is imperative to remember that *the measurement of ANY phenomenon ALWAYS contains a certain amount of chance error.* That, of course, is why we should be nervous about inferring the competency of any individual student from how s/he does on any one test. (Or on a string of unreliable tests.)

One day I went into the university's testing bureau to pick up the scored tests from several of my classes. In addition to simply scoring the tests, the bureau always ran, for the teachers' information, a statistical analysis to measure the tests' reliability. (There are several methods for computing this. Interested readers can consult any text on tests and measurement.) Perfect test reliability would result in a reliability score of 1.00, and zero reliability would yield a score of 0.0. Commercial tests are expected to yield reliability scores in the .90's; and good, teacher-made knowledge tests for classroom use yield reliability scores at least in the .80's. I mentioned to the bureau's director that I guessed that the science professors routinely got high reliability scores on their tests, since they were so proficient with numbers. There happened to be at that moment a stack of printouts on the counter waiting to be picked up by the chemistry department. The director smiled and read me the reliability scores of a dozen exams. To my amazement, the reliability scores ranged from .0 to .14. In other words, the test results were totally unreliable. Still, achievement on these totally unreliable tests determined most of the course grades for those hapless students.

Now that you are forewarned about some of the limitations of tests, let's look at four techniques to measure attitudes. Two of these approaches to measuring cross-cultural attitudes have been used especially extensively by social scientists for many years: social distance and semantic differential scales.

"Social distance" scales attempt to measure the degree to which one separates oneself socially from members of another culture (Bogardus, 1925). A modified social distance scale might look something like this:

Put an X after each nationality in as many of the five columns as your feelings dictate. Remember to give your *first* reactions to each nationality as a group. Do not give your reactions to the best or the worst members that you have known. Please work rapidly.

	1 Would marry one.	2 Would have one as close friend.	3 Would have one as next-door neighbor.	4 Would work with one.	5 Would have one as an aquaintance only.
French					
Spanish					
German					
Japanese					
Russian					
Arab					
Nigerian					
etc.					

The second approach measures the "semantic differential," or distance between two descriptors, with which the rater judges the defined culture group in terms of a number of bipolar traits (Osgood and Suci, 1955). A modification of this technique for use as a classroom attitude scale might result in something like this:

Put a check in the position which best indicates the direction and intensity of your feeling with regard to each pair of descriptors.

Tibetans in general tend to be:

good/	/	/	/	/	/bad
beautiful/	/	/	/	/	/ugly
clean/	/	/	/	/	/dirty
valuable/	/	/	/	/	/worthless
kind/	/	/	/	/	/cruel
pleasant/	/	/	/	/	/unpleasant
happy/	/	/	/	/	/sad
nice/	/	/	/	/	/awful
honest/	/	/	/	/	/dishonest
fair/	/	/	/	/	/unfair

The descriptors used in the above semantic differential proved to be useful in cross-cultural studies of many countries. Teachers may choose to identify the bipolar items by having the class/grade/school indicate in an open-ended exercise what the students feel to be the strengths and weaknesses of specified groups (e.g., Chicanos, blacks, French). The teacher then constructs from these descriptors the bipolar items for a semantic differential scale. This way, one uses terms that are in currency among the students and, presumably, mean something to them. (The psychometric properties of these scales, of course, will not be known.)

A third approach to measuring attitudes toward a defined group was developed by Grice (1934) and is still in use. This approach presents the respondents with a number of statements (over 40 in the original version). The respondent is asked to put a check in front of those statements with which s/he agrees. The following are sample items:

Following is a list of statements about the people of Gringolandia. Place a check before each statement with which you agree.

1. Show a high rate of efficiency in anything they attempt.
2. Can be depended upon as being honest.
3. Are noted for their industry.
4. Are envious of others.
5. Are highly emotional.
6. Are tactless.
7. Are a God-fearing group.
8. Are self-indulgent.
9. Are quick to understand.
10. Have an ideal home life.

Finally, a fourth approach illustrates another variation in attitude measurement. This forced-choice questionnaire was developed to measure annual changes in the self-esteem of bilingual program students in the primary grades. The items are presented orally and bilingually. Students are asked whether they "mostly agree" or "mostly disagree" with each statement.

1. I am happy with myself.
2. I am happy at home.
3. I like school.
4. My teacher likes me.
5. I am not nervous when my teacher asks me a question.
6. I can do many things well.
7. My friends like me.
8. I like to speak Arabic (or whatever their home language is).
9. I like to speak English.

10.   I like to read.
11.   I like to do arithmetic.
12.   I like music classes.
13.   I like art classes
14.   etc.

In a variation of this, brief, written questionnaires for elementary school bilingual children can be developed by making up your own items, and putting one item per page, written in big block letters (prime type) in both the students' home language and English. The students indicate their attitude toward each item by marking one of two faces, as the following examples taken from a student practice sheet illustrate.

A. QUIERO A MI MAMA. I LOVE MY MOTHER.

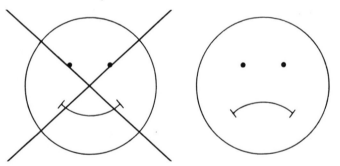

B. ME GUSTA EL DOLOR DE OIDO. I LIKE EARACHES.

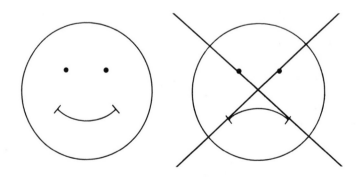

Shaw and Wright (1967) have prepared a compendium of attitudinal scales, along with examples and evaluations of each. There are sections devoted to the nature of attitudes, methods of scale construction, social practices, social issues and problems, international issues, abstract concepts, political and religious attitudes, ethnic and national groups, and social institutions. Two experienced foreign language teachers offer assistance in measuring attitudinal variables, Cooke (1970) for Spanish and Savignon (1972a) for French. Foreign language and bilingual education teachers will find the description of 342 oral and written tests, many of them attitude measures, which was compiled by the Northwest Regional Educational Laboratory (1978), to be helpful. Cohen's (1979) very useful book on evaluating bilingual programs contains a chapter on affective measurement. An exposition of virtually all of the social science postulates concerning ethnocentrism has been prepared by LeVine and Campbell (1972).

Most classroom testing focuses on cognitive learning rather than on student attitude. The rest of this chapter will examine different approaches to measuring cultural skills and knowledge.

Criterion-Referenced Tests

The performance evaluations elaborated in Chapter 4 are, in the jargon of the profession, a form of criterion-referenced testing in which the teacher clearly delineates the student competencies to be achieved. Whether the students do or do not achieve enough to pass the unit (or course) depends on whether they meet the criteria spelled out *before* they are evaluated.

This type of testing is the most useful in giving teachers and students relevant feedback on achievement as it relates to specific intercultural communication goals. Since this was covered at length in Chapter 4, I will go on to a discussion of the most popular form of classroom testing: norm-referenced testing.

"Standardized" Tests

"Norm-referenced" test scores are evaluated within the context of how an *individual student* scores *in relation to* how a *group* (the classroom or some national group) scores on the same test. These tests are often curved so that "average" achievement is awarded a "C," and so on. (Criterion-referenced tests, on the other hand, are evaluated in terms of what percentage of the test items the student answers correctly.) Two familiar examples of norm-referenced testing are the standardized college entrance exams and the teacher-made, end-of-course multiple-choice tests.

Several states have, from time to time, administered standardized culture tests to their secondary students. New York State, through the Regents Examinations, has the longest tradition of this. A dozen or so years ago I was one of several people invited by the New York Department of Education to critique these examinations. Based on a review of 83 test items appearing in six different Spanish exams, I found 82 of the items tested knowledge of the following five areas:

1. recognition of historical events and persons (22 items);
2. recognition of trivial facts (19 items);
3. recognition of toponyms (17 items);
4. ability to define vocabulary (13 items);
5. familiarity with plastic arts, especially architecture (11 items).

While the narrow scope reflected in the above breakdown may no longer be true of the Regents Examinations, it does highlight many endemic weaknesses in the few culture tests in recent use. Another common weakness, the confusion of literary knowledge with behavior patterns, is exemplified in the culture test of the MLA Proficiency battery, published by the Educational Testing Service. The Kansas Test of Spanish and Latin American Life and Culture, published by Kansas State Teachers College (Emporia), illustrates how dates, historical facts, and literary bits can be easily misused. The most common items appearing on most culture tests, unfortunately, can be correctly answered by a superficial familiarity with geographical and historical facts.

Most norm-referenced testing is not of the type described above. It is done by a classroom teacher in the form of end-of-semester exams. This type of testing is ideally suited for a department where two or more instructors teach the same levels and where a uniform evaluation criterion is desired.

The designer of a cross-cultural test begins, if s/he is a purist and follows the classical prescription, by defining his/her, specific objectives. The designer then elaborates on the various areas of culture that bear upon the stated objectives. This elaboration consists of mapping out the thematic character of the "universe" of relevant test items. Will the test objectives support items concerned with art and literature, for example? Will the items have to be tied directly to linguistic units?

One testing program (Seelye, 1968c), designed to measure the biculturation of the American colony in a Latin American country, divided test items into two major categories: (1) items that are associated with the ability to function in a society, and (2) items that measure knowledge not overtly associated with functioning in the society. Falling into the latter category are items based on abstract or implicit patterns of which the native is not aware (although these patterns may well indirectly affect behavior), erudite academic knowledge, and patterns for which there is not wide concordance in the target culture (patterns peripheral to the core culture). In addition, ideal patterns of belief that do not occur frequently (false patterns) and patterns that present a cultural anomaly in that they deviate from a major value of the culture (dysfunctional patterns) should probably be avoided unless they are clearly identified in the test as anomalous patterns. In this research, the ability to use the target cultural patterns to satisfy societal conventions was measured through items that have been shown to differentiate empirically the cultural stranger and the target native.

The seven cultural goals described in Chapter 4 provide an excellent frame for devising purposeful test items for the classroom.

Validating Test Items

It would seem to belabor the evident to observe that the correct response to a test item should itself be correct. Yet we are whimsically casual about requiring documentation to back up a "right" answer. This is especially easy to observe in tests of discrete units of culture where the student selects the correct response from among several choices offered. In spite of extensive experience over three decades in a number of countries of Latin America, Europe, Africa, and Asia, and almost 30 years as an educator, I still find myself making a few simple errors in designing cross-cultural test situations.

The most common error lies in generalizing beyond the legitimate extension of a cultural practice. Test questions that contain wording such as "In X situation, a Latin American would act in Y manner," have repeatedly been shown to be dangerous. The test designer who is drawing a situation from either personal experience or a written source should attempt to be specific in the wording of the item. More likely of success are items worded "A Mexican can be expected to do X in Y situation," or better still, "A middle-class Peruvian male living in Lima can be expected to do X in Y situation." Little work has been done to provide a "cultural atlas" of varieties in cultural patterning within any given geographic area, so the test designer had best tread with caution.

Certain patterns that have come to be regarded as "typical" offer a particular dilemma in test construction, for we want the test to avoid reinforcing clichés and half-truths. Groups are often stereotyped along the lines of several patterns of behavior that are infrequent in the group but may be even less frequent in other groups. Perhaps these infrequent patterns can be tested best within the context of in-group approval or disapproval, rather than in terms of the frequency of the pattern. For example, rather than ask whether German men often have mistresses, the item could be phrased, "Would a German politician running for office be discredited were it to become known that he supported a mistress in addition to his wife?"

Validation techniques vary in rigor from polling a representative sample of target subjects in order to establish the distribution of a cultural pattern to the simple acceptance of a generalization based on an anecdote of the classroom teacher or returning tourist. While the ultimate strength of the test will depend in great part on the rigor of the validation techniques employed, there are many occasions when the exigencies of the classroom relegate sophisticated methods to the realm of the impractical. Three quite different methods for documenting the validity of a cultural pattern—classroom authority, pretesting with the target people, and expert opinion—differ widely in their relevance for the classroom teacher.

Classroom Authority

In those cases where the classroom teacher is well-grounded in the target culture, the authority of his/her word usually suffices. This is probably satisfactory if one does not take oneself too seriously; most of us have discovered that what is accepted with adulation in the classroom often gets quite another reception at a staff meeting. The usefulness of an item validated solely by the classroom teacher is necessarily local. While this is obviously the most expedient technique for teachers at the battlements, it is important to recognize that great modesty becomes the teacher rash enough to insist on the validity of a pattern so documented.

Pretesting

The acid test of whether an item forms part of the explicit or conscious culture of a people is to administer it to them, controlling for relevant variables such as age, sex, residence, and social class differences. Although 95 percent agreement can be expected on the correct response to a language test administered to educated natives of a target culture, the best that can realistically be expected on a widely administered culture test is 65 percent agreement. In one study (Seelye, 1968c), items achieving 51 percent or more agreement (with a test group of varied composition) were retained when they were significantly contrastive with the performance of North Americans on the same items.

The obvious disadvantage of quantitative methods of validation is that they are difficult to implement. The method most accessible to teachers who want to document a cultural pattern by an independent source is to use the expressed opinions of specialists in the target culture as documentation.

Expert Opinion

As we all know, experts differ in opinion. Naroll (1962), an anthropologist, discusses an elaborate and highly sophisticated means of checking the credibility of a reporter by a method he calls data quality control (see especially his Chapters 1 and 7). He suggests, for example, a six-level classification reflecting the authority of the investigator or source depending on the nearness to the actual date ("source proximity"): (1) datum report, "where an artifact or a statement is itself the trait being studied"; (2) participant report, "where an event or culture pattern is described by a participating culture bearer"; (3) observer's report, "where an event or culture pattern is described by an eyewitness who is not himself a participant in the culture or subculture pattern involved"; (4) derivative report, "an account by a nonobserver based on a report of another which is no longer available for study"; (5) scholar's report, "an account by a nonobserver, based on existing primary sources which the comparativist does not find it convenient to consult directly"; (6) reader's report, "an account by a nonobserver based on other writings, in which specific passages in primary sources covering the data in question are not cited." The particular level of source proximity can be further evaluated for reporting bias by introducing such control factors as length of stay of the reporter in the target culture, explicitness and generality of the report, and familiarity with the target language.

A less rigorous method of validation along the lines of the technique just mentioned would be to document the accuracy of a cultural pattern with three independent sources, but without an elaborate assessment of source proximity and reporter bias.

Some Illustrative Mistakes

Some years ago in Guatemala a colleague, Tom Daiglé, and I began designing a culture test (we wanted to measure the acculturation of Americans there) by thinking of specific items of Guatemalan cultural behavior that differed in form, distribution, and meaning from an analogous United States pattern, then casting them into test form. As it became increasingly difficult to recollect from memory new contrastive items, we began working from mnemonic topics such as religion or death. As a third means of identifying contrastive patterns, we took statements made in anthropological reports and attempted to devise questions from them. Of the three methods, we found the first to yield the most successful test items, the second to be the next most productive attack technique, and the third to be the approach most fraught with problems of validation.

Each individual test item consisted of a stem and four multiple-choice responses based on analogy to the phonemic concept. That is, the correct response presented a situation totally unfamiliar to Americans or one that contrasted in form, distribution, or meaning to the pattern Americans recognize as their own.

Two bilingual Guatemalan groups of 20 each were used to pretest the English version of the questionnaire. The contrastive test item would be introduced to one group; then any changes which seemed to be warranted were made. It was then tested on the second group, changed again, retested on the first group, and so on. The main function of this pretest group was to give an indication of what items would be successful and to discover problems that limited their acceptability. The pretest groups also served to point out *faux pas.* For example, some of our "fictional" names conveyed too much meaning. Because these two groups became quite familiar with the questionnaire, their school was not used in the final testing.

Some of our *unsuccessful* items might illustrate the problems of writing cross-cultural tests. The following is an example of a pattern reported by anthropologists which we then cast into question form.

The most appropriate place for two businessmen to conclude a business transaction is
A.   a prestigious bar.
B.   an intimate soft-drink stand in the central market.
C.   the home of one of the businessmen.
D.   the stadium during a soccer game.

We expected Guatemalans to answer A, and Americans C. As it developed, however, three times as many Guatemalans answered C as A. We feel that in spite of this the reported pattern is accurate, that Latins do not transact business in the home, and we attribute the failure of the question to two factors. First, the wording is probably faulty. Perhaps a stem such as "What kind of atmosphere would (Latin American) businessmen look for in which to close a big business deal?" might have elicited a better response. Second, there is difficulty in finding a group of sufficient size sophisticated enough in the ways of businessmen to test the pattern.

Some questions brought out the differing social orientations of the subjects due to sex differences. Two examples will illustrate this.

The president of Guatemala offers Mr. Sánchez the position of Minister of Education, but he declines the offer because
A.   the salary of public servants is very low.
B.   he fears assassination.
C.   traveling would absent him from home too often.
D.   he fears permanent identification with the government in power.

It was expected that Guatemalans would answer D, and Americans would be spread over the other three choices, with a concentration on B. Guatemalan males did, in fact, generally answer as expected, but the females had a strong tendency to answer B. The reason for women's answering as they did would seem to be lack of political sophistication; although some of the ministry posts are dangerous—Minister of Defense, for example—ministers of education had met with controversy but not death as an occupational hazard. (Some years after this testing, Minister of Education became a more dangerous post.)

Another question on which males unexpectedly performed better than females is the following question that tests nursing customs.

A mother is nursing her infant in public. This would be
A.   infrequent and in poor taste.
B.   common, but only in one or two social classes.
C.   more or less common on all social levels.
D.   almost totally unheard of but not reprehensible.

Males generally answered the anticipated B, while females tended to select D. Males apparently are not oblivious to lovely women nursing in public. (The test results as a whole did not indicate a general tendency for one sex to be more alert to social forms than the other.)

The understandable impulse to see things as they should be ideally rather than as they are was exemplified by several questions. For example:

A young man has political ambitions. He would like, in fact, to become president of the country some day. In choosing a career to help realize his ambition, he would probably choose to go to
A.   the seminary and become a priest.
B.   the university and study medicine.
C.   the military academy and become an officer.
D.   the university and study political science.

The political history of Guatemala consists of a long procession of military governments. When this question was posed, in the previous 140 years only two constitutionally elected presidents had completed the period for which they had been elected. On the other hand, one military dictator this century was in power 13 years. There have been but a handful of civilian heads of state. But, in answer to our question, Guatemalans overwhelmingly answered D—and the university curriculum does not even offer a degree in political science! In fact, there isn't even a political science department.

Occasionally a question contained two or more responses, instead of just one, that appealed to Guatemalans. The following interesting situation affords an example.

> A pretty young woman is waiting for a bus on a busy street corner. A man comes up behind her and pinches her. She would
> A. tolerate it, but only during carnival time.
> B. call a policeman any time of the year.
> C. laugh and feel proud.
> D. pretend nothing had happened so people would not notice.

Although the largest concentration of Guatemalans chose D as expected, almost a third answered B. As yet, we have not heard of a Guatemalan woman who has called a policeman in this situation. Perhaps they think they should!

Another perplexing pattern of response was provoked by the following question.

> A volcano in Antigua erupts. The people of Guatemala City would
> A. ask the government for protection.
> B. rush to see the spectacle.
> C. deny the possibility of an eruption because the volcano has been inactive for many years.
> D. prepare to evacuate the city.

Most Guatemalans surprisingly answered D; about 30 percent answered B as expected. Possibly the D response is too ambiguously worded: It might not be clear which of the two cities, Antigua or Guatemala, is indicated. Also, we overstated the B response by using the word *rush* instead of a more temperate *go.*

Social classes occasionally replied differently to a question. The upper class, for example, tended to see public school teachers as members of the upper-low class, whereas the low class saw them as middle class.

One last example (patterned after an example from Lado [1961]) will illustrate the difficulty of writing successful questions.

> It is Sunday afternoon and the soccer game is very exciting. One of the players makes a vital play. The public whistles loudly. This indicates that they are
> A.   cheering the player.
> B.   asking for a repetition; more of the same.
> C.   showing their displeasure.
> D.   cheering the goal which has just been made.

The contestants were equally divided between C and D. This question appears to have four weaknesses in our wording: (1) The stem leads one to believe that a vital play was completed, rather than just attempted; (2) it is not specified whether the whistling public represents the home rooters or the visitors; (3) response C allows that the whistling is done to show displeasure, rather than to ridicule the player; and (4) it is possible the phenomenon of whistling might have more complex meaning and distribution than we realized.

To illustrate some objective test items that did work, I'll take four items from the final version of the test that measured knowledge of Guatemalan culture. All four items relate to food.

1.   When a Guatemalan gets up from the table after eating, he
     *A.   says thank you, or some other pleasantry.
     B.   just smiles.
     C.   says nothing, but does not smile.
     D.   says nothing, but taps his chest lightly.

2. Sometimes a store displays a red flag (about 1′ square) outside its door. This indicates
   A. the employees are striking.
   B. the store is closed for repairs or inventory.
   *C. they are selling fresh meat.
   D. none of the above.

3. Which of the following times would a Guatemalan traditionally eat tamales?
   A. Sunday noon
   *B. Saturday evening
   C. For breakfast
   D. There is no preferable custom

4. A lamp with a candle inside is covered with red paper or red cellophane and displayed outside a doorway. This indicates
   A. a party is in progress.
   B. it is a theater exit.
   *C. tamales are being sold.
   D. none of the above.

Recycling Trivial Items

Once the validity of the test items has been subjected to healthy skepticism, the test designer usually has a pile of factual but superficial items such as "What is the capital of France?" These trivial items can be converted into academically defensible items that test specific course objectives.

That testers think of so many trivial things to test is of no great concern. Creativity is not served by an inhibiting and premature preoccupation with quality. Ideas need to be welcomed in whatever form they initially appear; they can be refined later. That teachers actually *test* so many trivial things *is* of concern.

Trivial items can be reclaimed by reversing the "ideal" process of devising test items directly from specific goals. The tester can reclaim these weak items that seek to test superficial facts by resolving four questions:

1. How does the trivial fact relate to the lives of the target people?
2. What other behavior patterns come to mind when you think of the way the trivial item relates to the lives of people?
3. What, if any, additional facts can be given in the item to provide the raw material for testing skill in problem-solving?
4. Which of the seven goals listed in Chapter 4 most readily relates to the item as it evolves through the above three questions?

The test item should then be reworked to fit the goal's intention more closely. This process of converting trivial, purposeless items into respectable items is illustrated in the table at the end of Chapter 3, and by the "great belly button question" at the beginning of Chapter 8.

There are at least five limitations imposed upon any testing program by chance and circumstance: the aim of the examiner limits the test content; the validation technique employed further limits content; the time available for testing limits both content and the format of the test; the format of the test limits both content and the circumstances of the testing; and, finally, the imagination of the test designer limits everything.

Just as there is a need for culture tests to be more goal-oriented than is presently the case, there is a corresponding need for more experimentation with the format of culture tests. A variety of formats such as classroom checklists, simulation, objective questions, and audiovisual, oral, and tactile approaches may be used in constructing culture tests.

Classroom Checklists

Teachers who manage classrooms that involve students in individualized instruction often develop checklists of student activity.

When a student completes a specified activity, either s/he or the teacher checks the appropriate box on the checklist. The checklist, in effect, becomes a "test" of successful activities. (This technique also is used in "mastery learning.") The value of the checklist depends on how purposeful and goal-related the activities are.

An excellent, succinct discussion of the preparation of instructional objectives—the key to good testing—is provided by Mager (1962) in his programmed book. Exemplary curriculum materials incorporate purposeful student activities. An especially good high school series was developed under the direction of the anthropologist Malcolm Collier (ACSP, 1968). These multi-media materials focus on the teaching of a social studies unit on prehistory.

One of the prehistory units, by way of illustration, seeks to develop student ability to interpret evidence in the area of early human societies. To this end, Bushman culture is studied via filmstrips, site maps, readings, and so on. A number of specific student activities are identified: Use imagination and evidence to make inferences about the Bushman way of life; Identify factual evidence to support an inference; Challenge others' inference if evidence or reasoning suggests an alternative inference. For the last of the three mentioned activities, several measurement techniques are suggested which lend themselves to checklists. For instance, keeping a record during regular class of which students do challenge others' inferences. Another way to test the objective is by presenting the student with a question such as: "The Kalahari Bushmen eat only meat and other animal products. Can you tell by what evidence this is known?" When the student makes the desired response, this is noted on the checklist. (For this example, the proper response would be to challenge the statement and to give contrary evidence [e.g., nutshells]).

Collier's approach to introducing anthropology's insights into existing school curricula—rather than as an added course— has implications for other fields as well. Working with teachers from other disciplines can enhance the accomplishment of many culture goals.

Simulation

Ideally, the best way to test the ability to operate in a second culture would be to place the student in the target culture and then observe him/her in a series of "foreign" situations. But this method lacks economy and, in addition, would be fatiguing for the middle-aged examiner sentenced to observe the young at work and play.

Simulating certain controlled situations would seem to offer a viable alternative to placing the student in the target culture for test purposes. A role is assigned the subject, such as Latin American student leader, president of France, peasant, businessman, or Peace Corps volunteer. A series of problem-solving situations are then presented for resolution in a form consistent with the target reality. This method becomes more feasible the longer the time available for testing since only a few subjects can be tested concurrently during a 30-minute period. In the longer form the test itself, if intensely oriented to problem-solving situations, can afford an experience that would assist the subject in handling the inevitable "cultural fatigue" of residence abroad. Preparation of experiences of this type require a lot of work. For help in developing simulations, see Livingston and Stoll, 1973; Zuckerman and Horn, 1973; Stadsklev, 1974, 1975; Jones, 1982; and Lamy, et al., 1980.

Objective Tests

Although objective tests are somewhat difficult to compose, their ease in correction is especially appreciated when large numbers of students are tested. Once the test is designed, correction is completely objective and can be accomplished by practically anyone—and without prejudice (something that cannot be said for essay questions).

Besides the Guatemalan examples already given, another example, taken from the ACSP unit on "Culture as Adaptation to Complex Social Systems: Peasants," illustrates another approach to objective testing. The student is asked to study a sheet of dialogue typical of a peasant (examples from India and Italy are given). The class is divided into thirds, and each is assigned a different situation. One student from each group is selected to play the role of peasant and another the role of outsider. "First they read given lines, then ad lib as long as they can, trying to say kinds of things (and in a manner) typical of the part played." The student-oriented objective of this is: "Recognize two or more ways in which peasants usually adapt to outsiders and persons who control their lives and explain how they are adaptive: close-knit family, deference, shrewdness, caution, suspicion, humble appearance." The following ACSP test item is appropriate for measuring achievement of the student objective:

> Suppose a stranger entered a peasant village and told the first man he met that he was a new government official whose duty was to help the villagers find better ways to farm their land. Which of the following reactions would you expect from the peasant? (Choose three)
>
> _____Asking the stranger for his credentials
>
> _____Claiming that he already had the best farming methods in the village
>
> ___x___Showing a lot of respect for the stranger's authority
>
> _____Inviting the stranger home for dinner
>
> ___x___Caution in answering the official's questions
>
> _____Volunteering information about how lucky the village had been in its crops recently
>
> ___x___Appearing interested in the official's advice on farming

Visual Tests

Suppose a short story has been read in class and a lottery vendor figures in the plot. In testing recognition of a lottery vendor several slides of Latin Americans can be projected: one of a corner candy vendor, another of a businessman, a third of a boy selling chewing gum, and a fourth slide picturing a lottery vendor. The student would indicate the latter response on his answer sheet. Or, more economically, the student would be asked to identify all of a series of images for which s/he had been given some context from which to deduce the answers. Any pictorial image, such as slides, drawings, magazine clippings, will do.

Audio Tests

Here the principle is the same as for visual tests, except the student responds to audio stimuli. A taped section might contain a portion of the lottery vendor's spiel, a brief section of a radio announcer's reading of the articles that announce a state of siege, or a humanely brief portion of a radio commercial. Needless to say, the content of the test would depend on what the teacher wanted to measure; here the concern is with test technique, not content. Nostrand develops the audiovisual possibilities for the teaching of cultural content in language courses in a brief article replete with ideas (Nostrand, 1966b).

Oral Exams

The interview, or oral exam, has long been a device for eliciting information on almost any topic from a student. Structured interviews have the advantage of being easier to code and evaluate than open-ended interviews and are, consequently, more objective. However, what the structured interview usually amounts to is a multiple-choice test administered orally. Open-ended interviews often produce unexpected information, but sooner or later the mass of information collected has to be coded for appraisal. Then, too, the interviewers of open-ended exams have to be articulately aware of the object of their search, for unless the interview is recorded they will consciously or unconsciously be eliminating many data (most of which might well be extraneous to the purpose of the interview anyway.) The critical concept in developing interviews is K.I.S.S. (Keep It Simple, Stupid).

Tactile Tests

Object-using tests confront the subject directly with some aspect of the target culture, thus avoiding the abstract artifices that relegate the target culture, as many students perceive it, to the limbo of the lifeless. The student could be given a lottery ticket to check against a newspaper containing the winning numbers. In another situation s/he might be given a knife, fork, spoon, plate, and instructions to eat a Mexican taco which is thoughtfully provided him/her (eating it, to be culturally authentic, with his/her fingers). Primary and secondary teachers have used tactile devices (often curios of the airport variety with but limited potential) more than have college dons, but few teachers have explored the possibilities of tactile tests.

Technical Help

Finally, there are some excellent sources prepared by teachers to assist in the technical aspects of test construction. A wonderfully succinct (37 pages) introduction to teacher-made tests is available free from the Educational Testing Service in Princeton (Diederich, 1964). Lado's book (1961) on language testing contains two excellent chapters which are still entirely relevant to readers of this chapter. The testing manual by Valette (1977) also discusses cultural testing.

The nature of each specific test item determines the kind of inquiry it might be subjected to, but some general questions can be asked of most discrete test items to assess their strength:

1.   To what extent is the cultural pattern evident to a member of the target culture? (Does it represent an implicit or an explicit pattern?)
2.   To what social, sex, residential, and age groups would the pattern apply?
3.   What documentation has the teacher required to back up the "right" answer? Do native speakers of the

language—except for those involved in teaching the course—score the expected responses?

4. Is the answer to the question either too difficult or too facile for the intended testees? (Item analyses will give this information.)
5. Can the item be recast to test a skill rather than a fact?
6. What is the pedagogical justification for testing the item? Exactly which cultural goal is to be tested?
7. If test items from a number of different objectives are to be included in the same test, in what proportion is each to be represented?
8. Does each item measure just one cultural element?
9. Does test achievement indicate knowledge of the target culture, or does achievement depend mostly on some extraneous skill such as language or reading ability, general intelligence, or imitating the opinions of the teacher?
10. Can the test be objectively scored?
11. Are attitudes that are conducive to cross-cultural understanding measured in a way that will avoid confusing opinion with fact?
12. What is the reliability of the test as determined through item analysis?

Suggested Activities

1. Using the topic and activities developed in your performance objectives for the seven goals, compose a test with sample items using multiple choice, objective, audio, oral, and tactile techniques.
2. Try to validate your test using the criteria on pages 188-89.
3. Examine a commercial culture test and determine how many items relate to one of the seven cultural goals.
4. Develop a 10-item attitude scale, administer it to at least six people, and score the results.

10

If I'm Bicultural, Will the Real Me Please Stand Up?

Students who live in the U.S. and who come from homes where a language other than English is spoken are already well on the way to becoming bicultural. Biculturalism conveys important intellectual advantages, but it also entails stress, especially concerning self-identity. This chapter discusses issues relevant to the development of a strong sense of identity, issues such as pressures to conform and cultural relativism. The chapter tackles the question of how bicultural youths can "become themselves," and it presents models of how other people have become bicultural. Finally, problems and challenges in the school environment are discussed.

The Challenge

No one is born bicultural any more than anyone is born fluent in a language. "None is born wise," said Ptahhotep, in 24th century B.C. Egypt. With each skill that one acquires to facilitate communication with people from another culture, one becomes more bicultural.

Students with an enviable headstart in acquiring intercultural communication skills frequently enter our classrooms from homes where another language is spoken. ESL and bilingual education classrooms are populated almost solely by students who each day increase their skill in functioning appropriately in diverse cultural settings. Individuals who grow up with feet in two different cultures have a unique opportunity to view objectively what in most people is a conditioned reflex beyond easy scrutiny—the role convention plays in the formation of thought and behavior.

As is the dreary case with most opportunities for growth, biculturalism is not without its stresses. Cross-cultural contact inevitably provokes some degree of cross-cultural conflict, especially for students who are expected to internalize disparate—and sometimes conflicting—values. This chapter will focus on stresses that students from "minority" backgrounds often experience as they develop their own sense of self. Some of this stress may become counterproductive and lead to undesirable behaviors such as low self-esteem or drug abuse. Much of this excess pressure can be alleviated by teachers sensitive to the personal dilemmas commonly faced by bicultural individuals. Most of the stress, fortunately, acts as an incentive for the individual to make exciting discoveries about the interaction between self and the world beyond.

Teachers of bicultural students can deal with student identity problems in three ways: ignore the problems inherent in the integration of two separate world views and ways of doing things—and leave the student to his/her own resources; adopt regional and partisan positions and attempt to "sell" the slanted version of reality that one country or the other accepts as orthodoxy; or help students deal creatively with the effects of multicultural conditioning. The latter choice will appeal to any teacher who has read this far in this book.

Resisting Pressures to Conform to Provincial Standards

Although bicultural people are essential to the well-being of any society, to be bicultural in some societies (e.g., middle-class U.S.A.) may be to risk appearing a little "different." This is partly because a bicultural person's communicative patterns differ from those of mainstream members of either culture since bicultural people can and do talk to people with whom their peers cannot communicate.

Another reason why bicultural people are sometimes viewed with distrust in very provincial societies is that they cannot be counted on to have the values of the dominant culure. The hysterical internment of Japanese-Americans in the U.S. during World War II is an example of what can happen in this regard. Underlying much of the controversy regarding how far public financed schools should go in recognizing cultural and linguistic pluralism within their systems is a concern for how much diversity a nation can contain and still maintain its national unity and viability. Seelye and Wasilewski (1979) argue that biculturalism does not pose any threat to national viability. Quite the contrary, biculturalism can strengthen a nation.

In many societies everyone is expected to be able to function linguistically and culturally in *at least* two cultures. Europeans, perhaps pushed by their geopolitical circumstances, are examples of this expectation of multiculturalism. An educated person in India, to use another example, customarily is fluent in five or six languages. I am writing this chapter ten thousand feet up in Ecuador's Andes mountains, where many Spanish-speaking teachers confront classrooms populated almost solely by Quichua-speaking children. The survivors—both children and teachers—are those who can function biculturally. (Since one cannot function within a society without being able to communicate with its inhabitants, biliguality [or bidialectalism] is a prerequisite of biculturalism.)

One can escape appearing culturally different by forfeiting one of the two cultures—and there is always considerable pressure on economically and politically subservient groups to make this sacrifice—but trading one brand of monoculturalism for another seems an unnecessarily palid business. Besides, for one person to go from monocultural Chinese-speaking to monocultural Indonesian-speaking (or whatever) requires passing through a state of biculturalism—and that is where there is the most potential for social learning. To the extent that a culture group also is distinguishable physically from "mainstream" people, then "escape" from being regarded as different is often impossible. (On the other hand, escape from being just another pretty face is a lot easier.)

It is the expectation of many people in the U.S. that one's efforts will be amply rewarded when one loses the "annoying" vestiges of a "foreign" culture and becomes an A*l*l*-*A*m*e*r*i*c*a*n. The realization of this expectation would be as tragic for the intellectual development of the U.S. as for the person losing one of his/her cultural heritages. In becoming A*l*l*-A*m*e*r*i*c*a*n the child is expected, like Judas, to deny past associations and allegiances, rather than to build on them. Consider the Chicano first-grader, for example, suffering through reading in a language he does not yet know so that in high school he can suffer through classes in Spanish, a language he was made to forget. Extinction of minority cultures is an ill-thought-out wish of many "mainstream" peoples worldwide. In areas where pressures to acculturate and to conform have won out, society has inherited the bitter irony of rootless uniculture, with its attendant alienation and commerce in headache remedies.

It is not just mainstream society that resists cultural pluralism—parents, too, can pose a "generational" hurdle. To the extent that parents want Juanito to be a little replica of themselves, talking, acting, and thinking as they do, they are consigned to disappointment. The culture of the parents was a seasoned response to the conditions in which they lived. Often, they lived an agrarian, pre-industrial life that bears little resemblance to present urban life in Mexico City or San Juan. It was often a life lived before there were many opportunities for the occupation of the son to differ substantially from that of the father; it was a pre-women's liberation life that allowed the daughter few opinions that differed from those of the mother, and later, perhaps, from those of the mother-in-law; it was life where social classes "knew their place." It was a life enriched by folk art, strong beliefs, and wise adages. And the culture worked, witness the very existence of children from that cultural parentage in our classrooms. But it was a culture that in some regards is largely dysfunctional when transplanted to post-agrarian societies. An illustration of this is seen in the daily drama where thousands of rural people in Latin America flock to cities in hope of a better life. At any rate, it was the culture of another generation, and the prerogative—and necessity—of each generation is to modify the rules of the game.

Nor are children home free who emigrate from an *urban* culture outside the U.S. While the urban cultures of London, Buenos Aires, Mexico City, and Los Angeles probably have more in common with each other than with the rural peasant classes in their own country, there are still important differences in the life of each of these cities. The culture of each population is a response to present needs as seen through the many-colored but distorted prism of its own unique past experiences.

No, the culture of bilingual children cannot be precisely that of the parents. To be so would be to sacrifice the experience and independence of the children for the expediency of the status quo.

Cultural Relativism

Cultural relativism can be discussed in a classroom from several perspectives: if you wanted people to think you were brave, and you were a male living in the first half of this century as a Jívaro in Ecuador, what might you do? What ideas do you have that you would be willing to hurt someone else to keep? If someone from an unfamiliar culture came to your house for dinner and ate spaghetti with his fingers, what would you do? (For what it's worth, I eat pizza with my fingers in the U.S. and with a fork in Italy.)

What if it were against your beliefs to eat any kind of meat and you had not eaten anything for several days and you were invited to a friend's home for dinner and all they served was steak and potatoes?

Teachers can help their students develop insight into the part cultural conditioning plays in the formation of their own identity by having them talk about how large a family they want to have, and how much they want to march to the tune of a different drumbeat. Whose drumbeat? What type of person are they describing? Are they comfortable with the description? A puzzle in the interrelatedness of self-identity and societal feedback that may intrigue older students focuses on a literary dilemma: Is Don Quijote immortal because of Miguel de Cervantes Saavedra, or does Cervantes owe his immortality to Don Quijote?

The French intellectual André Malraux argues that the world is between cultures. Just as the fall of Rome ended one era, the end of European colonization (circa 1950) ended another. We are now living in the interim between a colonial era and a "decolonial" era, he says. David S. Hoopes, a founder of the Society for Intercultural Education, Training, and Research, refers to the potential that bilingual people have to "mediate" between cultures. Perhaps interim, bicultural man can put his/her mediating imprint on the next, more compassionate, era.

The cultural reality of the U.S. classroom forces its students to deal with the cultural heritage of their home vis-à-vis mainstream U.S. culture. Bilingual teachers can help students who are between cultures interpret both cultures honestly and sympathetically.

Most problems in interaction between an educator of one culture and a pupil or parent of another stem from the implicit, culturally conditioned assumptions each makes about the other. Preparing educators to deal with these "foot in mouth" problems is not an easy task. The most effective approach to date is the sophisticated training method developed by Alfred J. Kraemer. It teaches educators how to recognize and identify the subtle cognitive manifestations of *their own* cultural conditioning by observing how hidden cultural values affect the behavior of (videotaped) fellow Americans interacting with people from different cultures. This training increases one's ability to diagnose, and often prevent, the most pervasive problems in intercultural communication. At a more general level, the training greatly facilitates learning to understand another culture from a nonethnocentric perspective. (School systems that may want to have their teachers trained to use this method and its unique materials can directly contact Dr. A. J. Kraemer, Human Resources Research Organization, 300 North Washington Street, Alexandria, VA 22314.)

The following brief scenario illustrates how Kraemer uses one mainstream U.S. value (in this case, the tendency to define and describe people primarily in terms of their work and achievements) to bring American educators to an understanding of how their values affect intercultural communication.

MRS. RAMÍREZ: Yes, I'm sorry I couldn't come to the party. Did you enjoy it?

MRS. JONES: Oh, yes, I met so many interesting people there. There was one woman, Marlena, who used to be an English teacher, but now she is high up in the Office of Education. And, oh, there was another man who works for IBM as a computer engineer, and has just been assigned to the Paris office.

MRS. RAMÍREZ: Hmmm?

MRS. JONES: And, let's see, I talked for a long time with another gentleman who would never tell me what he was doing. I called him the mystery man.

MRS. RAMÍREZ: Why did you call him that?

Episodes such as this form part of the workshop exercises. Taken together, these exercises enable the participants to identify the often unspoken values behind Mrs. Jones' behavior and to see in themselves reflections of the same mainstream values. (The presence of a "contrast culture" person [Mrs. Ramírez] merely serves in these exercises to make it easier for American educators to see how their values are culturally conditioned.)

Becoming Yourself

Knowledge of how one's values and sense of self image can be helpful in itself to individuals who are dealing with identity issues.

There is a big difference in the way human and nonhuman life forms tend to make the adjustments needed to survive. In nonhuman life forms, many behavioral characteristics (e.g., where eagles build nests) are largely determined by genetic selection brought about through the interaction of the species with forces that selectively favor the propagation of certain genes—those favoring great eyesight in eagles, for instance, or tricky prehensile tails in monkeys or camels that can go a long time without drinking chocolate milk shakes.

In homo sapiens, it is man's culture—not his genes—that evolves to meet the exigencies of changing life conditions. Culture is the principal adaptive mechanism humans use to cope with life's circumstances. When the pace of the "hunt" is leisurely, one can dawdle over long meals. When these circumstances change, the adaptive mechanism must also change (e.g., fast food restaurants on every corner). These cultural changes help the individuals within that changing culture to continue as viable organisms. To the extent survival of a society is threatened by behavior that has become dysfunctional (e.g., thermonuclear arms buildups), traditional ways of doing things (e.g., national defense measured by the destructive power of its armaments) become a liability to the group. In homo sapiens there are no subspecies to evolve different genetic directions like there are in birds and bees and cinnamon trees. In mankind there are subcultures, not biological subspecies, that provide the wherewithal to help man adapt to his environment.

Were culture seen simply as an adaptive tool, to use or discard as needed, then cultural change would not evoke the emotional trauma associated with its occurrence. But because the culture of man, besides being pragmatically adaptive, also provides the vehicle for aesthetic and moral satisfaction, even minor changes sometimes evoke major crises by inducing anxiety in the gratification of the most subjective of basic needs, the psychological. An example of this is the consternation among the citizenry of San Francisco, California, when they learned that some of their Southeast Asian neighbors were eating unwanted dogs. Alas, cultures define beauty and truth as ethnocentrically as any other topic. Hall (1976) argues that man must learn to separate his perception of self from the cultural extensions of his self that he fabricates in response to adaptive pressures. These cultural responses can easily lose their functionality as circumstances change. People become bicultural in response to adaptive needs. Bicultural individuals are faced with the need to identify those belief forms that have cross-cultural validity in satisfying aesthetic and moralistic needs, and to differentiate the form from the need.

Any correlation between "race" and culture is coincidental, not causal. A child begins life with a genetic, chemical, neurological base that will be affected by age, disease, and nutrition. Physical anthropologists have not discovered any gene present in one race or ethnic group that is not found in other races or ethnic groups as well. Although the frequency of specific genes differs in different populations, humans share the same basic gene pool.

Nutrition, unlike race, is an important determinant of behavior and varies more widely from population to population than does the relative frequency of particular genes. To the extent that we are eating better food than our parents, our inborn genetic program acts out its development without as many debilitating hindrances. We are what we eat, some say. A child with an extra Y chromosome (Down's syndrome), will never have the intellectual capacity to be a nuclear physicist regardless of what he eats, but a person with genes that permit him or her to become a genius will never realize this potential if his/her first few years are spent in belly-swollen malnutrition. It is also unrealistic to expect a child from a ghetto environment, where the parents have been unable to resolve the essential problems of food and roof, to come to class disposed to reach for academic excellence for its own sake.

No matter how smart your mother was, or how much vitamin D-enriched milk you drink, you are not going to be a nuclear physicist if you are born—and stay—in a Kapauku Papuan village in New Guinea. Nor are you going to design a suspension bridge (a Pygmy invention) if you live in the Sahara Desert. One realizes potentials within a cultural setting. It is no genetic accident that different cultures experience a flurry of distinguished production in the arts—a Golden Age—at infrequent but discernible periods in their history. It is a *cultural* accident. Human talents fall in and out of fashion. Facilities for intellectual development in modern Latin America, as reflected by proffered government scholarships, go to bright children who want to become engineers, not poets. The intellectual capacity for both is there in the gene pool, but cultural elements engender one at the expense of the other. (Some would say that poets thrive in adversity.)

We see ourselves in relation to our environment. The way we perceive this relationship depends on the looking glass we use. Our inborn intelligence, our group-intelligence (the wisdom of the tribe), our language system, and the particular situations in which we find ourselves (including the kind of feedback we get from others) are the major determinants of what we see.

The brilliant Neanderthal who invented the knife did not see stone the same way that her neighbors, the Flintstones, did, although they adopted her insight readily enough. Individual intelligence is the source of the folk wisdom of a people. Alan W. Watts (1969) observed that "the stereotyped attitudes of a culture are always a parody of the insights of its more gifted members." Bicultural individuals will develop different world views because—but not only because—of differences in intelligence.

The collective wisdom of one's culture influences one's concept of self in such basic matters as whether we see ourselves as subject and the rest of the world as object (Western thought), or whether we see ourselves at one with the world, a pattern of energy interacting with all things and getting our form from this interaction (Eastern thought). Do we have an identity independent of our interaction with others and with nature? Social psychologists would say no. As products of Western, Protestant thought we rebel against the notion that we are not captains of our ship.

But the realization that our self is inseparable from its environment does not take away any of our uniqueness. Who has had the same genetic combination? Who has had the same experiences in life? The possibilities for human uniqueness are infinite both in spite of and because of our dependence on ". . . circumstances beyond our control."

Ironically, one of the least potent ingredients of self-identity in monolinguals is a sense of being part of a national political system. There are only a few occasions yearly when nationality is given ritualistic observance. Other than during an election year, or at times of celebrations such as Independence Day or birthdays for deceased statesmen, one hardly thinks of one's "national" identity. Much more powerful are subnational identities such as family, city, region, or roles such as woman, teenager, athlete, Mormon, steelworker, or high school teacher.

One's nationality becomes significant by contrast with another in much the same way that ethnocentrism comes into relief when its basic premises are challenged by a different value system. Governments often play upon this reality by making much ado about some political problem involving "outsiders," while at the same time muting criticism of internal affairs. Territorial disputes, for example, are bombastic occasions in which to sound the drums of national identity.

Focusing on a national level of identity can obscure important ethnic differences within any one nationality. Likewise, a narrower focus on ethnic background can overlook important attitudes and behavior that are shared with the national, or mainstream, culture. One blond, blue-eyed, prospective bilingual teacher was berated by an ethnically conscious community worker in Chicago who claimed, with much feeling and some sarcasm, that Puerto Rican students would not be able to identify with her because she was an "Anglo." There are, of course, Puerto Ricans from all kinds of backgrounds and this prospective Puerto Rican teacher heralded from one of them that did not match the stereotype.

For an individual residing within the country of his birth, ethnic background is more important than nationality. Where I lived for several years in Italy, people were first Vicentini (from the town of Vicenza), second from Veneto (the northeast region), third from Northern Italy, and only fourth, Italian. When we go abroad, however, national identity assumes greater importance —the Vicentino is Italian, the Alabaman in Mexico is a *yanqui*, and the Welshman in France is an *anglais*. One of the characteristics of living in a second country is that one finds oneself dealing frequently with what was hitherto a minor aspect of self-identity —nationality. One is generally, by consequence, ill equipped to deal with the national aspect of one's identity unless one is confronting the behavior of a different nationality.

The teacher may be more effective in buttressing the self-esteem of a child when ethnic identities are not lost in the national conglomerate. When the first student language census was taken in Illinois schools about ten years ago, teachers reported that their students spoke languages such as "Indian" instead of Urdu or Hindi or Tamil, or any of the other 500 languages spoken in India, 14 of which even have "official" status for governmental dealings.

A big step in liberating ourselves from the caprices of cultural conditioning is taken when we soberly perceive the immense importance it plays in the determination of our sense of identity. In discovering this sense of self, the bicultural person does not deny the influence of one or another culture on his character—he accepts that he is a product of all his experiences. The Spanish philosopher José Ortega y Gasset expressed the interaction of self and culture in this way: *Yo soy yo y mis circunstancias*. Once one knows how the game of life is played, and that it is a game— complete with arbitrary rules and plaster of Paris incentives—one is free to take, if one wishes, a more sporting attitude toward the human scene.

A powerful predictor of behavior is knowledge of a person's cultural background, especially when subcultural variables such as age, sex, social class, religion, occupation, and place of residence are taken into consideration. A useful outline for focusing on the cultural origins of ideas and behavior was prepared by Kraemer (1973), adopted from Kluckholm and Murray (1953):

Every person thinks and acts in *some* respects
- (a) like all other persons
- (b) like some other persons
- (c) like no other person

- (b1) like other persons of the same sex
- (b2) like other persons of the same occupation
- (b3) like other persons of the same age
- (b4) like other persons in the same role
- (b5) like other persons in the same situation

One way in which teachers can use this outline is to have students offer personal examples for each item on the outline.

If one is the product of cultural conditioning, then bicultural people are the product of two contrasting forms of cultural conditioning. This makes it harder to predict the behavior of bicultural people. It is fun to watch bicultural strangers interact at parties, when each knows the first-culture patterns of the other. In this situation, the conventions governing appropriate behavior forms are up for grabs. For instance, an American guest might bow to a Japanese guest at the same time that the latter extends his hand to shake the American's hand. Anthropologists have dubbed the resulting mix of behavior "bobbing." Each partygoer responds unexpectedly to the first-culture patterns of the other.

Classroom activities can provide explicit help in integrating conflicting values. There are activities to highlight these cross-cultural conflicts (Weeks, Pedersen, and Brislin, 1977), but there is no pat way to dispatch the confusion that accompanies the ensuing conflict. Tender loving care seems to be the response that inspires the most confidence. Uvaldo Palomares' (1974) technique of the magic circle may bring some of these affective confusions to light for subsequent discussion. (In this activity, a dozen or fewer children sit in a circle and share their personal feelings on a given topic. Topics cover areas such as: I can show you something I feel good about [kindergarten]; I didn't know I'd get in trouble [second grade]; I had a hard time choosing between two things [third grade].) For high school children, value clarification exercises may make the problem easier to deal with. Some value clarification exercises are described in Pfeiffer et al. (1969-1975), Simon et al. (1973), Weeks et al. (1977), and Seelye (1979).

How Other Bicultural People Cope

Looking at the behavior of people who have attempted to "make peace" with disparate cultural systems, molding conflicting experience into an integrated sense of self, it is clear that there are many different ways to accomplish this. The models that other people provide can help students see where they are in the process of biculturation. These models can also help students judge the usefulness that different forms of adaptation may have for their own lives.

Eight divergent ways in which individuals respond to situations of marginality or uprootedness were identified over three decades ago by Donald T. Campbell (1950), the eminent social psychologist, from descriptions found then in the social science literature: (1) to become an agent of change through a personal and creative deployment of innovation; (2) to have one's ego damaged, as characterized by neurotic indecisiveness, aimlessness, schizoid withdrawal, self-deprecation, cynicism, and destructiveness; (3) to convert a relativism of values into a stable standard of reference and a way of life; (4) to adapt to situations by focusing on the interplay between role and reference group, letting one's behavior be guided by several discrete "generalized others"; (5) to retain one's first cultural goals (e.g., money) while abandoning the culturally prescribed means of achieving them; (6) to reestablish an orthodoxy, often more rigid than the "natural born" variety, characterized, perhaps, by a reactionary return to the parental culture or by a return to the ghetto; (7) to overconform rigidly to the second culture, resulting sometimes in anti-egalitarian, anti-lower-class attitudes on the part of the socially mobile; (8) to adopt, in concert with other uprooted persons, a novel orthodoxy, differing from and probably hostile to all of the traditional cultures whose contact may have produced the marginality.

Real-life models cover the wide range of strategies suggested by Campbell: Amish farmers following the customs of rural farmers of two centuries ago—even though the descendants of their ancestors who remained in Germany no longer share that culture; Eskimo fishermen who return home after years of medical treatment in sanatoriums in urban Canada, never to mention anything that happened during those "foreign" years; nativistic South Sea Islanders who create a glorious, ancient culture the way they imagine it to have been; the person who changed his name from Hipólito Pérez Ramos to Hal Rome, and says he's of Italian descent if anyone asks; the angry militant who rejects all cultural values; the Buddhist bodhisattva, who sees life as a game in which one avoids confusion of social role with self-identity; the person who neatly compartmentalizes values into separate boxes, one for each culture; and so on.

A study which viewed second-culture coping strategies as healthy, nonpathological attempts to deal with daily exigencies, suggests that all intercultural coping, which includes the thousands of behavioral choices that are made, falls into one of five categories (Seelye and Wasilewski, 1979; also recounted in Brislin, 1981, pp. 277—79):

1. *Avoidance*, a nonacceptance of second-culture patterns. (Example: A woman from India moves to the U.S. and continues to wear a *sari*.)
2. *Substitution* of second-culture patterns for first-culture patterns. (Ex.: The Indian woman wears Western dress exclusively.)
3. *Addition* of second-culture patterns to first-culture patterns. (Ex.: She wears *saris* or Western dress, depending on the circumstances.)
4. *Synthesis*, or recombination of behavior from first and second cultures, where both cultural influences are simultaneously apparent. (Ex.: She wears a *sari*, but combines it with leather boots and a long-sleeved blouse or sweater.)

5. *Resynthesis*, where an *original* integration of the influences of two cultures is effected, resulting in a novel third-culture pattern. (Ex.: She designs *haute couture* based on abstractions from the dress designs of both cultures.)

(For adolescents from non-Western backgrounds, dress is an area that commonly provokes particular stress [Louden, 1978; Brah, 1978; Saunders, 1982].)

After interviewing 200 bicultural adults, Seelye and Wasileweski found that 75 percent reported using three or more different coping strategies to meet different demands at diverse times in their lives. These researchers stress that one does not begin by using "avoidance" as a response to all situations and then evolve toward "resynthesis" as the preferred strategy. Rather, one draws on many or all of the coping strategies; choice of a particular strategy depends on the nature and context of the cultural demand and on how one is disposed at the moment.

If a student can find "kindred spirits" among the school staff, perhaps someone of the same ethnic background, his/her attempts to find suitable models for emulation will be aided. But teachers should not make the mistake of thinking that they are all things to all students. Sensitive teachers can bring to the student's attention a wide range of models found in literature or in examples of people living in the student's community.

Students can be given the assignment of interviewing different people in their family or community who are bicultural to see how they describe their attempts at integrating cultural differences. Though there is no one right way to become bicultural, some ways are healthier than others. The healthier ways use all experience as a springboard to greater awareness of the interrelatedness of self and the universe; they do not deny experience.

To generate further insight into the dynamics through which minority persons effectively cope and adapt in multicultural environments, Jacqueline Howell Wasilewski (1982) described the strategies used by people who successfully adapted to life in the

U.S. and determined which strategies were prominent in the experiences of four major minority groups. Wasilewski based her ethnographic study on several hundred life histories that were published in English. Her study focused on three major domains: the *environments* in which interpersonal interaction takes place (both physical and psychological); the *competencies* of the actor (abilities to appraise social situations and to transform reality); and the *behaviors* exhibited in these particular environments by the actor (abilities to deploy behavior appropriately, to accept one's own diversity, to accept assistance from the dominant group). Wasilewski developed a checklist that can be used to indicate—from the perspective of the minority person doing the coping and adapting—the presence of important patterns.

Recurring patterns emerged from Wasilewski's study that are particularly helpful in enabling minority people to cope and adapt to multicultural conditions. Successful copers have:

1. A superordinate goal (e.g., concern for someone else's welfare, perhaps by participating in an organization or movement);

2. Role models and mentors;

3. The ability to choose (internally) to be one's complex self in the face of cultural and interpersonal pressures to simplify (e.g., "I'll never be Japanese enough for my grandmother or American enough for my friends, so I'll just have to be myself");

4. The ability to *behave* (externally) in accordance with one's complex self. (This leads, oftimes, to improvement in the environment's ability to accept the diversity inherent in culturally plural individuals);

5. The ability to transform negative energy (e.g., bitterness) into positive energy (e.g., deciding one is not going to spend energy in self-destructive ways, then going on to use one's energies to develop a skill or build something;

6.   A large repertoire of coping strategies from which to choose behaviors appropriate to a particular situation (e.g., when to behave actively, when to behave passively).

In other research (Seelye and Wasilewski, 1981) into how bicultural children develop the skills they need in order to function simultaneously in different cultural settings (a Spanish-speaking home, with black peers, and in an urban, all-English school), it was discovered that one of the most important correlates of success in school was whether they made a friend the first day of school. Further, success in the other domains was related to whether they had a close confidant with whom they could talk about anything.

In a school in Dearborn, Michigan, a teacher asked one sixth-grade ESL class to write what they felt about school. A winsome Arabic-speaking student, Terry Makki, emphasized in her brief essay the importance of friends.

I always want to be nice to people but I don't know how. I give people my stuff just so they can be my friends. I sometimes act like them so they can be my friends. I hate teasing people but if you want to have some friends, well that's what I did, but it didn't work. In Lebanon I used to be quiet and nice and did all my work and got good grades. These days I'm getting good grades. But in class people talk to me so I talk back to them so they don't get mad at me. I know I complain. I know I take some things serious but I'm trying not to. I cry because I try to be that person's friend, but then they start calling me names. Girls start coming to me and saying that some of the girls and boys are saying that I'm the ugliest girl and they all hate me. There is another way I try to be their friend, and that is acting like them but I think they don't like the way they act. The real me is nice, kind, generous, sweet, and quiet. But that is not the way I act in class. I'm just telling you on paper how I really feel and how I used to be and the truth.

Examples such as these of how others worked through typical bicultural problems let students know they are not alone and that there are many ways to accomplish cultural integration. By projecting his/her own concerns into someone else's problem, the student can retain privacy while effecting definitional clarity of some of his/her own frustrations.

"Messages" from School

A factor to be considered consciously by a bilingual student is the extent to which s/he receives satisfaction from group endeavor in comparison to individual accomplishment. Each society has people of every ilk, but some societies are oriented around one type more than another. In the U.S., for example, the Protestant Ethic, the frontier spirit, laissez-faire, high social class and geographic mobility, and the large size of the country have produced a lot of Captain Marvels who change the rest of the world to suit themselves by shouting, "SHAZAM!" In Mexico, on the other hand, the extended family often affords the setting within which one achieves psychological satisfaction. In some socialist countries a major attempt is being made to have individuals sublimate their own cravings into societal priorities so that the good of the group has more psychological force than drives toward individualization.

All societal institutions pit the group against the individual, but some societies do it with more efficiency than others. A person who is highly egocentered can expect frustration in a society whose institutions are based too efficiently on subordinating individual interests to group goals. Likewise, a person who feels comfortable in working for the good of the many will experience distress in a society where one is expected to contribute as an individual, without aid of family, friends, or work cohorts.

Schools, too, sometimes pit the institution against the individual, and they have six hours a day, nine months a year, for twelve years (or more) to get their message across. The dialects of academia sometimes serve as armaments in the employ of the institution in its struggle for student minds. Classification systems, especially those constructed by monocultural social scientists, often are biased against bicultural people. For example, the following continuum popular among Western psychologists is one semantic trap to avoid in a discussion of ego:

strong ego...weak ego

This dichotomy implies a positive value on "strong ego" and a negative value on "weak ego." Whenever a classification system places one in categories with negative overtones, it is time to counterattack with another classification more sympathetic to one's complexity. One antidotal continuum that might turn the tables here associates "weak ego" with a desirable quality:

weak sense of universe.............strong sense of universe

Here, strong ego is synonymous with weak sense of universe.

Some people view bilingualism, the most overt sign of biculturalism, as a desirable condition only of the upper class or of people from the non-English world. Middle- and working-class U.S. children and adults are expected to remain monolingual. This view, of course, negates the worth per se of bilingualism and would limit its utility to jet set peregrinations to the health spas of Europe or as a communicative tool for "foreign" or "minority" peoples to discourse with America, the Fabulous. The self-esteem of the bicultural student is enhanced by the presence of teachers, administrators, and peers of the mainstream culture who are fluent in the language and customs of the minority ethnic group. It is also positively affected by the presence of adult bilingual-bicultural models from the minority culture as well. It is a lot easier for a student to see the value of bilingualism and biculturalism when it is sought after by people from all cultural backgrounds.

The management style of U.S. classroom teachers constitutes another way in which the dominant culture sends "messages" to unsuspecting bicultural students. These messages constitute a "hidden curriculum" with which the students must successfully interact. Through intensive study of a small number of classrooms, Margaret LeCompte (1981) identifies five rules which students were expected to internalize and which were embedded in the teachers' "management-type behavior." These rules were:

1. Do what the teacher says.
2. Live up to teacher expectations for proper behavior.
3. Stick to the schedule.
4. Keep busy.
5. Keep quiet and don't move too much.

LeCompte suggests that schools teach children how to manage these "hidden" rules of classroom behavior.

All sorts of unintended (to give the benefit of the doubt) messages are conveyed by teacher behavior. In one bilingual education program that I evaluated the teachers (uncharacteristically for bilingual teachers) used Spanish solely for punitive purposes: "Shut up." "Sit down." "Be quiet." The medium for academic content and praise was English.

Tiedt and Tiedt (1979) suggest a number of practical ways teachers can help build a positive concept of self. The authors outline ideas for activities such as welcoming the student, the "me" collage, writing projects (e.g., What I Like about Me, Ten Things about Me), It's Okay to Be Afraid (students write fears on slip of paper, put in box anonymously, slips are drawn, and the whole class discusses the fear), the fantasy trip (close your eyes, think back to the time you first . . . How did you feel?; think of a time something unpleasant happened in school . . . what should the teacher have said to make it all right?), names (my name, what my parents call me, what my friends call me . . .), family roots.

These authors list teaching strategies that they recommend be avoided:

1. Activities in which there is only one winner.
2. Publicizing the "A" papers or those that got 100 percent on the spelling test. (This ignores the children who need a boost the most.)
3. Putting a grade on every paper a child completes.
4. Teaching to mastery. (Fluency and enjoyment [of reading] more important.)
5. Expecting the same answer to everything.

Ethnic minority students are exposed to the trials and trivia, heros and villains of *both* their home culture (or the culture of their parents) and U.S. mainstream culture. The challenge is for these students to *integrate* what they hear. I studied Mexican history in Mexico and U.S. history in the U.S. Only after several hours of history lectures about the U.S. Southwest did I realize that my U.S. teacher was talking about the same historical period that my Mexican teacher had addressed previously. In the area of overlap, there were two completely different histories! This observation—that each society puts its own interpretation on events —can be enlightening.

It is hard to feel good about yourself if everyone except your mother is telling you what a dud you are. From the age of six to 18 to 22, anybody who gets mediocre or worse grades in school suffers from loss of self-esteem. Successful school experiences are like jolts of energy that recharge the batteries of self-esteem. Efforts to strengthen pupils' self-esteem must include skill development. The concluding observation made by Lieberman, Yalom, and Miles (1973) in their impressive study of encounter groups is pertinent for all educators:

> The participant must be able to carry something out of the group experience that is more than a simple affective state. He must carry with him some framework, though by no means necessarily well-formulated, which will enable him to transfer learning from the group to his outside life and to continue experimenting with new types of adaptive behavior.

. . . Most small groups will spontaneously evolve into a social unit which provides the affective aspects of the intensive group experience; the leader's function is to prevent any potential obstruction of the evolution of the intensive experience, and in addition to be a spokesman for tomorrow as he encourages group members to reflect on their experiences and to package them cognitively so that they can be transported into the future (p. 439).

Success in the "noncultural" cognitive areas of the curriculum bolsters a healthy sense of self-esteem in bicultural students. So, in a real sense, the math or gym teachers are aiding the cause of self-identity when they ply their trades to get children to do things they could not do before.

We teachers tend to develop a very limited view of the accomplishments of our students. This is especially true for bilingual students. In one study (Seelye and Wasilewski, 1981), the teachers of 50 Hispanic children were asked to list the skills of the bilingual students they had in class. None of the monolingual teachers listed a single ethnically related skill such as fluency in Spanish, social graces, cooking and dancing abilities, abilities to function in culturally diverse settings. Another research study (Carrasco, 1981) concludes that "even the most conscientious teachers may have a limited view of their children's talents and abilities in the classroom."

Two mistakes commonly accompany cognitive skill development in programs aimed at students for whom English is a second language. The more common of the two is to assume falsely that the learning style of the "average" Anglo child, as embodied in course syllabi, will snugly fit the Hispanic (or other) child if only it is translated into Spanish (or other foreign language). The other mistake is to assume falsely that most Spanish-speaking children share the same learning style, even if it is seen as differing from the Anglo. The trick—and it does not matter which ethnic group you happen to be teaching—is to be prepared to help a student learn concepts and skills in the best way for him/her. One can expect nearly as much variance within ethnic groups as between them.

In recent years, schools have attempted to select instructional materials that portray people and problems with which students of diverse backgrounds can identify. A student booklet developed by the Peace Corps in Ecuador entitled, "Ñucanchi Mundoca Cashnami" ("This Is How Our World Is"), contains graphics of a Quichua woman nursing her child, of growing corn, of a carpenter at work, etc. It was made expressly for Quichua-speaking otaveleño children to learn about the world around them through images that really belong to their world. The book has been a success—among otaveleños. When the book was used with Quichua-speaking children in other locations in Ecuador, the pictures provoked laughter—the corn was all right, but the headdress of the woman looked weird and the long braid of the otavaleño carpenter struck them as even weirder. The teachers were faced with a dilemma: to publish different editions for each subcultural division of the Quichua world, or to broaden the child's world by including graphics of many different Quichua-speaking people at the expense of total relevance to any one regional group. The latter decision was made by the Peace Corps and the results are encouraging.

In the case of the excellent instructional materials developed by Ralph Robinett et al. (1973) in Florida, the decision was made to develop three versions of their materials: a Mexican version for the Southwest, a Cuban-Puerto Rican version for the East, and a version for use in areas such as Illinois where there is a mixture of Mexicans, Puerto Ricans, Cubans, and other Hispanic nationalities. The economics of the situation heavily weighs the decision. No one in the U.S., for example, is getting out versions of their materials that would allow a Guatemalan or Argentine child to relate immediately to them. However, to shrink the world that a child is exposed to unduly would duplicate the error of previous U.S. textbook writers and illustrators who thought the world was populated solely by WASPs. In deciding how culturally specific to make instructional materials, some compromise can be healthy. In fact, the only version of Robinett's materials that was published commercially was the multi-ethnic edition.

Knowledge of one's ethnic and/or national background serves to provide a sense of one's own continuity with the past and provides the feeling (some would say illusion) that the traditional ways are being retained, if only via memory. The Jívaro Indians of Ecuador are doing just this in their bilingual programs through transcriptions of stories told by old shamans. This is especially important where an awareness of continuity is threatened by loss of language or by a sudden, drastic change in what one does or how one dresses. These threats can be alleviated. Knowledge of historic accomplishments can instill pride in one's background and give one a sense of cultural roots. Examples taken from contemporary life have an immediate appeal to youth; they are a call to action. For some students of mathematical aptitude, modern mathematicians like Einstein may be more effective models than ancient giants like Aristotle.

Rapid cultural change breeds alienation if the change is imposed by outside forces. It is common for cultures to experience a confrontation-depression-revival syndrome as a result of contact with a culture perceived to be dominant. The whole process of evolution takes about 100 years. Teachers can help combat this particular source of alienation by involving parents and students in as many educational decisions as feasible. Alienation is reduced when one thinks of oneself as choosing the "best" of the second culture; the potential for alienation increases when one adopts wholesale a different way of life in place of one's own.

Educators have just begun to scratch the surface in helping bicultural students to realize their creative potential. This potential will remain elusive as long as teachers, current curricula, and curricula developers remain monocultural in experience and outlook. Everyday role changes manifest a subcultural flexibility that can aid both monocultural and bicultural educators to develop insight into the process of biculturation.

The critical integration in the process of becoming bicultural is a personal, psychological one that can be helped by teachers who themselves understand the process explicitly. At present, this understanding is intuitive and fragmentary.

Suggested Activities

1. Using Kraemer's outline for focusing on the cultural origins of ideas and behavior, give three examples from your own life of each of the nine items in Kraemer's outline.
2. Together with three or four of your colleagues, locate yourselves on a 10-point continuum: from strong sense of ego to strong sense of universe.
3. Tape-record or write an ethnic history of yourself, starting as far back as you can.

11

Sharing a Good Thing: Global Education

Intercultural educators can be on the cutting edge of a school-wide curriculum that thrives on cultural differences. Diverse, culturally conditioned learning styles can be recognized and learning enhanced by curricular innovations. Students of whatever ethnic background can develop the whole range of skills and understandings that are possible in a multicultural curriculum, but the testing of ethnically distinct children requires special sensitivity to cross-cultural differences in learning styles. This chapter offers many suggestions for implementing the kind of education that will result in the acquisition of intercultural communication skills by students of all ethnic backgrounds.

We live in a multicultural world. An education that helps students acquire intercultural communication skills is a necessity for everyone, not just for the culturally "deprived" or distinct, but for *all* children as cultural beings. A contemporary author expresses this in engagingly simple language:

This chapter has been coauthored by Jacqueline Howell Wasilewski.

I've often thought there ought to be a manual to hand to little kids, telling them what kind of planet they're on, why they don't fall off, how much time they've probably got here, how to avoid poison ivy, and so on. . . . And one thing I would really like to tell them about is cultural relativity. I didn't learn until I was in college about all the other cultures, and I should have learned that in the first grade. A first grader should understand that his or her culture isn't a rational invention; that there are thousands of other cultures and they all work pretty well; that all cultures function on faith rather than truth; that there are lots of alternatives to our own society. Cultural relativity is defensible and attractive. It's also a source of hope. It means we don't have to continue this way if we don't like it [Vonnegut, 1974, p. 139].

To adopt the perspective of cultural relativity is to recognize that different cultures provide different behavioral options for satisfying the universal physical and psychological needs of Homo sapiens. This point was the main thrust of Chapter 2 and underlies much of Chapter 10. An understanding that cultural conventions are created by people to serve ourselves lays the foundation for a kind of cultural literacy, the acceptance of man as a cultural being. Aristotle said man is a political animal, which is much the same thing. One eminent anthropologist (Hall, 1976) says that culture is dictatorial unless it is understood and examined. Just as a fish never discovers water as long as it remains immersed, so it is that only when we are called upon to function in another culture are our basic assumptions revealed. Until an alternate is known, the medium of life is an unexamined given.

Teachers can make a difference in the way we see ourselves. They can structure the curriculum so that students can examine the many ways cultural conditioning affects the quality of human thought and actions. This chapter provides teachers and teacher trainers with ideas culled from many sources to increase curricular relevancy in a multicultural world.

The Checkered History of Multicultural Education

O. Henry, that master of surprise endings, is reported to have said that the Statue of Liberty "offered a cast-ironical welcome to immigrants." These immigrants—and all American groups save one are of immigrant background—have affected the evolution of American education. Two books trace this effect. Weiss (1981) reconstructs the period between 1840 and 1940, and Gollnick (1980) focuses on the history of education from 1943 to the present. There have been many permutations ranging from education in ethnically specific private schools, through ethnic studies in public schools, to an emergent but beleaguered multicultural or global education.

Appel and Appel (in Weiss, 1981) observe, in an article entitled "The Huddled Masses and the Little Red School House," that in the early years of this century the U.S. changed from a largely rural, small-town, homogeneous, white, Protestant society to an industrial, urban, heterogeneous, ethnically diverse, secular society. These authors argue that the "little red school house" had always been a compelling symbol for education in that former era. But as yet there are no compelling symbolic substitutes for the little red school house in our present heterogeneous society. Appel and Appel reason that educational symbols are needed to "provide rallying points for what is strong, appealing, and excellent with respect to the education of minorities." These symbols "would help groups with divergent views to articulate shared ideas and values better than the ubiquitous symbol of recent history, the school bus!" The authors add that it is as difficult to live up to unsymbolized aspirations as it is to live down harmful stereotypes.

Berrol (in Weiss, 1981) states that in no case was school the central or most important acculturative experience for the ethnic groups. Rather, it was the *expanding economy* of the turn of the century that offered a job to even the greenest newcomer which provided a locus where the newcomer could learn how the American system worked. Fellow workers, bosses, and union leaders taught them. They learned politics from district leaders and ward bosses. Ethnic newspapers made them aware of all kinds of social developments, including how to play baseball. Mothers and children learned from the streets, the former while doing marketing, the latter while playing with peers. Settlement houses also made a profound contribution to immigrant adaptation.

A pithy history of multicultural education between 1924 and 1941 (Montalto, in Weiss, 1981) examines the "tolerance" professed during that period toward people of diverse ethnicity. Montalto notes that along with this "tolerance" came an accompanying fear that to foster greater awareness of cultural distinctiveness would also foster "minority chauvinism." This fear, along with World War II, effectively killed the movement toward multicultural education. Montalto states that the "persistence of our divisions, whether they be ethnic, regional or class in nature, is still a disturbing reality, a reality with which we have only begun to deal." (See also Ogbu, 1978; Seelye and Wasilewski, 1979; Walsh, 1979; Davis, 1980; Gollnick and Chinn, 1981; García, 1982.)

Two acute pressures inhibit the growth of global education—a wartime mentality and economic hard times. Since teachers cannot directly affect either, what can they do to help prepare students for the real world—a multicultural planet? The answer is obvious: they can implement a curriculum which enthusiastically acknowledges the polycultural setting of our species.

Curricula Adjustments

The adaptation of course content already in the curriculum is the best and most easily implementable way to achieve multicultural objectives. As one educator observes,

> ... every school subject, if taught truthfully and realistically, requires a plural culture perspective. Science, literature, the behavioral sciences, all must be freed from the monocultural

ethnocentric focus that characterizes most standard course work.... We can no longer tolerate nor afford to permit a subject area to be called generally "music," "history," "psychology," "political science," when it is really a *culture specific* music, history, psychology, or political science ... [Hilliard, 1975].

Course content can be made more global in two ways. First, teachers, with the help of specialists, can exploit opportunities to illustrate existing course objectives with examples that serve additionally to increase knowledge of other cultures. An example of this approach might be a math unit that rightly credits the Mayas of what is now Mexico and Guatemala with the world's first use of the zero, followed several centuries later by the Arabs.

A second approach involves developing new instructional objectives that allow multiculturally oriented units to fit into existing courses. Let's say, for example, that one such objective is to illustrate the interdependence of cultures. The math curriculum could cull many examples of cultural diffusion, such as why the invention of the zero by the Arabs (who got it from the East Indians) spread widely throughout the world, whereas the same invention by the Mayas did not diffuse widely.

Whichever of these two general approaches is employed to integrate cultural objectives into existing courses, curriculum development teams and teacher training institutions can greatly facilitate the process by aiding the identification and production of relevant objectives for all courses at all levels. One should not forget the potential inherent in sports and the arts. The former provides grist for understanding the relation between competition and cooperation, whereas the latter affords opportunities to experience and/or express cultural symbolism.

Any attempt to get school curricula to better articulate the multicultural world in which we live obviously must involve classroom teachers directly. Teachers, as well as students, learn by doing, and teachers learn side by side with their students. (Teachers usually learn more than students.) When classroom learning openly acknowledges its two-way nature, new instructional styles often place less emphasis on verbal exposition (the resplendent teacher-talk that occupies so much classroom time) and on narrowly focused teacher-student interactions ("Johnny, why do the Masai drink camel blood?" "Gee, I don't know, Miss Stern, I left my book at my cousin's last night and couldn't . . ."). More emphasis is placed on getting students to learn from one another, on developing group activities, and on cultivating a zest for learning by showing that the teacher shares in the excitement of learning. McLaughlin's (1976) study of how to implement change stresses that "mutual adaptation is the best way to ensure that change efforts are not superficial, trivial, or transitory."

The type of preservice and inservice teacher training that can best help teachers prepare for working in a global curriculum, therefore, is characterized by an emphasis on exploration and experimentation, in which much learning is accomplished through demonstrations, modeling, simulations, and deduction (Gay, 1977). John Dewey stated it simply: we learn by doing.

There is some controversy revolving around the proper focus of global education. (How could there possibly be global education without animated differences of opinion?) One informed position taken by the National Council for the Social Studies (Banks et al., 1976) argues that *ethnic pluralism* and not cultural pluralism should be the focus of curriculum reform. "Cultural pluralism suggests a type of education which deals with the cultural contributions of all groups within a society. Consequently, that concept is far too broad and inclusive to set forth effectively the boundaries of an area encompassing both the contributions of ethnic groups and the problems resulting from ethnic discrimination in American society." Still, it is not yet clear that this distinction is a necessary one once we begin dealing with specific skills on operational levels. This chapter will focus on the broader concept of cultural pluralism. (The last chapter included a discussion of ethnic identity vs. national identity.)

An easy to read, nuts-and-bolts aid to classroom activities relevant to intercultural education is presented by Tiedt and Tiedt

(1979). These authors cover topics such as building positive self-concepts, determining the role of language (including various dialects of English), fostering intergroup relations, developing activities around a multicultural calendar, creating teacher materials, and identifying available resources. For other activities appropriate to a multicultural curriculum, see Baldwin and Wells (1980), Hicks (1981), King (1980), Lurie (1982), and Baker (1983).

A brief look at the "hard core" curricula areas will generate additional ideas and illustrations of how adjustments can be effected to exploit the multicultural content implicit in all curricular areas.

Math, Science, and Technology

Mathematics is perhaps the only world language of the present day. The Western hegemony during the last several centuries has been largely due to the preeminence of science and technology: Spanish guns in Mexico and Peru in the fifteenth century and English steam engines 300 years later. (This latter development of industrial technology was perhaps ultimately dependent on the fact that sixteenth-century Britain ran out of firewood and turned to coal to heat the foggy isle, and this adoption of a new fuel set in motion the chain of events which culminated in the Industrial Revolution [Nef, 1977].)

Yet the development of a technological culture is fraught with ironies. The Arabic concept of zero, which resolved a mathematical problem that neither the Greeks nor the Romans had been able to solve and which facilitated the mathematical description of the world, sprang from the Hindu culture which perceived the world quite differently from the Greek. The Greeks demarcated space, described and measured the dimensions of shapes and volumes, had their eye caught by the concrete, the discrete, the something. The spaces between "somethings" were seen as vacuums, as the opposite of "somethings." Hindu culture, on the other hand, saw the world as pattern on pattern, as cyclic and blending, and as kaleidoscopically transforming. Space was a manifesting field, the universe played hide-and-seek with itself, nothing was something, potentially anything (Dass, 1974).

The West puzzles as to why the Chinese used gunpowder only for fireworks, while it took the West 1,000 years to adopt the wheelbarrow from China. And speaking of wheels, the Mayas used wheels but only on toys (Casson et al., 1977).

Or a completely different tack might be taken by teachers to introduce "culture" into technical subjects. For instance, the principles of probability might be demonstrated through use of card games popular with different ethnic groups represented in the classroom (Gay, 1977).

Social Studies

Social studies is, of course, the "natural" arena for introducing multicultural content since virtually every social studies objective can be illustrated by examples from hundreds of cultures.

Simulations are particularly effective with elementary school children. Some fourth grade children in California regularly turn their classrooms into the haciendas of the Spanish Colonial Era. They take Spanish names, answer roll call in Spanish, study Spanish as well as English spelling and vocabulary words, make clothes like those worn during the period, learn songs, dances, and games, tan hides, dip candles, make donkey carts, grind corn and try to prepare tortillas, read of Father Sierra, visit the local mission and dream of a different world within its cool, thick walls, then visit the local center of present-day Chicano life. Students often combine everything they have learned in student-created plays about the era. These can be vivid means of evoking the flavor and the feel of another era and another way.

Older students, if they like, can be more analytic and can begin to develop sociological and anthropological skills. One superlative introduction to field research is Robert M. Coles' *Children of Crisis* series (1967-78) on the children of Mexicans, blacks, Native Americans, and Eskimos as well as those of white

sharecroppers and plantation owners, children of both the power-
less and the powerful.

A good source of material for social problems that typically
are faced by ethnic groups is the ethnic press. Murphy (1974) lists
black, Chicano, and Native American newspapers (186 publications for Native Americans alone), and Seelye and Day (1982) and
Day (1977) suggest student activities based on Spanish-language
newspapers. An excellent text on minority relations in the U.S. is
available in Vander Zanden (1983). For help in identifying or
developing simulations, see Livingston and Stoll (1973), Zuckerman and Horn (1973), and Stadsklev (1974; 1975).

Language and Literature

Language can serve as the core curriculum of a multicultural
school. Language is, of course, a major vehicle for the transmission of culture. Learning the cultural roots of a language is essential for meaningful fluency. The preceding chapters of this book
have provided innumerable exercises and activities for revealing
the patterns of culture while learning a second (or third) language.

A plural society is an intercultural society, a society which
effectively communicates across cultural boundaries. A crucial
skill in such a society is the ability to be expressive and articulate,
whether on behalf of oneself or one's group (Freire, 1974). The
clearest form of communication is usually accomplished through
language.

In mainstream U.S. society, the value placed on the ability to
manipulate language in many of its forms, oral and written, has a
great deal to do with student achievement which, in turn, affects
subsequent success in the workplace (Massad, 1972; Goodenough,
1976). Further, researchers generally believe that positive self-
concept can best be nurtured in an environment which respectfully
accepts a child's first culture (e.g., Seelye and Wasilewski, 1981).
Of course, inherent in this situation there may be a conflict: What
if a child's first culture does not value expressive, articulate
children?

In U.S. society, even a child from a cultural background which does not value articulation and expressiveness will have to be articulate and expressive enough to communicate that very characteristic of his or her group. In fact, a curriculum focus on cross-cultural communication patterns may contribute to the child's ability to cope on his or her own terms, so that s/he can "...understand himself and his behavior in a social context and learn to make wise choices with which he can live . . ." (Ammons, 1969).

The techniques teachers develop to help individual students learn a pattern of responses appropriate to varying contexts are likely to be quite idiosyncratic. Self-concept cannot be evaluated independently of the standard used: the standard of the mainstream culture, of the child's first culture, or of the child himself (Saville-Troike, 1973). Llabre, Ware, and Newell (1977) indicate that even the structures underlying the self-concept of children are not the same across sex and ethnic groups.

Langdon (1966) developed a language arts program in which children were encouraged to write about emotional experiences, gradually refining their style so that their written compositions matched their enthusiasm for telling their stories orally. (See also Ashton-Warner, 1963; Richardson, 1964.)

It is in using language to communicate that children learn a language well, whether it is their first, second, or third language (Paulston, 1974), especially if what they are communicating is "purposeful and significant" to them. One student in a bilingual program that encouraged writing about things of deep significance to the students themselves said, "This is the first time that anybody in a course like this ever asked me to tell them what I know" (Rivers, 1975).

Students are, above all else, interested in themselves and their friends. Every student, no matter what his or her level of ability, is an expert in at least one thing, their own feelings. An intriguing challenge for older students in creative writing courses lies in developing ethnic identity in a world where even the most disparate of cultures are coming into daily contact. Such courses can help students develop the ability to articulate the difficulties and opportunities they may experience in living on cultural boundaries.

The ability to enter a literary world may be akin to the ability to enter another culture. In both, one suspends "usual" conventions to accept a different set of premises. The ways in which a novelist builds his literary world, the techniques of literary analysis, the use of literature by anthropologists as a social science tool: these are topics that can stimulate fruitful classroom discussion. A number of books can help the teacher to enrich his or her students by illustrating literary responses to life's dramas (Hsu, 1969; Booth, 1967; Peckham, 1967; Kahler, 1967; Watts, 1969; Goonetilleke, 1977).

In operation, a classroom activity to assist student entry into a literary world may look like this: The students prepare two products: (1) an essay, drama, song, or painting on the major themes of a recently read novel (e.g., the individual as a stranger, solitude, lack of known parentage or ancestry); and (2) a personal statement, through prose, poetry, visual, impression, or analysis of one's own background. Both products can be shared with the class at large and discussed. The final class product would be a "bound" edition of the students' work, along with photographs and "reviews" of the non-print products. The volume can also include notes of some points made by classmates. One group of students named their "book" The I I Know.

After World War II, a girl of Chinese immigrant parents entered public elementary school in Stockton, California. Today she teaches college English. Her book, The Woman Warrior: Memoirs of a Girlhood among Ghosts (1976) won the National Book Critics Award for the best book of nonfiction published that year. This book is a chronicle of Maxine Hong Kingston's own particular experiences growing up on the Chinese-American cultural boundary and of her continued attempts to find an American song that can be accompanied by Chinese instruments. The "ghosts" of the title are not ancestral memories of China, rather, they refer to anyone who is not Chinese. You see, only the Han people are real. "You must not tell anyone," my mother said, "what I am about to tell you . . ."

Classroom activities such as a personal statement of one's background may help future "warriors" to understand in themselves a process that too often ends dialogue rather than begins it.

New Courses

The approaches to achieving multicultural objectives mentioned above are not the only ways to add global perspectives to the curriculum. Sometimes secondary schools are tempted to add a new course (universities practically always see this as the solution) to achieve objectives not already being addressed.

An example of a new course developed by classroom teachers is Dimitriou's (1977) "Suburban Ethnicity: A Case Study of the American-Greek Experience in Southern California," a teaching and resource manual for an intercultural studies curriculum developed for junior and senior high school students at Palos Verdes High School, Palos Verdes Estates, California. It was developed to reveal the Greek immigrant experience in Southern California and includes slide and tape materials. This general format can serve teachers as a model for developing materials about other ethnic groups in either English or the ethnic language. Activities include:

(1)   student preparation of three-generation family trees;
(2)   an inquiry into ethnic characteristics and ethnic stereotyping, both positive and negative, which begins with each student listing five positive and five negative stereotypes for his/her ethnic group (or, for the student who is multiethnic, the group with which s/he selects to study);
(3)   an introduction to sociological and anthropological field research by having each student conduct interviews of (a) an older acquaintance or relative with a strong ethnic background; (b) a second generation American; and (c) a third generation "ethnic";

(4)   visits to a church, mosque, Buddhist temple, or syna-
gogue to be reported on orally or in writing by
responding to a predeveloped list of study questions;

(5)   an investigation of ethnic dances as a means of exploring different worlds (e.g., what do the dance configurations tell about the values of the culture?); and

(6)   preparation of an ethnic cookbook (a particularly
savory assignment in multiethnic classes) which can be
handed out or sold to the rest of the school (the dishes
can be prepared by volunteers and eaten by the entire
school and accompanied by any folk songs and dances
that have been learned).

The manual also includes suggested research questions, notes
on religious and folk beliefs, and an extensive compendium of
Greek resources in the Los Angeles area.

Such activities create opportunities in which evaluation techniques other than written examinations can be employed: for
example, oral interviews, audio recordings of student performances, peer evaluations, diaries, and "demonstration" evaluations.

An example of a "demonstration" activity is a student production of a play based on the ethnic experience (see Dimitriou,
1977; Gay, 1977). A multiethnic sociodrama of *Manchild in a
Promised Land, Down These Mean Streets*, "I Am a Woman," "I
Am Joaquin," "The American Dilemma," or "It Bees That Way"
are some specific instances of a demonstration activity. These can
give evidence of ability to understand ethnic cultures and experiences, to select and organize a variety of materials, to present different ethnic perspectives on the same issues, and to use
knowledge gained from many disciplines, multimedia techniques,
and multiethnic perspectives to develop an idea, issue, and/or
event into a coherent message.

Field Experiences

The dramatic break in routine afforded by field trips can be used to advantage by teachers who avoid the common pitfalls that tend to trivialize this type of academic experience. Besides visits to *things* of interests, visits to people are exciting when students are prepared for the event ahead of time. Simply bringing people into contact is not enough. The history of education in U.S. overseas dependent schools is a case in point. Though these schools are often, geographically speaking, right in the middle of a foreign culture, the curricula barely reflect this. Almost no use is made of the fact that Germany, Spain, or Japan is just quite literally outside the school door. Frequently, classes in the host language are not even offered.

For field experiences to be effective, careful liaison should be developed between the schools and the communities by people comfortable working outside their own ethnic and social class enclaves.

Thinking Cross-Culturally

Lurking in the shadows of consciousness is the "hidden curriculum," the values, assumptions, and managerial techniques used in schools to implement the formal program. It has many origins.

Mitchell and Watson (in Baptiste, Baptiste, and Gollnick, 1980) observe that the style of interaction that female teachers tend to adopt with their students is often derived from the style in which they themselves were mothered. This style sometimes is frustrating for students whose expectations of appropriate female behavior with children are conditioned by a contrastive cultural background. Compare, for example, a black authoritarian mother, a white-Anglo-middle-class pal, and an affectionate and warily respectful Hispanic mother—as nurturant sources of positive affect for various students.

More and more, the task of teaching is to discover ways to elicit the behaviors we are interested in developing. Cole, Gay, Glick, and Sharp (1971), Glick (1974), and Cole and Scribner (1974) show unequivocally that cognition is not culture free, that it is not a trait, but a process, "an adaptive instrument suited to the demands of an environment as seen by the subject." Finding out which environmental demands elicit which behaviors can generate "positive statements relating behavior to occasions" (Glick, 1969). Many of the most surprising of these "statements" have originated with the hapless experiences of teachers and researchers as they attempt to test knowledge and skills cross-culturally.

One interesting approach to measuring cognition was developed when a given test did not elicit the desired performance. The test was changed until it fit the social situation in which the skills to be tested were usually exhibited so that the desired performance could be elicited. Seemingly minor variations in contextual variables sometimes affect even the kinds of tasks that "all rational people" would perform reasonably.

> ...we wanted to use everyday objects as things to sort. Accordingly, we chose something that was highly familiar to our African subjects—beer bottles of various heights and colors.... Our African subjects, though familiar with these objects and their differentiae, refused to sub-classify them— all bottles were heaped in a single category. We had made the mistake of using empty bottles, which were clearly garbage and nothing else. Preliminary observations with filled bottles shows that these can be classified [Glick, 1974].

The performance measures were not so much related to the ability to classify as to the culturally conditioned constraints of reasonability that would allow the subjects to use the classification to be tested.

There have been many fascinating studies done in cross-cultural settings that have yielded interesting hypotheses.

Two famous theories of cognition have received extensive cross-cultural treatment, Piaget's theory of cognitive development and Witkin's theory of cognitive style. Both literatures are thoroughly reviewed in Cole and Scribner (1974) and in Scribner and Cole (1981). Extensive reviews of Piagetian research in cross-cultural areas are available in Dasen (1972) and Goodnow (1969), and of cognitive style research as it applies to cross-cultural areas in Dawson (1967) and Berry (1966). The former theory stresses universal stages of development, whereas the latter stresses differences in style.

Cole and Scribner (1974) extensively review the research literature on the interrelationships between culture, cognition, language, perception, conceptual processes, learning, memory, and problem-solving. In almost every area of research reviewed, the research subjects have been shown to be sensitive to a whole host of factors connected with the research problem: the specific demands of the task; the materials used in the performance of the task; the way the problem is worded; what responses are requested. Because little attention has been paid to these factors, researchers have, according to Cole and Scribner, "altogether neglected motivational, attitudinal, and other factors" in their studies of how people think.

Witkin et al. (1977), in an article on the educational implications of field-dependent and field-independent cognitive styles, caution "against using the relations now found to exist between cognitive style and . . . performance to perpetuate a self-fulfilling prophecy." (In essence, a field-dependent person is one who is especially sensitive to the characteristics and desires of those with whom s/he must interact; a field-independent person is more self-actualized and ego centered, and, therefore, more independent of environmental concerns.)

Research in cross-cultural contexts has generated questions about just how to respond to differences in cognitive style. U.S. school systems are thought to favor field-independent cognitive modes with positive reward accruing to self-seeking, aggressive students who are able to work independently. Yet most hunting-gathering peoples—the epitome of field-independence—have been among the worst academic performers in the learning environments we provide. The sophisticated study by Cole and Means (1981) demonstrates how cognitive differences have led to prejudicial interpretations which result in mental differences being perceived as mental defects.

Ramírez and Castañeda (1974) point out that just because a child has a Hispanic name does not mean that his/her preferred cognitive style is field-dependent. There is great diversity in the Hispanic community; the child's early environment may be traditional, dualistic, or atraditional.

Cole and Scribner (1974) stressed the importance of assuming nothing when teaching children from another culture. A test of simple inference in which an apparatus consisted of a key, a locked box with three compartments, and a piece of candy (the goal) presented all sorts of difficulties for the subjects in their study. In different permutations of this experiment, it became apparent that

> the difficulty that young children and tribal Liberians experience with our simple inference task is that they do not know how to begin. For some reason, the process involved in obtaining a key from the side panel of the original apparatus interferes with later phases of the response sequence. Cultural differences seem in this case to reside in the kinds of initial situations that promote a good beginning for problem solution, not in the ability to link separately learned elements in order to solve the problem [Cole and Scribner, 1974].

Preferred cognitive style is also supposed to be related to which hemisphere of the brain is dominant in mental operations, the left hemisphere for field-independence, the right hemisphere for field-dependence. According to this theory, verbal-analytical processes are carried out in the left hemisphere, and nonverbal, spatial skills are right-brained phenomena. Cross-cultural research on brain-damaged individuals has revealed some interesting wrinkles in this sharply dichotomous picture, however. Frenchmen suffering from aphasia lose their written language if damage occurs to the left hemisphere, their spoken language if the damage is more to the right. Japanese aphasics, however, lose their spoken language if damage is more to the left, their written language if the damage is more to the right (Stewart, 1977). It is also interesting to note that dyslexic Japanese children are unusually dyslexic in the Katakana alphabet (the phonetic alphabet), and almost never in Kanji (the ideographic alphabet) (Samples, 1977). What does this all mean in terms of our conventional dichotomies about the verbal and the nonverbal, about alphabets and art? It means that we still have a lot to learn.

Research indicates that humans have extraordinary powers of recovery and that even "the mind may have some of the qualities of an elastic surface, easily deformed by shearing forces, but able to rebound when those forces are removed" (Kagan, 1978).

So many aspects of human personality that used to be considered as fairly stable "traits" now appear to be learned behaviors. For instance, altruism, generosity, personal consideration, and sharing are all prosocial behaviors that are learned (Mussen and Eisenberg-Berg, 1977). Different cultures and different child-rearing practices help or hinder to varying degrees the development of these behaviors. However, because prosocial behavior is learned, it can also be modified. And more and more we are seeing how different environments elicit different behaviors. Even a value as universal as ethnocentrism is context bound (Brewer, 1977).

The fruitfulness of perceiving cognition as an adaptive process responsive to context, and the desirability of concentrating on what people can do rather than on what they cannot do, are powerfully demonstrated by Fraiberg's (1977) book, *Insights from the Blind: Comparative Studies of Sighted and Blind Infants*. Fraiberg noted that despite the absence of communicative expression in the faces of blind children, they do convey expression—in their hands. "The hands give meaning to emotional experience," Fraiberg says of blind children. Sighted children get so locked into reading faces that they miss the expressiveness of the blind. (When Fraiberg showed film clips to Piaget of blind Robbie adaptively pursuing a sound-making toy to the place where it was "lost," thereby demonstrating that he had reached the level of "object permanence," Piaget threw his beret in the air and cheered.)

This necessity of discovering ways of enabling children to grow is also exemplified in the work of Maria Montessori, who provides a model for those instances where "a genuine cultural difference can interfere with academic process . . ." (Carlson, 1976). Her system of education, developed for Roman slum children at the turn of the century, assumes no previous knowledge, even of basic concepts. Everything is taught from scratch in its most concrete form, from what is round to how you hang up your coat. This formal learning occurs in a highly structured environment in which the hidden curriculum also reinforces the cognitive patterns (problem solving, independence of action, responsibility) being developed in the formal part of the curriculum. (It is interesting to note in view of our present difficulty in teaching people to read, that Montessori believed in teaching children to write before they learned to read. Expressive functions first!)

The multicultural child begins life less able than the monocultural child to indulge in "thinking as usual" because already s/he is the inheritor of a cultural pattern which provides alternative "recipes" for "typical solutions for typical problems available for typical actors" (Schutz, 1964). Nothing is given. Everything must be negotiated. "A common domain of activity" and "shared congruent objectives" (Stewart, in press) must be established. In a multicultural context a child is always learning new responses to old stimuli, old responses to new stimuli, and totally new stimulus-response patterns. The child is always engaged in trying to figure out when to generalize a response across situations and when to contextualize responses—that is, how to behave appropriately in different contexts. This enriching experience is, in a multicultural curriculum, available to "ethnics" and mainstream students alike.

The optimum environment for doing all this effectively is one that is characterized by a high tolerance for flexibility, ambiguity, and paradox. Most cultural environments are not so constituted, since one of the main functions of culture thus far in human history has been to provide those nice comfortable "recipes" for action within the boundaries of one's culture.

Once again, the importance of situation-specific variables cannot be emphasized enough.

> The familiar nursery school activity of having children mix flour and water to make paste . . . fails completely when Native American children refuse to make the paste because flour is food and one does not play with food [Rivlin, 1977].

A teacher unfamiliar with this prohibition would have great difficulty "extracting" this piece of cultural information from these students, especially early in the school year, because of the additional social custom of keeping silent initially with unfamiliar people in unfamiliar situations (Saville-Troike, 1978).

An extended discussion of student rights within a multicultural classroom appears in García (1982). Several points made by García are particularly salient: (1) Students must know what their rights are before they can practice them; (2) majority rule should not quell individual student rights; (3) students have the right to be different; and (4) students have the right to a positive self-concept.

Some students may feel pressure to conform because of an American penchant for decision making. Perhaps one reason for the emphasis on making decisions and choices in American society is the tension arising from a dominant cultural tradition which assumes that, once all the information is in and all the data processed, one is able to choose the one right answer. (Black is black and white's right.) However, India, another culturally diverse society, presents us with a contrasting dominant pattern, one with an opposite assumption: that it is *not* necessary to make choices. "The Westerner's choice is to make choices; the Hindu's is to lose his choosing self . . ." (Gilliat, 1972). And to do that the Indian has developed a "habit of ignoring the obvious [and] making a detour to preserve his calm" (Theroux, 1975).

So, in the words of Maxine Hong Kingston, we are left with the problem of how we can learn "to make [our] mind large, as

the universe is large, so that there is room for paradoxes..."
(Kingston, 1976). When is choice simply a strategem for avoiding
difference (Stewart, in press)? Adler (1976) says that a
multicultural style can evolve when an individual is capable of
negotiating the conflicts and tensions inherent in cross-cultural
contacts. This ability to negotiate is greatly facilitated in pluralistic societies with their many "alternatives and equivalent ways of
reaching the top" (King, 1975).

Children who are multicultural can realize that theirs is a situation largely without precedent. They are heirs to a fledgling tradition which offers the possibility of seeing the world whole. They
will perhaps have the chance to build a future which allows for
more complex kinds of wholeness. At present the people who are
engaged in this task are a growing community of poets, writers,
dancers, scientists, teachers, lawyers, scholars, philosophers,
entrepreneurs, students, and citizens for whom the old boundaries
are irrelevant (H. Taylor, 1969b; Gordon, 1964).

Ackermann (1976) believes that perhaps the challenge of our
time is "helping man to relate to unknown man." Intercultural
skill is thus the ability to function as a stranger and to interact
with strangers (Bochner, 1973; Schutz, 1964).

The cultural pattern of the approached group is regarded by
multicultural people as "not a shelter but a field of adventure, not
an instrument for disentangling problematic situations, but a
problematic situation itself." This pattern is not a refuge but a labyrinth in which one has lost all one's bearings (Schutz, 1964).

In this encounter with strangeness, the stranger tries to define
the new fact; tries to catch its meaning; and then begins to transform it little by little so that the strange fact is compatible and consistent with all his other facts. Experience has been enlarged and
adjusted.

We know very little about this "relating with unknown
man." There are tribes today in the Amazon basin who kill strangers on sight because the concept of a stranger who is also a
human being is lacking. There has been little research into the conditions needed for creating trust among strangers, or the develop-

ment of cultural perception, that is, the way in which people differentiate the important from the unimportant patterns in a strange culture. For instance, in U.S. society use of the left hand is purely idiosyncratic; an individual just happens to be left handed. In Muslim culture, however, what one does with which hand is a matter of formal culture with severe consequences if one transgresses the rules. (The left hand is used for personal hygiene; therefore it is considered unfit to use for eating, for example.) How does one learn what is a "rule" and what is not and in which cases to apply the rule? In a given social situation, an American might act as an individual whereas a Japanese might act in terms of his role, or vice versa. Chapter 10 described how some of these confusions can be dealt with effectively.

Connected with multiculturalism but different from it is the question of intercultural skill. One may grow up multicultural in the sense that if one's parents belonged to two different cultural groups one may have learned to function in both. However, unless one has *generalized* those processes which enable one to participate effectively in two cultures to learning how to interact with cultures as yet unknown, one could conceivably tolerate the dissonances which are "all in the family," so-to-speak, but not be so tolerant of those that appear when interacting with "strange" cultures.

Alternate Pedagogies

There are some really different—some would say bizarre—approaches to learning that can be explored in adventuresome, globally oriented classrooms.

In an integration of Piagetian cognitive developmental and Witkenian cognitive-style theories, Samples (1977) characterizes mentality as consisting of four different modes. (These he describes—in social science "dialect"—as: the symbolic, which takes two forms, the abstract and the visual; the synergetic comparative; the integrative; and the inventive.) There is a natural capacity to perform in all the modes throughout all the Piagetian stages of development (sensory-motor, pre-operational, concrete operational, and formal operational), but formal schooling consistently rewards only the symbolic-abstract mode. Test materials, curriculum emphasis, and pressure on teachers and administrators for skill in the three Rs—"a return to the basics"—exclude all other modes. Yet it is ironic that at the most profound stage in learning, children are learning holistically, particularly during Piaget's preoperational stage when they are acquiring language simultaneously with learning to walk upright. Jonas Salk defines wisdom as "the use of both sides of the mind, the analytic and the analogic" (quoted in Samples, 1977, p. 692). What are some strategies for exercising the whole mind?

One method of broadening the range of learning modes is to develop instructional materials that are descriptive rather than prescriptive, that encourage students to cull structures from experience rather than imposing structures upon experience (Samples, 1977). A simple example of such strategies is to allow symbolic-visual expression if a student falters with symbolic-abstract expression, to encourage him or her to paint, draw, or sculpt his or her response. Later the student would be encouraged to express the idea through speech or writing. (The opposite journey from symbolic-abstract to symbolic-visual expression would be equally as interesting for those with an analytic preference.)

Pedagogies that are truly alternatives to the "symbolic-abstract-mode" that Samples among others finds prevalent in most formal school systems are currently being discovered or, in many cases, rediscovered. *The Centering Book: Awareness Activities for Children, Parents and Teachers* (Hendricks and Wills, 1975), for example, suggests activities from ouside the Western logical linear cognitive tradition. These activities may introduce yoga, Zen, the dream work of the Senoi people of the Central Malay Peninsula, or the Muslim Sufi tradition. Hendricks and Wills have produced an almost programmed text with chapters on basic centering, relaxing the mind, expanding perception, relaxing the body, working with dreams, imagery, stretching the body, movement and dance, and storytelling. It is essentially an elementary text for what has come to be called "transpersonal education." It seeks a synthesis in education of intellect and intuition, mind and body, fact and feeling.

Houston and Master's (1973) book, *Mind Games*, presents specific alternative methods of teaching and learning. For instance, it suggests ways to teach mathematics rhythmically, as patterns of sound and movement rather than as symbolic-abstract patterns: clapping, tah-teh-tah-teh-tah, tah-teh-tah-teh-tah, instead of saying, "Five and five are ten." This method recognizes that mathematical and musical skills often coincide, but opts to approach this linked universe through the music rather than through the geometry of the spheres. Hall (1983) argues that rhythm is the fundamental ingredient of all human interaction. Rhythm, like love and comedy, is a matter of timing. When people feel uncomfortable in an interaction it may be, according to Hall, because their cultural rhythmic styles are different. Learning to communicate across cultures involves developing the appropriate cultural rhythms.

Perhaps the best description of a truly alternative pedagogy in a modern setting (from a U.S. perspective) appears in Rohlen (1978) in which the author describes the methods of "spiritual education" ("Seishin Kyoiku") which form part of the corporate training programs for many medium and large Japanese companies. In the course of this training, young executives run marathons, meditate, and do unpaid labor.

Multicultural Environments

What are the characteristics of those settings which elicit multicultural behavior and thereby facilitate the acquisition of intercultural communication skills? How are these settings created in a school?

Environments that engender intercultural skills provide an atmosphere in which children can expand their repertoire of behaviors. No child is forced into an either/or position, where, for instance, he or she must give up speaking Pidgin in order to speak English. Rather, s/he is encouraged to use all behaviors appropriately. It is an environment which values uniqueness and idiosyncracy and facilitates the individual's interaction with the world at large. The microcosm of the school becomes attuned to the community in which it exists.

What does good teaching in a multicultural context look like? Two highly idiosyncratic New Zealand teachers provide possibilities—Sylvia Ashton Warner who taught in Maori schools for twenty-four years and Elwyn Richardson who took a job as schoolmaster in a mixed Maori/European school in an isolated rural area when he could not find a job as a marine biologist. Neither had special funding, just necessities and time.

Sylvia Ashton-Warner (1963) developed an approach based on the simple notion that children learn to read and write more readily from materials affectively important to themselves, preferably those they have written themselves. In Ashton-Warner's school it all began in kindergarten. When each child arrived in class s/he would tell the teacher which word s/he would like to learn. The word was written on two cards, one to keep at school and one to carry around all day, take home, and learn. Next morning the words kept at school were dumped onto the floor. Everyone scrambled for their own word. Then the children paired off and taught each other their words. Eventually, the words became sentences and the sentences stories, and the children learned to read by reading their own and each other's stories.

Meanwhile, in Oruaiti School, a square wooden room built in 1889, roofed with red-painted corrugated iron, gable-ended, weather-boarded, and with three windows, Elwyn Richardson was creating a community of artists and scientists out of rural Maori and European schoolchildren, children whose only "academic" resource at home was the Bible. They set about learning by collecting specimens—words, seashells, different spellings, new thoughts—gradually sorting out observations, discarding stock responses, testing generalizations, and evaluating their inventions over long periods.

The primary demand on the child was that he should think through exactly what he observed, felt, or believed . . . a great deal of careful training went into eliminating the merely stock response and the expected answer. But combined with this demand for . . . a personal view, and of course necessary to it, was the filling acceptance of idiosyncracy and the affectionate acceptance of the strengths and limitations of each member of the group . . . [Richardson, 1964].

There are, in addition, at least one German and two American schools described in the literature that seem to be providing promising environments for diversity. Frances Sussna's multicultural school in San Francisco uses bicultural teachers to assist in the teaching of specialized knowledge and skills in a context where both the accomplishments of one's own group and interaction with other groups are stressed. The program thus fosters individual self-confidence and situations of meaningful intergroup contact. In the mornings the students interact in mixed groups to learn basic skills, and in the afternoon they meet in their ethnic groups for history and language. When each group has a holiday, the others are invited to help celebrate it. Stress is on pride in one's own heritage and respect for the heritage of other groups. The aim is to stimulate interaction among groups who feel themselves to be equal (D. Lewis, 1976).

There is a public school in Urbana, Illinois, the Martin Luther King School, in which half the students speak one of 21 different languages (Bouton, 1975). One striking point about this school is that every person on the staff, from the principal to the janitor, is culturally "literate." They all have intercultural skills. On one occasion, for example, the janitor was able to take care of an East Indian boy who in his first week at school had an attack of diarrhea on the playground. The janitor handled the situation with such sensitivity that the boy's considerable embarrassment was greatly alleviated despite a language barrier. In another case, aides were able to help a new Japanese student understand that the boy who had hit her had done so accidentally. She thought she had been attacked.

Another interesting school in a rapidly changing, heterogeneous community is in Schonhausen in the Remstal in West Germany (Spindler, 1974). Since World War II, Schonhausen's population has almost doubled. What was a homogeneous, agricultural, folk community is now heterogeneous, partly agricultural, but largely suburban community. Some Catholics have come into the formerly totally Protestant area, and many do not speak the local dialect of German. Yet Schonhausen has assimilated this diverse influx while maintaining a low incidence of crime, suicide, and juvenile delinquency.

Longstreet (1978) gives teachers the tools for doing their own observational action research on the effect of ethnicity on their students' scholastic experience. She includes sample profiles and checklists which critically define the impact of ethnicity on verbal and nonverbal communication, on intellectual styles, and on social value patterns. Renwick (1980) provides an extensive and practical elaboration of how to evaluate multicultural education programs.

Duane Campbell (1980) suggests that teachers develop their own curriculum packages and gives examples based on an inquiry approach to learning. One package, for example, deals with the dynamics of values and social action.

In a study of classroom integration, Slavins (1979) makes the startling observation that there was only one strategy that led to improved interpersonal relations and increased academic performance, measured by more time-on-task behavior: the assigning of interracial partners on schoolwork teams. This strategy was found to be much more effective than workshops, biracial student advisory committees, minority history courses, or multiethnic texts.

A study of effective teachers of Eskimo and Indian students (Kleinfeld, 1975) identified two teacher factors that were associated with student success: the establishment by the teacher of an atmosphere of emotional warmth which encouraged students to develop personalized relationships; and teacher demand for high-quality academic work.

If there is an overriding theme to the examples of successful implementation of multicultural education cited in this chapter, it is that in each case the reality of where the children are at that particular time is being responded to. It is no good wishing they were someplace else. Adventurous teachers are designing a creative curriculum that fits the multicultural world in which we live.

Coaxing students into an international perspective is made much easier by a series of publications sold by the Center for Teaching International Relations, University of Denver (Denver, CO 80208). Of the many exciting titles in the CTIR Publications catalog, our own favorites include *Demystifying the Chinese Language* (by a Stanford University team, 1982), *Teaching About Cultural Awareness* (Smith and Otero, 1982), *Japan Meets the West: A Case Study of Perceptions* (by a joint Stanford and University of Washington team, 1983), *Teaching About Diversity: Latin America* (Switzer and Redden, 1983), and *A Comparative View of the Roles of Women and Men* (Miller, Johnson, and Foster, 1982). These publications come complete with lesson plans and classroom handouts. We have used some CTIR lessons with undergraduate students which were designed for elementary school children and have found the lessons appropriate after making a few simple modifications.

Global perspectives cannot develop in ignorance of how the globe is partitioned into nation states. *The New World Atlas* (Kidron and Segal, 1984), in conjunction with *Activities Using 'The State of the World Atlas'* (Hursh and Prevedel, 1983; this needs some revision to fit with the latest edition of the *Atlas*), offers secondary and tertiary students a graphic way to become acquainted (through maps) with many interesting issues. Both publications are available through CTIR Publications (see previous paragraph).

Suggested Activities

1. Take a basal text in a subject area such as math or science (or any curriculum area of special interest to you) and identify ten locations where a relevant multicultural mini-unit could be developed.
2. Develop one of the multicultural mini-units you identified above.
3. Briefly sketch out a plan to incorporate *Seishin Kyoiku* methods in a course you teach or plan to teach; or, if you are not planning to teach, apply them to some other job-related area.

12

What Are the Sources?

There are so many sources to help us understand a foreign culture that it is necessary to develop a method for cutting the number down. We cannot assign four hundred titles to our students. Modern teachers who see their role as that of preparing students to survive future shock, the trauma that results from having to face too much change in too short a time (see Toffler, 1970), seek to avoid having students develop an undue respect for obsolescent "facts."

The misspent search for an authoritative tome of the "50 most important facts" of the foreign culture brings to mind a parlor game popular in some circles, Trivia. Trivia requires the successful participant to be the first to respond correctly to a question whose answer is not worth knowing. Some teachers play the game of "Filling Freddie Farkle Full of Fickle Facts." This is commonly accomplished through superficial units on art, food, the market place, the War of Independence, and above all, on the principal navigable rivers and their seamy ports. These teachers ask questions such as "What is the principal river of Germany and what is its principal port?" or "In what country of Latin America is tin the principal product?" Trivia gives the illusion of learning something. Any educational objective that promotes the learning of facts for their own sake is enhancing the probability of a severe case of future shock. It takes more than the illusion of learning to justify schooling.

Before pertinent sources are identified, the student must learn to ask intelligent questions. The real issue is: What's worth knowing? Only after this is answered can we go about the task of assembling sources to respond to the questions. The two previous chapters which most rigorously have attempted to say what is worth knowing are Chapter 3 (The Seven Goals of Cultural Instruction) and Chapter 8 (Asking the Right Questions).

Teachers who want to get a feel for what has been written from 1966-1977 on the teaching of culture can turn to four review articles that put 400 relevant publications into perspective (Seelye, 1969b; Morain, 1971; Nostrand, 1974; Jarvis, 1977). My own review article states that the identification of "specific cultural objectives in operational and measurable terms" should now be the main task of the profession. Morain's article makes the point that "an understanding of culture—anthropological and traditional—can provide the missing component in the language student's search for relevancy." Looking ahead, Morain says that "a seer with even a cloudy crystal ball could predict that the future will hold increased emphasis on teaching for cross-cultural understanding." Nostrand also sees a growing concern for cross-cultural understanding and notes that "interest in superficial details is being replaced by a greater sensitivity to differences in people's values, assumptions, and modes of thought and feeling." Jarvis notes that the "number and quality" of culture materials integrated into beginning texts is increasing, but that the lecture method is "still used far too frequently, despite indications of [its] inefficiency in developing cross-cultural effectiveness."

Svobodny (1973) has written the best article to date which discusses the techniques of data retrieval in foreign language education. Articles and books are not, of course, the only source of information. Magazines, newspapers, radio, TV, movies, LP records, and comic books offer much up-to-date data for cultural analysis.

What help can classroom teachers get in their efforts to develop in their students the particular type of reading skills needed to penetrate the mass media? A sample of available materials in Spanish includes units to develop skill in reading newspaper headlines (Seelye and Day, 1974; 1982) and newspaper content in general (Smith, 1981). For French print media, one recent publication aims at presenting the feminine view (Steele and Bourlon, 1980), another looks at a cross-section of *la vie quotidienne* (Paoletti and Steele, 1981). Visits to the exhibitors' booths at professional conferences will turn up many more.

One of the best sources of information is somebody who lives or who has lived in the target culture.

The references that have been cited in this book, along with many other pertinent sources of information, are listed in the following bibliography.

Bibliography

Aarons, Alfred, Barbara Gordon, and William Stewart (eds.) *Linguistic-Cultural Differences and American Education. Florida FL Reporter* 7 (1969):1-175.

Abraham, Sameer Y., and Nabeel Abraham (eds.) *The Arab World and Arab Americans: Understanding a Neglected Minority.* Detroit, MI: Center for Urban Studies, 1981.

Ackermann, Jean Marie. "Skill Training for Foreign Assignment: The Reluctant U.S. Case." In Larry A. Samovar and Richard E. Porter (eds.). *Intercultural Communication: A Reader.* Belmont, CA: Wadsworth Publishing Co., 1976, pp. 298-306.

ACTFL. *ACTFL Provisional Proficiency Guidelines.* Hastings-on-Hudson, NY: American Council on the Teaching of Foreign Languages, 1982.

Adams, Henry E. (ed.). *Handbook of Latin American Studies: No. 35: Social Sciences.* Gainesville: University of Florida Press, 1983.

Adler, James P. *Ethnic Minorities in Cambridge,* Vol. I (Summary), *The Portuguese.* Cambridge, MA: City Department of Planning and Development, 1972.

Adler, Peter S. "Beyond Cultural Identity: Reflections on Cultural and Multicultural Man." In Larry A. Samovar and Richard E. Porter (eds.). *Intercultural Communication: A Reader.* Belmont, CA: Wadsworth Publishing Co., 1976, pp. 362-80.

Afful, Elizabeth. *A Study of Ghanaian Language Teaching in Three Primary Schools in Accra.* Paper submitted to the Language Centre, University of Ghana, in Partial Fulfillment of the Requirements for Diploma in Ghanaian Language. Legon: University of Ghana, 1976.

Aguirre Beltrán, Gonzalo. *La población negra de México: estudio etnohistórico.* Segunda edición aumentada. México, D.F.: Fondo de Cultura Económica, 1972.

Alameda County School Department. *Cultural Understanding: French, Level I.* Hayward, CA, 1971.

Alameda County School Department. *Cultural Understanding: Spanish, Level I.* Hayward, CA, 1969.

Albert, Ethel M., and Clyde Kluckhohn. *A Selected Bibliography on Values, Ethics and Esthetics in the Behavioral Sciences and Philosophy.* Glencoe, IL: Free Press, 1959.

Allen, Edward D., and Rebecca M. Valette. *Modern Language Classroom Techniques: A Handbook.* New York: Harcourt, Brace, Jovanovich, 1972, pp. 260-61.

Allport, Gordon. *The Nature of Prejudice.* New York: Anchor Books, 1958.

Althen, Gary L. *Human Relations Training and Foreign Students.* Washington, DC: National Association for Foreign Student Affairs, 1970 (EDRS: ED 048 084).

Altman, Howard B., and Victor E. Hanzeli (eds.). *Essays on the Teaching of Culture: A Festschrift to Honor Howard Lee Nostrand.* Detroit, MI: Advancement Press of America, 1974.

American Association of Colleges for Teacher Education. *No One Model American: A Statement on Multicultural Education.* Washington, DC: American Association of Colleges for Teacher Education, 1972.

Ammons, Margaret. "Communication: A Curriculum Focus." In Alexander Frazier (ed.). *A Curriculum for Children.* Washington, DC: National Education Association, Association for Supervision and Curriculum Development, 1969.

Anderson, Beatrix, and Maurice North. *Cassell's Beyond the Dictionary in German.* New York: Funk & Wagnalls, 1969.

Andersson, Theodore, and Mildred Boyer (eds.). *Bilingual Schooling in the United States.* Washington, DC: United States Government Printing Office, 1970.

Ansre, Gilbert. "Madina: Three Polyglots and Some Implications for Ghana." In Sirarpi Ohannessian, Charles A. Ferguson, and Edgar C. Polomes (eds.). *Language Surveys in Developing Nations.* Arlington, VA: Center for Applied Linguistics, 1975.

Anthropological Curriculum Study Project (ACSP). *Modern and Traditional Societies* (Kit and student readings); *Origins of Humanness* (Kit and student readings). New York: Macmillan, 1968 (out of print).

Arendt, Jermaine D., and Percy Fearing (eds.). *The Extended Foreign Language Sequence: With Emphasis on New Courses for Levels IV and V.* St. Paul: Minnesota State Department of Education, 1971.

Ariès, Philippe. *L'enfant et la vie familiale sous l'Ancien Régime.* Paris: Plon, 1960. (Translated as *Centuries of Childhood.* New York: Knopf, 1962. Updated in "Les ages de la vie," *Contrepoint* 1 [1970]:23-30, and in his chapter in *Encyclopédie de la Pléiade. La France et les Français.* Paris: Gallimard, 1971.)

Armstrong, Robert G. "Language Policies and Language Practices in West Africa." In Fishman, Ferguson, and Das Gupta (eds.). *Language Problems in Developing Nations.* New York: Wiley, 1968, pp. 227-36.

Arnott, Peter. *An Introduction to the Greek World.* London: Macmillan, 1967.

Aronoff, Joel. *Psychological Needs and Cultural Systems: A Case Study.* Princeton, NJ: Van Nostrand, 1967.

Ashton-Warner, Sylvia. *Teacher.* New York: Bantam, 1963.

Asrael, Jeremy R. "Soviet Union." In James S. Coleman (ed.). *Education and Political Development.* Princeton, NJ: Princeton University Press, 1965, pp. 261-75.

Avery, Harry C. "Academic Reports: Conference on the Teaching of Latin in Inner City Schools." *Modern Language Journal* 54 (1970):424-25.

Baker, Gwendolyn C. *Planning and Organizing for Multicultural Instruction.* Reading, MA: Addison-Wesley, 1983.

Baldwin, J., and H. Wells. *Active Tutorial Work,* Books 1 to 4. London: Basil Blackwell, 1980.

Ballesteros, David. "Toward an Advantaged Society: Bilingual Education in the 70's." *The National Elementary Principal* 50, ii (1970):25-28.

Bamgbose, Ayo. *Mother Tongue Education: The West African Experience.* London: Hodder and Stoughton, 1976.

Banathy, Bela H. "Current Trends in College Curriculum: A Systems Approach." In Emma M. Birkmaier (ed.). *Foreign Language Education: An Overview,* ACTFL Review of Foreign Language Education, Vol. 1, Skokie, IL: National Textbook Co., 1972.

Banks, James A., Carlos E. Cortés, Geneva Gay, Ricardo L. García, and Anna S. Ochoa. *Curriculum Guidelines for the Social Studies.* Arlington, VA: National Council for the Social Studies (1515 Wilson Blvd.), 1976.

Banks, James A. (ed.). *Teaching Ethnic Studies.* Washington: National Council of the Social Studies, 1973.

Baptiste, H. Prentice Jr., Mira L. Baptiste, and Donna M. Gollnick. *Multicultural Teacher Education*. Washington, DC: Commission on Multicultural Education, American Association of Colleges for Teacher Education, 1980.

Barbour, Alton, and Alvin A. Goldberg. *Interpersonal Communication: Teaching Strategies and Resources*. Urbana, IL: ERIC Clearinghouse on Reading and Communication Skills (1111 Kenyon Rd.), 1974.

Barnlund, Dean C. (ed.). *Intrapersonal Communications Survey and Studies*. New York: Houghton Mifflin, 1968.

Baron, Bruce G. "The Humanities and the Curriculum." *Educational Leadership* 27 (1969):287-95.

Barrutia, Richard. "Overcoming Cultural Barriers." *Forum* 6 (Dec. 1967) (ED 019 901).

Bauer, Camille. *La France actuelle*. Rev. ed. Boston: Houghton Mifflin, 1971.

Bautista, Maria Lourdes. *Patterns of Pilipino Radio Drama: A Sociolinguistic Analysis*. Study of Languages or Cultures of Asia or Africa, Monograph Series No. 13, 1979.

Bawcutt, G. J. *Spanish Sign Language: Reading Comprehension Activities*. London: Harrap, 1977.

Bawcutt, G. J. "A Semiotic Approach to Culture." *Foreign Language Annals* 1 (1967):152-63.

Beaujour, M., and J. Ehrmann. *La France contemporaine*. Paris: Armand Colin, 1967.

Becker, Tamar. "Patterns of Attitudinal Changes among Foreign Students." *American Journal of Sociology* 73 (January 1968):431-41.

Behmer, Daniel E. "Cultural Mini-Skits Evaluated." *American Foreign Language Teacher* 2, iii (1972a):37, 43, 48.

Behmer, Daniel E. "Teaching with Wayne State Cultural Mini-Skits." *American Foreign Language Teacher* 3, i (1972b):3, 38-39.

Benson, Philip G. "Measuring Cross-cultural Adjustment:The Problems of Criteria." *International Journal of Intercultural Relations* 2, i, (1978):21-26.

Berelson, Bernard, and Gary A. Steiner (eds.). *Human Behavior: An Inventory of Scientific Findings*. New York: Harcourt, Brace & World, 1964.

Bernage, Berthe. *Convenances et bonnes manières*. Paris: Gautier-Langereau, 1964.

Bernstein, B. *Class, Codes, and Control*, Vol. 1. London: Routledge and Kegan Paul, 1971.

Berry, J. W. "Ecological and Cultural Factors in Spatial Perceptual Development." *Canadian Journal of Behavioral Science* 3, iv (1971):324-36.

Berry, J. W. "Temme and Eskimo Perceptual Skills." *International Journal of Psychology* 1, iii (1966):207-29.

Bibliography of Paperback Books Translated from the German and of Works on Germany. 2nd ed. Bonn: Inter Nationes, 1965.

Birdwhistell, Ray L. *Kinesics and Context: Essays on Body Motion Communication.* Philadelphia: University of Pennsylvania Press, 1970.

Birdwhistell, Ray L. *Introduction to Kinesics.* Washington, DC: Foreign Service Institute, Department of State, 1952.

Birkmaier, Emma, and Dale L. Lange. "Selective Bibliography on the Teaching of Foreign Languages, 1920-1966." *Foreign Language Annals* 1 (1968):318-53.

Bishop, Claire Huchet. *Here Is France.* New York: Farrar, Strauss and Giroux, 1971.

Bishop, G. Reginald (ed.). *Culture in Language Learning.* Report of the Northeast Conference on the Teaching of Foreign Languages. New York: MLA Materials Center, 1960.

Blauner, Robert. *Racial Oppression in America.* New York: Harper and Row, 1972.

Bochner, S. "The Mediating Man and Cultural Diversity." In *Topics In Culture Learning,* Vol. 1, 1973:23-27.

Bogardus, E. S. "Social Distance Scale," *Sociological Social Research,* 17 (1925):265-71.

Bolinger, Dwight. *Aspects of Language.* New York: Harcourt, Brace and World, 1968.

Booth, Wayne C. *The Rhetoric of Fiction.* Chicago: University of Chicago Press, 1967.

Boudon, Raymond. "Analyse secondaire et sondages sociologiques." *Cahiers internationaux de sociologie* 47 (1969):5-34. Trans. as "Secondary Analysis and Survey Research..." *Information sur les sciences sociales* 8, vi (1969):7-32.

Bouraoui, Hédi A. *Créaculture I. Créaculture II.* Philadelphia: Center for Curriculum Development, 1971.

Bouraoui, Hédi A. *Parole et action.* Philadelphia: Center for Curriculum Development, 1971.

Bourque, Jane M. "Study Abroad and Intercultural Communication." In Gilbert A. Jarvis (ed.). *The Challenge of Communication: ACTFL Review of Foreign Language Education,* Vol. 6. Lincolnwood, IL: National Textbook Co., 1974.

Bourque, Jane M. *The French Teen-Ager.* Detroit: Advancement Press of America, 1973.

Bouton, Lawrence F. "Meeting the Needs of Children with Diverse Linguistic and Ethnic Backgrounds." *Foreign Language Annals* 8, iv (Dec. 1975):306-16.

Brah, Artar. "South Asian Teenagers in Southall," *New Community*, 6, iii (1978):197-206.

Bransford, Louis A. (ed.). *Cultural Diversity and the Exceptional Child.* Chicago: Council on Exceptional Children, 1974.

Brault, Gerard. "Kinesics and the Classroom: Some Typical French Gestures." *French Review* 36 (1963):374-82.

Brein, Michael, and K. H. David. "Intercultural Communication and the Adjustment of the Sojourner." *Psychological Bulletin* 76 (1971):215-30.

Brembeck, Cole S. *Social Foundations of Education: Environment Influence in Teaching and Learning.* New York: Wiley, 1973.

Brembeck, Cole S. *Social Foundations of Education: A Cross-Cultural Approach.* New York: Wiley, 1966.

Brembeck, Cole S., and Walker H. Hill (eds.). *Cultural Challenges to Education: The Influence of Cultural Factors in School Learning.* Lexington, MA: Lexington Books, D.C. Heath, 1973.

Brewer, Marilynn B. "Perceptual Processes in Cross-Cultural Interaction." In D. S. Hoopes, P. B. Pederson, and G. W. Renwick (eds.). *Overview of Intercultural Education, Training and Research: Volume I, Theory.* Chicago: Intercultural Press, 1977, pp. 22-31.

Brewer, Marilynn B., and Donald T. Campbell. *Ethnocentrism and Intergroup Attitudes: East African Evidence.* New York: Wiley, 1976.

Brichant, Collette D. *Perspectives sur la civilization française; l'héritage culturel.* New York: American Book Co., 1964.

Brinton, Crane, John B. Christopher, and Robert L. Wolff. *A History of Civilization.* Vol. 1: *Prehistory to 1715.* Englewood Cliffs, NJ: Prentice-Hall, 1960.

Brislin, Richard W. *Cross-Cultural Encounters: Face-to-Face Interaction.* New York: Pergamon Press, 1981.

Brislin, Richard W. "Structured Approaches to Dealing with Prejudice and Intercultural Misunderstanding." *International Journal of Group Tensions*, 8, cxlii (1978):33-47.

Brislin, Richard W., and Michael P. Hamnett (eds.). *Topics in Culture Learning,* Vol. 2 (1974), Vol. 3 (1975), Vol. 4 (1976), Vol. 5 (1977). Honolulu, HI: East-West Center.

Brislin, Richard W., and Paul B. Pederson. *Cross-Cultural Orientation Programs.* New York: Gardner Press, 1976.

Brodin, Pierre, and Frédéric Ernst. *La France et les Français.* New York: Holt, Rinehart and Winston, 1967.

Brogan, D. W. *Parameters of Culture.* Hartford: Connecticut State Department of Education. *(FL News Exchange* 19, Special Supplement, February 1973.)

Brogan, D. W. "The Rung and the Ladder." In Joseph A. Tursi (ed.). *Foreign Languages and the "New" Student.* Reports of the Working Committees of the Northeast Conference on the Teaching of Foreign Languages. New York: MLA Materials Center, 1970.

Brogan, D. W. "Teaching Culture in the Foreign Language Classroom." *Foreign Language Annals* 1 (1968):204-17.

Brogan, D. W., and the editors of *Life. France.* New York: Time, Inc., 1960.

Brooks, Nelson D. *Language and Language Learning: Theory and Practice.* New York: Harcourt Brace Jovanovich, 1968.

Brown, George I. *Human Teaching for Human Learning: An Introduction to Confluent Education.* New York: Viking Press, 1971.

Brown, Ina C. *Understanding Other Cultures.* Englewood Cliffs, NJ: Prentice-Hall, 1963.

Bruck, Margaret, et al. *The 1968 NDEA Institute Follow-Up Evaluation.* Mimeographed. Montreal: McGill University, Department of Psychology, 1973.

Bureau of Educational and Cultural Affairs. *International Exchange—1968.* Washington, DC: Bureau of Educational and Cultural Affairs, 1969 (EDRS: ED 036 211).

Burger, Henry G. *Ethno-pedagogy: A Manual in Cultural Sensitivity, with Techniques for Improving Cross-Cultural Teaching by Fitting Ethnic Patterns.* Albuquerque: Southwestern Educational Laboratory, 1968. Available only from ERIC Documentation Service, Washington, DC: U.S. Office of Education (SP 001 971).

Bryde, J. F. *Indian Students and Guidance.* Boston: Houghton Mifflin, 1971.

Caldwell, Oliver J. "The Need for Intercultural Education in Our Universities." *Phi Delta Kappan* 52 (1971):544-45.

The California State International Programs: The Official Study Abroad Program...: France, Germany, Italy, Japan, Spain, Sweden, Taiwan. San Francisco: California State Colleges, Office of International Programs, 1968 (EDRS: ED 026 925).

Campa, Arthur L. *Teaching Hispanic Culture through Folklore.* ERIC Focus Report No. 2. New York: MLA/ACTFL Materials Center, 1968.

Campbell, Duane E. *Education for a Democratic Society.* Cambridge, MA: Schenkman Publications, 1980.

Campos Martínez, Luis. *Lo cinematográfico como expresión*. Bogotá, Colombia: Ediciones Paulinas, 1975.

Canfield, D. Lincoln. *Spanish with a Flourish*. AATSP Culture Unit #1, 1968. (See a current issue of *Hispania* for ordering information.)

Capelle, Janine, Guy Gilbert Quénelle, and Francis Grand Clément. *La France en direct*, 3. Paris: Hachette, 1971. *La France en direct*, 4. Paris: Hachette, and Lexington, MA: Ginn, 1972.

Cappelluger, E. M. *Guidance and the Migrant Child*. New York: Houghton Mifflin, 1971.

Carlisle, A. E. *Cultures in Collision: U.S. Corporate Policy and Canadian Subsidiaries*. Ann Arbor: University of Michigan, 1967.

Carlson, Elliot. *Learning Through Games: A New Approach to Problem Solving*. Washington, DC: Public Affairs Press (419 New Jersey Ave., S.E.), 1969.

Carlson, Paul E. "Toward a Definition of Local Level Multicultural Education." *Anthropology and Education Quarterly* 7, iv (Nov. 1976): 26-30.

Carmines, Edward G., and Richard A. Zeller. *Reliability and Validity Assessment*. London: Sage, 1979.

Carroll, John B. "Foreign Language Proficiency Levels Attained by Language Majors Near Graduation from College." *Foreign Language Annals* 1 (1967):131-50.

Carroll, John B. (ed.). *Language, Thought, and Reality: Selected Writings of Benjamin Lee Whorf*. Cambridge: MIT Press, 1956.

Casmir, Fred L. (ed.). *International and Intercultural Communication Annual*, Vol. 1. New York: Speech Communication Association (Statler Hilton Hotel), 1974.

Casmir, Fred L., and L. S. Harms (eds.). *International Studies of National Speech Education Systems*. Minneapolis: Burgess Publishing Co., 1970.

Casse, Pierre. *Training for the Cross-Cultural Mind: A Handbook for Cross-Cultural Trainers and Consultants*. Washington, DC: Society for Intercultural Education, Training, and Research, 1979.

Casson, Lionel, Robert Claiborne, Brian M. Fagan, and Walter Karp. *Mysteries of the Past*. Marion, OH: American Heritage Books, 1977.

Casteel, J. Doyle, and Miriam Williford. *Planning Cross-Cultural Lessons*. Gainesville, FL: National Seminar, 1976.

Casteel, J. Doyle, and Clemens Hallman. *Cross-Cultural Inquiry: Value Clarification Exercises*. Gainesville: University of Florida (Center for Latin American Studies), 1974.

Castle, Pat, et al. "An Explanation of Three 'Levels' of Competence for Spanish Classes." In H. Ned Seelye (ed.). *Perspectives for Teachers of Latin American Culture.* Springfield, IL: State Superintendent of Public Instruction, 1970, pp. 150-60.

Chamberlain, Jane S. *Source Materials for Teachers of Foreign Languages.* Washington, DC: National Education Association, 1968.

Chandra, Satish. "A Note on the Decentering of History and Apprehension of All People(s) of Their History." *Diogenes* 77 (1972):92-109.

Chao, Yuen Ren. *Language and Symbolic Systems.* New York: Cambridge University Press, 1968.

Choldin, Hannah W. "Foreign Language Day Houses." *Modern Language Journal* 52 (1968):88-89.

Chomsky, Noam. "A Review of *Verbal Behavior* by B. F. Skinner." *Language* 35, i (1959):26-58.

Christensen, J. A. "Education and the Delphic Oracles." *Media and Methods* 7, vi (1971):48-60.

Christian, Chester C., Jr., and John M. Sharp. "Bilingualism in a Pluralistic Society." In Dale L. Lange and Charles J. James (eds.). *Foreign Language Education: A Reappraisal.* ACTFL Review of Foreign Language Education, Vol. 4. Lincolnwood, IL: National Textbook Co., 1972, pp. 341-75.

Christian, Chester C., Jr., and John M. Sharp. "Literary Representation and Sociological Analysis: Social Class in Latin America." *Dissertation Abstracts* 28 (1967):2239A (TX).

Clapper, William O. (ed.). *Workshop on Teaching Culture.* ACTFL-FLAM (Foreign Language Association of Missouri). Jefferson City: Missouri Department of Education, 1972.

Clark, John L. D. *Foreign Language Testing: Theory and Practice.* Skokie, IL: Rand McNally, 1972.

Cleveland, Harlan, G. J. Mangone, and J. C. Adams. *The Overseas Americans.* New York: McGraw-Hill, 1960.

Cohen, Andrew, and Luis M. Laosa. "Second Language Instruction: Some Research Considerations." *Curriculum Studies,* 8, ii (1976):149-65.

Cohen, Bernard H. *Evaluating Bilingual Education Programs.* Hingham, MA: Teaching Resources Corporation, 1979.

Cohen, David (ed.). *Multi-Ethnic Media: Selected Bibliography in Print.* Chicago: American Library Association, 1975.

Cohen, Maurice. "Reflections on the Role of Philosophy in Studying Other Cultures." *Culture* 29 (Sept. 1968):240-51.

Cohen, Monroe D. (ed.). *That All Children May Learn We Must Learn.* Washington, DC: Association for Childhood Education International (3615 Wisconsin Ave., NW), 1971.

Cole, Michael, et al. *The Cultural Context of Learning and Thinking: An Exploration in Experimental Anthropology.* New York: Basic Books, 1971.

Cole, Michael, and Barbara Means. *Comparative Studies of How People Think: An Introduction.* Cambridge, MA: Harvard University Press, 1981.

Cole, Michael, and Sylvia Scribner. *Culture and Thought: A Psychological Introduction.* New York: Wiley, 1974.

Cole, Michael, John Gay, Joseph A. Glick, and Donald W. Sharp. *The Cultural Context of Learning and Thinking: An Exploration in Experimental Anthropology.* New York: Basic Books, 1971.

Coles, Robert. *Children of Crisis, Vol. IV: Eskimos, Chicanos and Indians.* Boston: Little, Brown, 1977.

Coles, Robert. *Children of Crisis, Vol. III: The South Goes North.* Boston: Little, Brown, 1971a.

Coles, Robert. *Children of Crisis, Vol. II: Migrants, Sharecroppers, Mountaineers.* Boston: Little, Brown, 1971b.

Coles, Robert. *Children of Crisis, Vol. I: A Study in Courage and Fear.* Boston: Little, Brown, 1967.

Commager, Henry Steele. *Meet the U.S.A.* Rev. ed. New York: Institute of International Education, 1970.

Concheff, B. *Cartas de España.* Lincolnwood, IL: National Textbook Co., 1982.

Condon, E. C. *Acculturation Problems in Adult Education.* Stenciled. (Series C, Teacher Training Materials, Reference Pamphlets on Intercultural Communication.) Rutgers, NJ: Rutgers Graduate School of Education, 1973a.

Condon, E. C. *Conflicts in Values, Assumptions, Opinions.* Stenciled. (Series C, Teacher Training Materials, Reference Pamphlets on Intercultural Communication.) Rutgers, NJ: Rutgers Graduate School of Education, 1973b.

Condon, E. C. *Introduction to Cross-Cultural Communication.* Stenciled. (Series C, Teacher Training Materials, Reference Pamphlets on Intercultural Communication.) Rutgers, NJ: Rutgers Graduate School of Education, 1973c.

Condon, E. C. *Nonverbal Communication.* Stenciled. (Series C, Teacher Training Materials, Reference Pamphlets on Intercultural Communication.) Rutgers, NJ: Rutgers Graduate School of Education, 1973d.

Condon, E. C. *Selected Bibliography on Culture and Cultural Materials.* Stenciled. (Series A, Teacher Training Materials, Reference Pamphlets on Intercultural Communication.) Rutgers, NJ: Rutgers Graduate School of Education, 1973e.

Condon, John C. *Semantics and Communication*. New York: Macmillan, 1966.

Condon, John C., and Fathi S. Yousef. *An Introduction to Intercultural Communication*. New York: Bobbs-Merrill, 1975.

Cooke, Madeline A. "Suggestions for Developing More Positive Attitudes toward Native Speakers of Spanish." In H. Ned Seelye (ed.). *Perspectives for Teachers of Latin American Culture*. Springfield, IL: State Superintendent of Public Instruction, 1970, pp. 118-39.

Cooney, D. *German Culture through Performance Objectives*. Detroit: Advancement Press of America, 1973.

Costner, Herbert L. "Varieties of Content Analysis." Mimeographed. 1964. (Available from H. L. Nostrand, Department of Romance Languages and Literature, University of Washington, Seattle.)

Council on International Educational Exchange. *Guidelines on Developing Campus Services for Students Going Abroad*. New York: Council on International Educational Exchange, Student Advisory Committee, 1972.

Crook, John. *Julius Caesar and Rome*. London: English University Press, 1968.

Cronbach, L. J., and P. J. D. Drenth (eds.). *Mental Tests and Cultural Adaptation*. The Hague: Mouton, 1972.

Crosbie, Kieth (comp.). *Project FLITE: Foreign Language Idea and Technique Exchange*. Olympia, WA: State Superintendent of Public Instruction, 1972.

Cudecki, Edwin, et al. "Teaching of French Culture in the Classroom." In Charles Jay and Pat Castle (eds.). *French Language Education: The Teaching of Culture in the Classroom*. Springfield, IL: Superintendent of Public Instruction, 1971, pp. 11-20.

Cullen, Arthur J. "A New Option for Foreign Language Students?" *Foreign Language Bulletin* 9, ii (1971):13-15.

Culture Contact. Cambridge, MA: Abt Associates, Inc. (56 Wheeler St.), 1969. (A simulation for grades 6-12)

Culver, Anke I. *The Magazine: A Reflection of Life-styles in the German-Speaking World*. Lincolnwood, IL: National Textbook Co., 1982.

Curt, Carmen Judith Nine. *Teacher Training Pack for a Course on Cultural Awareness*. Fall River, MA: National Assessment and Dissemination Center for Bilingual Education, 1976.

D'Alleva, Josephine. *Incontri Culturali: Cross-Cultural Mini-Dramas*. Lincolnwood, IL: National Textbook Co., 1982.

Dalby, David. "The Linguistic Map of Africa." Lecture delivered at the School of Oriental and African Studies, University of London, March 1977.

Damoiseau, R., and E. Marc. "La chanson moderne: Etude de civilisation et de langue." *Le Français dans le Monde* 47 (1967):40-44.

Darrow, Kenneth, and Bradley Palmquist (eds.). *The Trans-cultural Study Guide.* 2nd ed. Stanford, CA: Volunteers in Asia (Box 4543), 1977.

Dasen, P. R. "Cross-Cultural Piagetian Research: A Summary." *Journal of Cross-Cultural Psychology,* 3 (1972):23-29.

Dass, Ram. *The Only Dance There Is.* Garden City, NY: Anchor Books, 1974.

Davis, Martha. *Understanding Body Movement: An Annotated Bibliography.* New York: Amo Press, 1972.

Davis, Renee. *Cultural Pluralism as a Social Imperative in Education.* New York: Vantage Press, 1980.

Dawson, J.L.M. "Cultural and Physiological Influences Upon Spatial-Perceptual Processes in West Africa, Part 1." *International Journal of Psychology,* 2 (1967):115-28.

Day, J. Laurence. *The Sports Page: Based on Selections from Major Newspapers from the Spanish-Speaking World.* Lincolnwood, IL: National Textbook Co., 1977.

Debyser, Francis. "The Relation of Language to Culture and the Teaching of Culture to Beginning Language Students." *Language Quarterly* 6 (1968):i-ii.

Debyser, Francis. "Le rapport langue-civilisation et l'enseignement de la civilisation aux débutants." *Le Français dans le Monde* 48 (1967):21-24 (Part 1); 49 (1967):16-21 (Part 2).

Decaigny, T. "L'approche des cultures étrangères dans les cours de langues vivantes." *Revue des Langues Vivantes* 34, iii (1968):277-93.

Decaroli, Joseph. "What Research Says to the Classroom Teacher: Simulation Games." *Social Education* 36 (1972):541-43.

DeCrow, Roger. *Cross Cultural Interaction Skills: A Digest of Recent Training Literature.* Syracuse, NY: ERIC Clearinghouse on Adult Education, 1969.

Dee, Rita (ed.). *Planning for Ethnic Education.* Rev. ed. Chicago: Illinois Office of Education, Ethnic Studies Section, 1977.

Dekovic, Gene. *A Tu Per Tu: Contemporary Italy as Seen through Actual Interviews.* Lincolnwood, IL: National Textbook Co., 1979.

Dekovic, Gene. *Unterredungen aus Deutschland: Contemporary Germany as Seen through Actual Interviews.* Lincolnwood, IL: National Textbook Co., 1978.

Deusch, Karl W. *Nationalism and Social Communication: An Inquiry into the Foundations of Nationality.* Cambridge, MA: MIT Press, 1966.

Devereaux, G. *Reality and Dream: Psycho-Therapy of a Plains Indian.* New York: New York University Press, 1969.

Dewey, John. *Democracy and Education.* New York: Macmillan, 1961.

Dewey, John. *Freedom and Culture.* New York: Capricorn Books, 1939.

Dewey, John. *Experience and Education.* New York: Macmillan, 1938.

Dewey, John. "My Pedagogic Creed." *The School Journal* 54 (1897):77-80. Reprinted in Kahil I. Gezi and James E. Myers (eds.). *Teaching in American Culture.* New York: Holt, 1968, pp. 408-11.

Dezly, Glen Caudill. *The Public Man: An Interpretation of La América and Other Catholic Countries.* Amherst: University of Massachusetts Press, 1977.

Diederich, Paul B. *Short-cut Statistics for Teacher-made Tests.* 2nd ed. Princeton, NJ: Educational Testing Service, 1964.

Diéguez, Junior, Manuel, and Bryce Wood (eds.). *Social Science in Latin America.* New York: Columbia University Press, 1967.

Dil, Anwar S. (ed.). *Language, Psychology, and Culture: Essays by Wallace E. Lambert.* Stanford, CA: Stanford University Press, 1972.

Dimitriou, James F. *Suburban Ethnicity: A Case Study of the American-Greek Experience in Southern California.* A Teacher's Manual and Curriculum Guide for Activities and Resources. Palos Verdes Estates, CA: Palos Verdes High School, 1977.

Dimitriou, James F. *Other Words, Other Worlds: Language-in-Culture.* Reports of the Working Committees, Northeast Conference on the Teaching of Foreign Languages. New York: MLA Materials Center, 1972.

Dodge, James W. (ed.). *The Case for Foreign Language Study.* New York: MLA Materials Center, 1972.

Donoghue, Mildred R. *Foreign Languages and the Elementary School Child.* Dubuque, IA: William C. Brown, 1968.

Downs, James G. *Cultures in Crisis.* Beverly Hills, CA: Glenco Press, 1971.

Dow, Tsung I. *The Impact of Chinese Students Returned from America, with Emphasis on the Chinese Revolution, 1911-1949.* 1971 (EDRS: ED 062 228).

Ducan, Hugh D. *Communication and Social Order.* New York: Oxford University Press, 1970.

Dumont, Robert V. Sr., and Murray L. Wax. "Cherokee School Society and the Intercultural Classroom." In Joan I. Roberts and Sherrie K. Akinsanya (eds.). *Schooling in the Cultural Context.* New York: David McKay, 1976, pp. 205-16.

DuVerlie, Claude. "The Disappearance of the Academic Foreign Language Program." *American Foreign Language Teacher* 3, iii (1973):16-18.

Ebling, Benjamin. "Toward the Teaching of Authentic French Culture at the Secondary Level." *French Review* 46 (1973):927-30.

Echols, John M. "A Bibliography of Morris Opler." In Mario D. Zamora et al. (eds.). *Themes in Culture: Essays in Honor of Morris E. Opler.* Quezon City, Philippines: Kayumanggi, 1971.

Ehrlich, Howard J. *The Social Psychology of Prejudice.* New York: Wiley, 1973.

Eisenstadt, Shmael Noah (ed.). *The Protestant Ethic and Modernization: A Comparative View.* New York: Basic Books, 1968.

Eisenstadt, Shmael Noah. *Modernization, Protest and Changes.* Englewood Cliffs, NJ: Prentice-Hall, 1966.

El Habla de la Ciudad de México: materiales para su estudio. México, DF: Universidad Nacional Autónoma de México (Centro de Lingüística Hispánica), 1971.

Elkins, Robert J., Theodore B. Kalivoda, and Genelle Morain. "Teaching Culture through the Audio-Motor Unit." *Foreign Language Annals* 6 (1972):61-72.

English, Peter. *West Germany in Pictures.* New York: Sterling, 1967.

Epps, Edgar C. (ed.). *Cultural Pluralism.* New York: McCutchan, 1974.

Epstein, Noel. "The Bilingual Battle: Should Washington Finance Ethnic Identities?" *The Washington Post,* Sunday, June 5, 1977, CI & 4.

Erassov, Boris S. "Concepts of 'Culture and Personality' in the Ideologies of the Third World." *Diogenes* 78 (1972):123-40.

Esteves, O. P. "A Problem-Finding Approach to the Teaching of Social Studies." In H. Ned Seelye (ed.). *A Handbook on Latin America for Teachers: Methodology and Annotated Bibliography.* Springfield, IL: Office of Public Instruction, 1968, pp. 3-5.

Fagen, Richard R. *Politics and Communication.* Boston: Little, Brown, 1966.

Fantini, Mario, and Gerald Weinstein (eds.). *Toward Humanistic Education: A Curriculum of Affect.* New York: Praeger, 1970.

Farb, Peter. *Word Play: What Happens When People Talk.* New York: Knopf, 1973.

Fersh, Seymour (ed.). *Learning about Peoples and Cultures.* Evanston, IL: McDougal Littel and Company, 1974.

Fiedler, Fred E., Terence Mitchell, and Harry C. Triandis. "The Culture Assimilator: An Approach to Cross-Cultural Training." *Journal of Applied Psychology* 55 (1971):95-102 (EDRS: ED 042 343).

Fishman, Joshua A. *Bilingual Education: An International Sociological Perspective.* Rowley, MA: Newbury House, 1976.

Fishman, Joshua A. "The Breadth and Depth of English in the United States." In Alfred Aarons, Barbara Gordon, and William Stewart (eds.). *Linguistic-Cultural Differences and American Education. Florida FL Reporter* 7, i (1969):41-43, 151.

Fishman, Joshua A. *Language Loyalty in the United States.* The Hague: Mouton, 1966a.

Fishman, Joshua A. "Italian Language Maintenance Efforts in the United States and the Teaching of Italian in American High Schools and Colleges." *Florida FL Reporter* 4 (Spring 1966b).

"FL Commercials Readied for Schools." *Accent on ACTFL* 3, i (1972):10.

Fleming, Gerald. "Gesture Significances Then and Now: In Honor of Albrecht Dürer's 500th Anniversary." *Lebendiges Wort* (Grillparzerinstitut, Vienna) Heft 2, iii (1971a):26-30.

Fleming, Gerald. "Gestures and Body Movement as Mediators of Meaning in Our New Language Teaching Systems." *Contact* 16 (1971b):15-22.

Fleming, Gerald. "The Role of Gesture in Language Teaching." *Pensiero e linguaggio* (Milan) 2, v (1971c):31-43.

Fleming, Gerald. *Grammaire visuelle de Français.* London: Macmillan, 1970.

Flori, Monica. "The Hispanic Community as a Resource for a Practical Spanish Program." *Foreign Language Annals* 15, iii (1982):213-18.

Forges, Jack D. *The Education of the Culturally Different: A Multi-Cultural Approach.* Berkeley, CA: Far West Laboratory for Educational Research and Development, 1967 (EDRS: ED 013 698).

Forker, Jack D. *Apache, Navaho and Spaniard.* Norman: University of Oklahoma Press, 1960.

Four Families [of France, India, Japan, and English-speaking Canada]. Documentary film with comments by Margaret Mead. Montreal: Canadian Film Board (P.O. Box 6100), n.d.

Fraiberg, Selma. *Insights from the Blind: Comparative Studies of Blind and Sighted Infants.* New York: Basic Books, 1977.

France: Comparative Culture and Government. Lincolnwood, IL: National Textbook Co., 1971.

Franco, Jean. *The Modern Culture of Latin America: Society and the Artist.* Rev. ed. Baltimore, MD: Penguin Books, 1970.

Frazier, Alexander. "The Larger Question: A New Sense of Common Identity." *Educational Leadership* 27 (1969):215-17.

Freeman, Stephen A. "Let Us Build Bridges." *Modern Language Journal* 52 (1968):261-68.

Freire, Paulo. *Pedagogy of the Oppressed.* New York: Seabury Press, 1974.

Gaarder, A. Bruce. "Statement...Before the Special Subcommittee on Bilingual Education of the Committee on Labor and Public Welfare, United States Senate, Thursday, May 18, 1967...." *TESOL Newsletter* 2, i, ii (January, March 1968):21-22,28.

Gaarder, A. Bruce. "Bilingualism and the Schools." In Mildred R. Donoghue (ed.). *Foreign Languages and the Schools: A Book of Readings.* Dubuque, IA: William C. Brown Co., 1967, pp.123-32.

Galbreath, Robert. *Cultural Pluralism Project.* Report Number 1 to the Director. Milwaukee: University of Wisconsin-Milwaukee, 1972.

García, Ricardo L. *Teaching in a Pluralistic Society.* New York: Harper & Row, 1982.

Gardner, Robert C., and Donald M. Taylor, "Ethnic Stereotypes: Their Effects on Person Perception." *Canadian Journal of Psychology* 22, iv (1968):267-76.

Garfinkel, Alan. "Teaching Languages via Radio: A Review of Resources." *Modern Language Journal* 56 (1972):158-62.

Garfinkel, Alan, Robert J. Nelson, Sandra Savignon, and Philip D. Smith, Jr. (eds.). *LBRIG Newsletter* (Language-By-Radio Interest Group). Lafayette, IN: Department of Modern Languages, Purdue University.

Gay, Geneva. "Curriculum for Multicultural Teacher Education." In Frank H. Klassen and Donna M. Gollnick (eds.). *Pluralism and the American Teacher: Issues and Case Studies.* Washington, DC: American Association of Colleges for Teacher Education, 1977, pp. 31-62.

Gebser, Jean. "The Foundations of the Aperspective World." *Main Currents in Modern Thought* 29, ii (1972):80-88.

Geno, T. H. (ed.). *Northeast Conference on the Teaching of Foreign Languages.* Middlebury, VT: Northeast Conference, 1980.

Gezi, Kahil I. "Factors Associated with Student Adjustment in Cross-Cultural Contact." *California Journal of Educational Research* 16 (May 1965):129-36; also in Kahil I. Gezi, James E. Myers (eds.). *Teaching in American Culture.* New York: Holt, 1968, pp. 254-61.

Ghosh, Samir K. (ed.). *Man, Language, and Society.* The Hague: Mouton, 1972.

Gibson, Margaret Alison. "Approaches to Multicultural Education in the United States: Some Concepts and Assumptions." *Anthropology and Education Quarterly* 7, iv (Nov. 1976):7-18.

Giles, Raymond. Lecture on "The Anglo-Saxon Bureau of Immigration," University of Southern California's Washington Education Center, August 1977.

Gill, Clark C., and William B. Conroy (eds.). *The Treatment of Latin America in Social Studies Instruction Materials.* Latin American Curriculum Project, Bulletin 5. Austin: University of Texas, 1968.

Gill, Clark C., and William B. Conroy. *The Social Scientists Look at Latin America: Six Position Papers.* Latin American Curriculum Project, Bulletin 3. Austin: University of Texas, 1967a (EDRS: ED 012 365).

Gill, Clark C. and William B. Conroy. *Teaching about Latin America in the Secondary School: An Annotated Guide to Instructional Resources.* Latin American Curriculum Project, Bulletin 2. Austin: University of Texas, 1967b (EDRS: ED 012 833).

Gill, Clark C., and William B. Conroy. *Teaching about Latin America in Social Studies Instructional Materials.* Latin American Curriculum Project, Bulletin 1. Austin: University of Texas, 1967c (EDRS: ED 012 832).

Gill, Clark C., William B. Conroy, and Catherine Cornbleth. *Key Ideas about Latin America.* Latin American Curriculum Project, Bulletin 4. Austin: University of Texas, 1967c.

Gilliat, Penelope. "The Current Cinema: Self-Colloquy. About a Sub-continent." (Review of Malle's *Phantom India.*) *The New Yorker,* July 8, 1972.

Girod, Roger, and Francis Grand-Clement. *Comment vivent les Français.* Paris: Hachette; New York: Gessler, 1969.

Glazer, Nathan, and Daniel P. Moynihan. *Beyond the Melting Pot,* 2nd ed. Cambridge, MA: MIT Press, 1970.

Glenn, Edmund S. "Meaning and Behavior: Communication and Culture." *Journal of Communication* 16 (1966):248-72.

Glenn, Edmund S. "Toward a Theory of Intercultural Communication." *Kultura* (Belgrade) 17 (1972):55-69: English ed.:51-66.

Glick, Joseph. "Culture and Cognition: Some Theoretical and Methic Order. New Concerns." In George D. Spindler (ed.). *Education and Cultural Process: Toward an Anthropology of Education.* New York: Holt, Rinehart and Winston, 1974, pp. 373-81.

Goffman, Erving. *Relations in Public: Microstudies of the Publançais.* Paris: York: Basic Books, 1971.

Gollnick, Donna M., and Philip Chinn, (eds.). *Multicultural Education in a Pluralistic Society.* St. Louis: C.V. Mosby, 1983.

Gollnick, Donna M. *Multiculturalism in Contemporary Education.* Bloomington, IN: School of Education, Indiana University, 1980.

Gómez, Samuel. "The Teaching of Other Cultures." In Joseph S. Roucek (ed.). *The Study of Foreign Languages.* New York: Philosophical Library, 1968, pp. 293-309.

González Casanova, Pablo, et al. *Sociología del desarrollo latinoamericano: Una guía bibliográfica para su estudio.* México, D. F.: Universidad Nacional Autónoma de México (Instituto de Investigaciones Sociales), 1970.

Goodenough, Ward H. "Multiculturalism as the Normal Human Experience." *Anthropology and Education Quarterly,* 7, iv (Nov. 1976):4-6.

Goodenough, Ward H. *Description and Comparison in Cultural Anthropology.* Chicago: Aldine Publishing Co., 1970.

Goodenough, Ward H. *Cooperation in Change.* New York: Russell Sage Foundation, 1963.

Goodnow, J. J. "Research on Culture and Thought." In D. Elkind and O. H. Flavell (eds.). *Studies in Development.* New York: Oxford University Press, 1969.

Goonetilleke, D.C.R.A. *Developing Countries in British Fiction.* New York: Macmillan, 1977.

Gorden, Raymond L. *Interviewing: Strategy, Techniques, and Tactics.* Homewood, IL: Dorsey Press, 1980.

Gorden, Raymond L. *Living in Latin America: A Case Study in Cross-Cultural Communication.* Lincolnwood, IL: National Textbook Co., 1974.

Gorden, Raymond L. *Contrastive Analysis of Cultural Differences which Inhibit Communication between Americans and Colombians.* 1968a (EDRS: ED 023 337).

Gorden, Raymond L. *Cross-Cultural Encounter in a Latin American Bank.* Yellow Springs, OH: Antioch College, n.d., cir. 1968b.

Gorden, Raymond L. *Initial Immersion in the Foreign Culture.* Yellow Springs, OH: Antioch College, 1968c (EDRS: ED 023 339).

Gorden, Raymond L. *Spanish Personal Names as Barriers to Communication Between Latin Americans and North Americans.* Yellow Springs, OH: Antioch College, 1968d.

Gordon, Milton M. *Assimilation in American Life: The Role of Race, Religion, and National Origins.* New York: Oxford University Press, 1964.

Greelev, A. M. *Why Can't They Be Like Us? America's White Ethnic Groups.* New York: E. P. Dutton, 1971.

Green, Jerald R. "Kinesics in the Foreign Language Classroom." *Foreign Language Annals* 5 (1971):62-68; reprinted in Jerald R. Green (ed.). *Foreign Language Education Research: A Book of Readings.* Chicago: Rand McNally, 1973.

Green, Jerald R. *A Gesture Inventory for the Teaching of Spanish.* Skokie, IL: Rand McNally, 1968.

Greenberg, Joseph H. (ed.). *Universals of Language,* 2nd ed. Cambridge, MA: MIT Press, 1966.

Grice, H. H. "The Construction and Validation of a Generalized Scale Designed to Measure Attitudes Toward Defined Groups." *Bulletin Purdue University* 25 (1934):37-46.

Grittner, Frank M. (ed.). "Course Content, Articulation, and Materials: A Committee Report to the National Symposium on the Advancement of German Teaching." *Die Unterrichtspraxis* 2, i (1969):53-72.

Grove, Cornelius Lee (ed.). *Annotated Bibliography on Cross-Cultural Problems in Education.* New York: ERIC, 1979.

Gudykunst, William B. (ed.). *Intercultural Communication Theory: Current Perspectives.* Beverly Hills, CA: Sage Publications, 1983.

Guidelines for the Evaluation and Selection of Ethnically Valid Instructional Materials. Chicago: Illinois Office of Education (Urban and Ethnic Education Section, 188 West Randolph), 1975.

Gumperz, John J., and Dell Hymes (eds.). *The Ethnography of Communication.* Special Publication. *American Anthropologist* 66, vi, Part 2 (Dec. 1964).

Hage, Madeline Cottenet. *The Relationships and Rules of Social Life in France.* Mimeographed. Madison, WI: Department of Public Instruction, 1972.

Hall, Edward T. *The Dance of Life: The Other Dimension of Time.* Garden City, N J: Anchor Press/Doubleday, 1983.

Hall, Edward T. *Beyond Culture.* New York: Anchor Press/Doubleday, 1976.

Hall, Edward T. *Handbook for Proxemic Research.* Washington, DC: Society for the Anthropology of Visual Communication, 1974.

Hall, Edward T. *The Hidden Dimension.* New York: Doubleday, 1966.

Hall, Edward T. *The Silent Language.* New York: Fawcett, 1961.

Hall, Wendell, and Enrique Lafourcade. "Teaching Aspects of the Foreign Culture through Comic Strips." In H. Ned Seelye (ed.). *Perspectives for Teachers of Latin American Culture.* Springfield, IL: State Superintendent of Public Instruction, 1970.

Hammel, E. A. (ed.). *Formal Semantic Analysis.* Special Publication. *American Anthropologist* 67, v, Part 2 (Oct. 1965).

Hammond, Patricia, and Alan Garfinkel (eds.). *Recipes for Teaching Foreign Languages in Oklahoma.* Oklahoma City: State Department of Education, 1972.

Hancock, Charles R. "Student Aptitude, Attitude, and Motivation." In Dale L. Lange and Charles J. James (eds.). *Foreign Language Education: A*

Reappraisal. ACTFL Review of Foreign Language Education, Vol. 4. Lincolnwood, IL: National Textbook Co., 1972.

Harmes, L. S. *Intercultural Communication.* New York: Harper and Row, 1973.

Harris, David P. *Testing English as a Second Language.* New York: McGraw-Hill, 1969.

Harris, J. *Identity, A Study of the Concept in Education for a Multicultural Australia.* Canberra: Australian Gov. Pub. Service, 1980.

Harrison, Roger, and Richard L. Hopkins. *The Design of Cross-Cultural Training, with Examples from the Peace Corps.* 1966 (EDRS: ED 011 103).

Hatton, Robert W., and Gordon L. Jackson. "Fiesta Brava Wins the Ears." *Accent on ACTFL* 3, iv (1973):14-15.

Haukebo, Gerhard K. *Summer Foreign Language Programs for School Students.* MLA/ERIC Focus Report on the Teaching of Foreign Languages, Number 10. New York: MLA/ERIC, 1969.

Havighurst, P. J. "A Cross Cultural View of Adolescence." In J. F. Adams (ed.). *Understanding Adolescence: Current Developments in Adolescent Psychology.* Boston: Allyn and Bacon, 1968.

Hawkins, E. W. "'Language Lab' Should Be the Foreign Environment." *Dialogue* 9 (1971):8-9.

Haynes, Maria S. *Deutsch in drei Ländern.* New York: Odyssey, 1968.

Heinlein, Robert. *Stranger in a Strange Land.* New York: Putnam, 1961.

Hendon, Ursula S. "Introducing Culture in the High School Foreign Language Class." *Foreign Language Annals* 13, iii (1980):191-98.

Hendricks, Gay, and Russel Wills. *The Centering Book: Awareness Activities for Children, Parents and Teachers.* Englewood Cliffs, NJ: Prentice-Hall (Spectrum), 1975.

Henry, Jules. *Culture against Man.* New York: Random House, 1963.

Henry, Jules. "A Cross-Cultural Outline of Education." *Current Anthropology* 1, iv (July 1960). Also in Joan I. Roberts and Sherrie K. Akinsanyas (eds.). *Educational Patterns and Cultural Configurations: The Anthropology of Education.* New York: David McKay, 1976, pp. 100-70.

Herrera, Diane (ed.). *Puerto Ricans in the United States: A Review of the Literature.* Austin, TX: Dissemination Center for Bilingual Bicultural Education, 1973.

Hester, Ralph M. (ed.). *Teaching a Living Language.* New York: Harper & Row, 1970.

Hickey, Leo. "Ethnography for Language Learners." *Foreign Language Annals* 3, vi (1980):475-80.

Hicks, D. W. *Minorities: A Teacher's Resource Book for the Multiethnic Curriculum.* London: Heinemann, 1981.

Hill-Burnett, Jacquetta. "Commentary: Paradoxes and Dilemmas." *Anthropology and Education Quarterly* 7, iv (Nov. 1976):37-38.

Hilliard, A. "Cultural Pluralism: The Domestic International Connection." Paper presented at the American Association of Colleges for Teacher Education Conference, Fort Lauderdale, Florida, 1975.

Hocking, Eldon. *Toute la bande.* Film Program for Beginning and Intermediate French. Englewood Cliffs, NJ: Scholastic Magazines, 1970.

Hofstede, Geert. *Culture's Consequences: International Differences in Work-Related Values.* London: Sage, 1980.

Hogg, Thomas C., and Marlin R. McComb. "Cultural Pluralism: Its Implications for Education." *Educational Leadership* 27 (1969):235-38.

Hoijer, Harry (ed.). *Language in Culture: Conference on the Interrelations of Language and Other Aspects of Culture.* Chicago: University of Chicago Press, 1954.

Hollingshead, A. B., and F. C. Redlich. *Social Class and Mental Illness.* New York: Wiley, 1958.

Holt, Robert, and John Turner (eds.). *The Methodology of Comparative Research.* New York: Free Press, 1970.

Hoopes, David S. (ed.). *Readings in Inter-Cultural Communication,* Vol. I (1971) and Vol. II (1972). Chicago: Intercultural Press.

Hoopes, David S., and Paul Ventura. *Intercultural Sourcebook: Cross-Cultural Training Methodologies.* Chicago: Intercultural Press, 1979.

Hopkins, Robbins S. *Defining and Predicting Overseas Effectiveness for Adolescent Exchange Students.* Doctoral dissertation, University of Massachusetts, 1982.

Houston, James. *White Dawn: An Eskimo Saga.* New York: Harcourt, Brace, Jovanovich, 1971.

Houston, Jean, and Robert E. L. Master. *Mind Games.* New York: Dell, 1973.

Howe, Harold, II. "Cowboys, Indians, and Americans." *TESOL* Newsletter 2, iii (May 1968):3-6.

Howlett, Frederick G. "Le rôle de la télévision dans l'enseignement des langues modernes." *Canadian Modern Language Review* 28, ii (1972):42-49.

Hoxeng, James. *Hacienda.* Stencil, 23 pp. Amherst: University of Massachusetts (Center for International Education, School of Education), n.d., circa 1972.

Hsu, Francis L. K. *Americans and Chinese: Reflections on Two Cultures and Their People.* Garden City, NY: Doubleday, 1970.

Hsu, Francis L. K. *The Study of Literate Civilizations.* New York: Holt, Rinehart and Winston, 1969.

Hsu, Francis L. K. *Aspects of Culture and Personality: A Symposium.* New York: Abelard-Schuman, 1954.

Hsu, Kai-yu. "The Teacher as an Architect of Learning." *Foreign Language Annals* 3 (1970):377-82.

Hucker, Charles O. *China, a Critical Bibliography.* Tucson: University of Arizona Press, 1962.

Huizenga, Jann. *Looking at American Food: A Pictorial Introduction to American Language and Culture.* Lincolnwood, IL: National Textbook Co., 1983.

Huizenga, Jann. *Looking at American Signs.* Lincolnwood, IL: National Textbook Co., 1982.

Humphrey, Grace. *Stories of the World's Holidays.* Highland Park, NJ: Gryphon Press, 1971.

Hutchinson, Joseph. *Draft Standard for Five Levels of Proficiency in Cross-Cultural Communications.* Unpublished. Bethesda, MD: Defense Language Institute.

Hymes, Dell. "The Scope of Sociolinguistics." Social Science Research Council *Items* 26 (1972):14-18.

Hymes, Dell (ed.). *Language in Culture: A Reader in Linguistics and Anthropology.* New York: Harper & Row, 1964.

Ilbek, Jacques. "A Case of Semantic Interference." *The French Review* 41 (1967):368-76.

Imhoof, Maurice. "Controlling Cultural Variations in the Preparation of TESOL Materials." *TESOL Quarterly* 2 (1968):39-42.

Integrating Black Studies into Existing Social Studies Curriculum: A Model Unit. Chicago: Illinois Office of Education (Urban and Ethnic Education Section, 188 West Randolph), 1975.

Isaacs, Harold R. *Deseg: Change Comes to a Boston School.* (A report of an inquiry made for The Citywide Coordinating Council—Boston.) Boston: Citywide Coordinating Council, 1977.

Isaacs, Harold R. *Idols of the Tribe: Group Identity and Political Change.* New York: Harper & Row, 1975.

Jackson, Mary. "Let's Make Foreign Language Study More Relevant." *Today's Education: NEA Journal* 60, iii (1971):18-20.

Jakobovits, Leon A. "Motivation in Foreign Language Learning." In Joseph A. Tursi (ed.). *Foreign Language and the "New" Student.* Reports of the Working Committees, Northeast Conference on the Teaching of Foreign Languages. New York: MLA Materials Center, 1970, pp. 62-75.

Jameson, Brent L. *Student Attitudes in Culture Capsule Usage.* Master's thesis. Provo, UT: Brigham Young University, 1972.

Jarvis, Donald K. "Making Crosscultural Connections." In J. K. Phillips (ed.). *The Language Connection: From the Classroom to the World.* Lincolnwood, IL: National Textbook Co., 1977.

Jay, Charles. "Study of Culture: Relevance of Foreign Languages in World Affairs Education." In Pat Castle and Charles Jay (eds.). *Toward Excellence in Foreign Language Education.* Springfield, IL: Office of Public Instruction, 1968, pp. 84-92.

Jazayery, M. A. "Persian Language Instruction." *Middle East Studies Association Bulletin 6,* i (1972):9-29.

Jencks, C. S. *Inequality: A Reassessment of the Effect of Family and Schooling in America.* New York: Basic Books, 1972.

Jenks, Charles L., Nancy G. Bostick, and J. Gregory Otto. *Deriving Objectives Training Unit 3,* Rev. ed. Berkeley, CA: Far West Laboratory for Education Research and Development, 1971.

Jenks, Frederick L. "Any Fifteen-year Old Student CAN Do Socio-Cultural Research." *Careers, Communication and Culture.* Lincolnwood, IL: National Textbook Co., 1974, pp. 65-71.

Jenks, Frederick L. *Planning to Teach Culture: An Instructional Manual.* Detroit: Advancement Press of America, 1972.

Jenks, Frederick L. "Teaching Culture through the Use of American Newspapers." *American Foreign Language Teacher 2,* iv (1972a):28-29, 40.

Jenks, Frederick L. "Toward the Creative Teaching of Culture."*American Foreign Language Teacher 2,* iii (1972b):12-14, 42.

Jenks, Frederick L. *A Schema for the Generation of Educational Objectives Related to the Teaching of Culture in the Foreign Language Classroom.* Doctoral dissertation, Wayne State University, 1971.

Jessor, Richard, Theodore D. Graves, Robert C. Hanson, and Shirley L. Jessor. *Society, Personality, and Deviant Behavior: A Study of a Triethnic Community.* New York: Holt, Rinehart and Winston, 1968.

Jonas, Sister Ruth. *African Studies in French for the Elementary Grades: Phase II of a Twinned Classroom Approach to the Teaching of French...*1972 (EDRS: ED 066 994).

Jones, Earl, and Frances Dean (eds.). *The Americas and Self-Identification.* Intercultural Education Series, 1970 (EDRS: ED 052 100).

Jones, J. Allen. "English Language Teaching in a Social/Cultural Dialect Situation: 1." *English Language Teaching* (London) 22, iii (1968):199-205.

Joncich, Geraldin M. (ed.). *Psychology and the Science of Education: Selected Writings of Edward L. Thorndike.* New York: Teachers College, Columbia University, 1962.

Jorstad, Helen L. *The Magazine: French Mini-Culture Unit.* Lincolnwood, IL: National Textbook Co., 1976.

Juaire, Dennis. "The Use of Folksongs to Develop Insight into Latin American Culture." In H. Ned Seelye (ed.). *Perspectives for Teachers of Latin American Culture.* Springfield, IL: State Superintendent of Public Instruction, 1970.

Kagan, Jerome. "The Baby's Elastic Mind." *Human Nature* 1, i (Jan. 1978):66-73.

Kahler, Erich. *Out of the Labyrinth: Essays in Clarification.* New York: Brazillier, 1967.

Kany, C. E. *American-Spanish Euphemisms.* Los Angeles: University of California Press, 1960a.

Kany, C. E. *American-Spanish Semantics.* Los Angeles: University of California Press, 1960b.

Kany, C. E. *American-Spanish Syntax.* Chicago: University of Chicago Press, 1951.

Kaplan, Bert. "Personality and Social Structure." In R. A. Manners and D. Kaplan (eds.). *Theory in Anthropology: A Sourcebook.* Chicago: Aldine, 1968.

Kaplan, Bert (ed.). *Studying Personality Cross-Culturally.* New York: Harper and Row, 1961.

Kaplan, Fran, Lorraine Zinn, and Helene Aqua. *Community Orientation: Survival in the City.* Mimeographed. Milwaukee: United Migrant Opportunity Services, Adult Basic Education, United States Office of Economic Opportunity, 1970.

Katcher, Roberta. *Culture Shock: What Problems in Acculturation Can Occur in a New Society?* 1971 (EDRS: ED 066 987).

Keesing, R. "Theories of Culture." In Bernard Siegel (ed.). *Annual Review of Anthropology.* Palo Alto, CA: Annual Review, 1974.

Kelly, L. G. *25 Centuries of Language Teaching.* Rowley, MA: Newbury House, 1969.

Kenworthy, Leonard S. *The International Dimension of Education. Background Paper II.* Washington, DC: Association for Supervision and Curriculum Development, 1970 (EDRS: ED 039 202).

Khanbikov, Ia. I. "Folk Pedagogy," *Soviet Education* 9, i (1967):32-41.

Kiev, Ari. *Transcultural Psychiatry.* New York: Free Press, 1973.

Kilpatrick, Franklin P. (ed.). *Explorations in Transactional Psychology.* New York: New York University Press, 1961.

King, Edith W. *Teaching Ethnic Awareness.* Glenview, IL: Scott, Foresman, 1980.

King, Edith W. *Worldmindedness: The World Context for Teaching in the Elementary School.* Dubuque, IA: William C. Brown, 1971 (EDRS: ED 052 094).

King, Edmund J. "Education for Uncertainty." Inaugural Lecture in The Faculty of Education, University of London King's College, Feb. 1976.

King, Edmund J. *Other Schools and Ours: Comparative Studies for Today.* New York: Holt, Rinehart and Winston, 1975.

King, Edmund J., C. H. Moor, and J. A. Mundy. *Post-Compulsory Education II: The Way Ahead.* Beverly Hills, CA: Sage Publications, 1975.

King, Edmund J., C. H. Moor, and J. A. Mundy. *Post-Compulsory Education I: A New Analysis in Western Europe.* Beverly Hills, CA: Sage Publications, 1974.

Kingston, Maxine Hong. *The Woman Warrior: Memoirs of a Girlhood Among Ghosts.* New York: Knopf, 1976.

Kleinfeld, Judith S. *Eskimo School on the Andreafsky: A Study of Effective Bicultural Education:* New York: Praeger, 1975.

Kliebard, Herbert M. "Bureaucracy and Curriculum Theory." In Vernon F. Haubrich (ed.). *Freedom, Bureaucracy, and Schooling.* Washington, DC: Association for Supervision and Curriculum Development, National Education Association, 1971, pp. 74-93.

Kliebard, Herbert M. "Curriculum Differentiation for the Disadvantaged." *The Educational Forum* 32 (1967):47-54.

Kluckhohn, F., and F. Strodbeck. *Variations in Value Orientations.* Evanston, IL: Row, Peterson, 1961.

Kohlberg, Lawrence, and Rochelle Mayer. "Development as the Aim of Education." *Harvard Educational Review* 42 (1972):449-56.

Kohls, L. Robert. *Survival Kit for Overseas Living.* Chicago: Intercultural Press, 1979.

Kraemer, Alfred J. *Teacher Training Workshop in Intercultural Communication: Instructor's Guide.* Alexandria, VA: Human Resources Research Organization, 1976.

Kraemer, Alfred J. *Workshop in Intercultural Communication: Handbook for Instructors.* Alexandria, VA: Human Resources Research Organization (300 North Washington St.), 1974.

Kraemer, Alfred J. *Development of a Cultural Self-Awareness Approach to Instruction in Intercultural Communication.* Alexandria, VA: Human Resources Research Organization, 1973.

Kroeber, Alfred L., and Clyde Kluckhohn (eds.). *Culture: A Critical Review of Concepts and Definitions.* New York: Random House, 1954.

LaBarre, Weston. *The Human Animal.* Chicago: University of Chicago Press, 1954.

Lado, Robert. "Language, Thought, and Memory in Language Teaching: A Thought View." *Modern Language Journal* 54 (1970):580-85.

Lado, Robert. "How to Test Cross-Cultural Understanding." In Robert Lado, *Language Testing: The Construction and Use of Foreign Language Tests.* London: Longmans, Green, 1961; New York: McGraw-Hill, 1964, pp. 275-89.

Lado, Robert. *Linguistics Across Cultures: Applied Linguistics for Language Teachers.* Ann Arbor: University of Michigan Press, 1957.

Ladu, Tora T. *What Makes the Spanish Spanish, and their New-World Descendants Different.* Detroit, MI: Advancement Press of America, 1974.

Ladu, Tora T. *Draft of New Guidelines for Foreign Language Teachers.* Presented for discussion at State Conference of Foreign Language Teachers. Raleigh, NC: Department of Public Instruction, 1967.

Ladu, Tora T., et al. *Teaching for Cross-Cultural Understanding.* Raleigh, NC: Department of Public Instruction, 1968.

Lafayette, Robert C. *Language in Education: Theory & Practice.* Arlington, VA: Center for Applied Linguistics, 1978.

Lafayette, Robert C. (ed.). *The Culture Revolution in Foreign Language Teaching: A Guide for Building the Modern Curriculum; Selected Papers from the 1975 Central States Conference.* Lincolnwood, IL: National Textbook Co., 1975.

La France, Marianne, and Claro Mayo. "Cultural Aspects of Nonverbal Communication." *International Journal of Intercultural Relations* 1, ii (1978):71-80.

Laird, Charlton. *The Miracle of Language.* Cleveland: World Publishing Co., 1953.

Lambert, Richard D. *Americans Abroad*. A Special issue of *The Annals*, 368 (Nov. 1966).

Lambert, Wallace E. "Motivational Variables in Second-Language Acquisition." *Canadian Journal of Psychology* 13 (1969):266-72 (EDRS: ED 031 968).

Lambert, Wallace E. "Psychological Approaches to the Study of Language." In Joseph Michel (ed.). *Foreign Language Teaching*. New York: Macmillan, 1967, pp. 215-50.

Lambert, Wallace E., Alison d'Anglejan, and G. Richard Tucker. "Communicating across Cultures: An Empirical Investigation." Mimeographed. Montreal: Dept. of Psychology, McGill University, 1972.

Lambert, Wallace E., Howard Giles, and Omer Picard. "Language Attitudes in a French-American Community." Mimeographed. Montreal: McGill University, 1973.

Lambert, Wallace E., and Otto Klineberg. *Children's Views of Foreign Peoples*. New York: Appleton-Century-Crofts, 1967.

Lander, Herbert. *Language and Culture*. New York: Oxford University Press, 1966.

Langdon, Margaret. *Let the Children Write*. London: Longmans, Green, 1966.

Lange, Dale L. (ed.). *Annual ACTFL Bibliography (1969 to 1975)*. Published in May issues of *Foreign Language Annals;* also available through ERIC.

Latin America: A Catalog of Dissertations. Ann Arbor, MI: Xerox University Microfilms, 1974.

Latin America: Intercultural Experiential Learning Aid. Provo, UT: Brigham Young University (Language Research Center), 1976.

Lawton, Denis. *Social Class, Language and Education*. New York: Schocken Books, 1968.

Leamon, M. Phillip. *Foreign Study for High School Students*. MLA/ERIC Focus Report on the Teaching of Foreign Languages, Number 5. New York: MLA/ERIC, 1969.

Lee, Irving J. *Customs and Crises in Communications*. New York: Harper and Row, 1954.

Lee, Irving J. *How to Talk with People*. New York: Harper and Row, 1952.

Leñero Otero, Luis. *Investigación de la familia en México*. México, D.F.: Impresora Gálvez, S.A. (Instituto Mexicano de Estudios Sociales), 1969, Segunda edición 1971.

Lerner, Daniel, and Wilbur Schram (eds.). *Communications and Change in the Developing Countries*. Honolulu, HI: East-West Center Press, 1967.

Lesser, G. S., G. Fifer, and D. H. Clark. "Mental Abilities of Children From Different Social-Class and Cultural Groups." *Monographs of the Society for Research in Child Development*, 30 (4, Serial No. 102), 1965.

LeVine, Robert A., and Donald T. Campbell. *Ethnocentrism: Theories of Conflict, Ethnic Attitudes and Group Behavior.* New York: Wiley, 1972.

Levno, Arley W. *Rencontres Culturelles: Cross-Cultural Mini-Dramas.* Lincolnwood, IL: National Textbook Co., 1977.

Lewald, H. Ernest. *Latino América: sus culturas y sociedades.* New York: McGraw-Hill, 1973.

Lewald, H. Ernest. "A Tentative Outline in the Knowledge, Understanding, and Teaching of Cultures Pertaining to the Target Language." *Modern Language Journal 52* (May 1968):301-9.

Lewis, Diane K. "The Multicultural Education Model and Minorities: Some Reservations." *Anthropology and Education Quarterly 7*, iv (Nov. 1976): 32-37.

Lewis, E. Glyn. "Bilingualism and Bilingual Education: The Ancient World to the Renaissance." In Joshua A. Fishman (ed.). *Bilingual Education: An International Sociological Perspective.* Rowley, MA: Newbury House, 1976.

Lieberman, Morton A., Irvin D. Yalom, and Matthew B. Miles. *Encounter Groups: First Facts.* New York: Basic Books, 1973.

Lieberman, Samuel. "Ancient Greek and Roman Culture." In James W. Dodge (ed.). *Other Words, Other Worlds: Language-in-Culture.* Reports of the Working Committees, Northeast Conference on the Teaching of Foreign Languages. New York: MLA Materials Center, 1972.

Lindzey, Gardner, and Elliot Aronson. *The Handbook of Social Psychology.* Reading, MA: Addison-Wesley, 1969. 4 vols.

Linton, Ralph. *Cultural Background of Personality.* New York: Appleton-Century-Crofts, 1945.

Lipton, Gladys. "Curricula for New Goals." In Dale L. Lange and Charles J. James (eds.). *Foreign Language Education: A Reappraisal.* ACTFL Review of Foreign Language Education, Vol. 4. Lincolnwood, IL: National Textbook Co., 1972, pp. 187-218.

Livingston, Samuel A., and Clarice Stasz Stoll. *Simulation Games: An Introduction for the Social Studies Teacher.* New York: Free Press, 1973.

Llabre, Maria M., William B. Ware, and John M. Newell. "A Factor Analytic Study of Children's Self-Concept in Three Ethnic Groups." Paper presented at the Annual Meeting of the National Council on Measurement in Education, April 1977.

Lockland, George T. *Grow or Die: The Unifying Principle of Transformation.* New York: Random House, 1973.

Loew, Helene. "FL Magazines Plus Planning Equal Up-to-Date Culture Units." *Accent on ACTFL* 3, iv (1973):6-8.

Lohnes, Walter F. "The Training of German Teachers in the United States." *Die Unterrichtspraxis* 2, ii (1969):69-76.

Longstreet, Wilma. *Aspects of Ethnicity: Understanding Differences in Education.* New York: Teachers College Press, 1978.

Louden, D. "Self-esteem and Locus of Control." *New Community*, 6, iii (1978):218-34.

Love, William, et al. *Options and Perspectives: A Sourcebook of Innovative Foreign Language Programs in Action, K-12.* New York: MLA Publications Center, 1973.

Loy, Jane M. *Latin America: Sights and Sounds, A Guide to Motion Pictures and Music for College Courses.* Gainesville, FL: Consortium of Latin American Studies Programs, 1973.

Lurie, Walter A. *Strategies for Survival.* New York: Ktav, 1982.

Lynch, Frank, and May Hallensteiner. *Understanding the Philippines: A Study of Cultural Themes.* Quezon City: Ateneo de Manila, Institute of Philippine Culture, 1967.

Mackey, William F. "A Typology of Bilingual Education." In Joshua A. Fishman (ed.). *Advances in the Sociology of Language II.* The Hague: Mouton, 1972, pp. 413-32.

Madrid-Barela, Arturo. "Towards an Understanding of Chicano Experience." In Larry A. Samovar and Richard E. Porter (eds.). *Intercultural Communication: A Reader.* Belmont, CA: Wadsworth Publishing Co., 1976, pp. 98-106.

Mager, Robert F. *Preparing Instructional Objectives.* Palo Alto, CA: Fearon, 1962.

Malraux, André. *La Tête D'Obsidienne.* Paris: Gallimard, 1974.

Mandelbaum, David G. (ed.). *Edward Sapir: Culture, Language and Personality, Selected Essays.* Berkeley: University of California Press, 1962.

Mangers, Dennis H. "Education in the Grapes of Wrath." *The National Elementary Principal* 50, ii (1970):39-40.

Manners, Robert A., and David Kaplan (eds.). *Theory in Anthropology: A Sourcebook.* Chicago: Aldine, 1968.

Marquardt, William F. "Informant-Interaction as Training in the Foreign Language Classroom." In David S. Hoopes (ed.). *Readings in Intercultural Communication*, Vol. II. Pittsburgh: Regional Council for International Education, University of Pittsburgh, 1972, pp. 36-40.

Marquardt, William F. "Criteria for Selecting Literary Texts in Teaching Cross-Culture Communication, Especially in English as a Second Language." In *Actes du Xe congrès international des linguisties, 1967.* Bucharest: Editions de l'Académie de la République Socialiste de Roumani, 1970, pp. 1019-27.

Marquardt, William F. "Creating Empathy through Literature between the Members of the Mainstream Culture and the Disadvantaged Learners of the Minority Cultures." *Florida FL Reporter*, Vol. 7, i (Spring/Summer 1969):134-35. (Special anthology issue entitled *Linguistic-Cultural Differences and American Education.)*

Marquardt, William F. "Literature and Cross-Culture Communication in English for International Students." *The Florida FL Reporter* 5, ii (1967):9-10.

Maslow, A. H. *The Farther Reaches of Human Nature.* New York: Viking Press, 1971.

Maslow, A. H. *Motivation and Personality.* New York: Harper, 1954.

Massad, Carolyn Emrick. "The Developing Self: World of Communication." In K. Yamamoto (ed.). *The Child and His Image.* New York: Houghton Mifflin, 1972, pp. 26-53.

Mathiot, Madeleine. "An Approach to the Study of Language-and-Culture Relations." *Dissertation Abstracts* 27 (1967) 3765B, Catholic University of America, Washington, D.C.

Mattelart, Armand. *La cultura como empresa multinacional.* Buenos Aires: Editorial Galerna (Talcahuano 487), 1974.

Mayers, Marvin K. *A Look at Latin American Lifestyles.* Dallas, TX: International Museum of Cultures, 1982.

Maynard, Richard A. *The Celluloid Curriculum: How to Use Movies in the Classroom.* New York: Hayden, 1971.

McLaughlin, Milbrey Wallin. "Implementation as Mutual Adaptation: Change in Classroom Organization." *Teachers College Record* 77, iii (Feb. 1976):339-51.

Mead, Margaret. *Culture and Commitment: A Study of the Generation Gap.* New York: Natural History Press, 1970.

Mead, Margaret. "National Character." In A. L. Kroeber (ed.). *Anthropology Today: An Encyclopedic Inventory.* Chicago: University of Chicago Press, 1953, pp. 642-67.

Mead, Margaret, and Rhoda Metraux. *The Study of Culture at a Distance.* Chicago: University of Chicago Press, 1959.

Mead, Robert G., Jr. "Reassessing the Ph.D. in Foreign Languages." *Bulletin of the Association of Departments of Foreign Languages* 4, iii (1973):26-29.

Mead, Robert G., Jr. *The United States Image in Latin America: A Select Bibliography.* Mimeographed. Storrs: University of Connecticut, 1972.

Mead, Robert G., Jr. "Let Students Live It Out." *Accent on ACTFL* 3, i (1972a):11.

Meade, Betsy, and Genelle Morain. "The Culture Cluster." *Foreign Language Annals* 6, 3 (March 1973):331-38.

Mehl, Bernard. "Academic Colonialism—A New Look." *Educational Leadership* 27 (1969):243-46.

Meyer, Philip. *Precision Journalism: A Reporter's Introduction to Social Science Methods.* Bloomington: Indiana University Press, 1973.

Meyers, Jerome Keeley, and Lee L. Bean. *A Decade Later: A Follow up of Social Class and Mental Illness.* New York: Wiley, 1968.

Michelli, James A. "Students Abroad Studying Their Own Thing." *Improving College and University Teaching* 20, 3 (1972):160-61.

Miller, Frank C. *Old Villages and a New Town: Industrialism in Mexico.* Menlo Park, CA: Cummings, 1973.

Miller, J. Dale. "Proverbs Supply Gems of Culture." *Accent on ACTFL* 3, iv (1973):9.

Miller, J. Dale, and Russell H. Bishop. *USA-Mexico Culture Capsules.* Rowley, MA: Newbury House, 1979.

Miller, J. Dale, and Maurice Loiseau. *USA-France Culture Capsules.* Rowley, MA: Newbury House, 1974.

Miller, J. Dale, John Drayton, and Ted Lyon. *USA-Hispanic South America Culture Capsules.* Rowley, MA: Newbury House, 1979.

Mimiague, Michel, et al. *Indicateurs de changements d'opinions et d'attitudes dans les jeunes générations, 1957-1970.* Mimeographed. Paris: C.N.R.S. Groupe d'Etude des Méthodes de l'Analyse Sociologique, Maison des Sciences de l'Homme, 1972.

Miner, Horace. "Body Ritual Among the Nacirema." *American Anthropologist* 58, (June 1956):503-7.

Modiano, Nancy. *Indian Education in the Chiapas Highlands.* New York: Holt, Rinehart and Winston, 1973.

Montagu, Ashley. *Culture and Human Development: Insights into Growing Human.* Englewood Cliffs, NJ: Prentice-Hall, 1974.

Morain, Genelle G. *Language in Education: Theory & Practice.* Arlington, VA: Center for Applied Linguistics, 1978.

Morain, Genelle G. "Visual Literacy: Reading Signs and Designs in the Foreign Culture." *Foreign Language Annals* 3 (May 1976):210-16.

Morain, Genelle G. "Teaching Culture Through the Audio-Motor Unit." *Foreign Language Annals* 6 (Oct. 1972):61-67.

Morain, Genelle G. "Cultural Pluralism." In Dale L. Lange (ed.). *Pluralism in Foreign Language Education.* ACTFL Review of Foreign Language Education, Vol. 3. Lincolnwood, IL: National Textbook Co., 1971, reissued in 1973, pp. 59-95.

Morain, Genelle G. "French Folklore: A Fresh Approach to the Teaching of Culture." *The French Review* 41 (April 1968):675-81.

Morris, Desmond. *Manwatching: A Field Guide to Human Behavior.* New York: Harry N. Abrams, 1977.

Morris, Marshall. *Saying & Meaning in Puerto Rico: Some Problems in the Ethnography of Discourse.* New York: Pergamon Press, 1981.

Muegge, Richard L. "The Teaching of *Prometheus Bound.*" *American Foreign Language Teacher* 2, iv (1972):31-33.

Mueller, Klaus A., and William Wiersma. "The Effects of Language Laboratory Type upon Cultural Orientation Scores of Foreign Language Students." *Modern Language Journal* 51 (1967):258-63.

Mueller, Theodore H. *Impression d'Amérique: Cultural Commentary.* Mimeographed. Lexington: University of Kentucky, 1972.

Mueller, Theodore H. *Cultural Notes on Jules Romains' Donagoo.* Mimeographed. Lexington: University of Kentucky, Department of French, 1968.

Murdock, George P., et al. *Outline of Cultural Materials,* Rev ed. New Haven: Human Relations Area File, 1982.

Murphy, Sharon. *Other Voices: Black, Chicano, and American Indian Press.* Dayton, OH: Pflaum/Standard, 1974.

Mussen, Paul, and Nancy Eisenberg-Berg. *The Roots of Caring, Sharing and Helping: The Development of Prosocial Behavior in Children.* San Francisco: W. H. Freeman, 1977.

Naroll, Raoul. *A Handbook of Method in Cultural Anthropology.* Garden City, NY: Natural History Press, 1970.

Naroll, Raoul. *Data Quality Control: A New Research Technique.* New York: Free Press, 1962.

National Council of State Supervisors of Foreign Language. "Guidelines for Evaluating Foreign Language Programs Abroad for High School Students: A

Reappraisal." *Foreign Language Annals* 6 (1973):453-56; also in Connecticut *FL News Exchange* 18, v (June 1972):2-5.

Nef, John U. "An Early Energy Crisis and Its Consequences." *Scientific American* 237, v (Nov. 1977):140-42, 146-51.

Nesbitt, William A. *Simulation Games for the Social Studies Classroom.* 2nd ed. New York: Foreign Policy Association, 1971.

Nierenberg, Gerald I., and Henry Calero. *Metatalk: Guide to Hidden Meanings in Conversation.* New York: Trident Press, 1973.

Niyekawa-Howard, Agnes. *A Psycholinguistic Study of the Whorfian Hypothesis Based on the Japanese Passive.* Honolulu: Educational Research and Development Center, University of Hawaii, 1968.

Northwest Regional Educational Laboratory. *Assessment Instruments in Bilingual Education: A Descriptive Catalog of 342 Oral and Written Tests.* Los Angeles: National Dissemination and Assessment Center (Calif. State Univ., L.A., 5151 State University Dr.), 1978.

Nostrand, Frances. "Review of *A Language-Teaching Bibliography.*" *Modern Language Journal* 54 (1970):39.

Nostrand, Frances, and Howard L. Nostrand. "Testing Understanding of the Foreign Culture." In H. Ned Seelye (ed.). *Perspectives for Teachers of Latin American Culture.* Springfield, IL: Superintendent of Public Instruction, 1970, pp. 161-70.

Nostrand, Howard L. "The 'Emergent Model' (Structured Inventory of a Sociocultural System) Applied to Contemporary France." *Contemporary French Civilization* 2, ii (Winter, 1978): 277-94.

Nostrand, Howard L. "Empathy for a Second Culture: Motivations and Techniques." In Gilbert A. Jarvis (ed.). *Responding to New Realities.* ACTFL Review of Foreign Language Education, Vol. 5. Lincolnwood, IL: National Textbook Co., 1974, pp. 263-327.

Nostrand, Howard L. "French Culture's Concern for Relationships: Relationism." *Foreign Language Annals* 6 (1973):469-80.

Nostrand, Howard L. "The Language Laboratory and the Sociological [read: Sociocultural] Context." *NALLD Journal* 4, iii (1970):23-38.

Nostrand, Howard L. "Theme Analysis in the Study of Literature." In Joseph Strelka (ed.). *Problems of Literary Evaluation: Yearbook of Comparative Criticism.* University Park and London: Pennsylvania State University Press, 1969, pp. 182-97.

Nostrand, Howard L. "Levels of Sociocultural Understanding for Language Classes." In H. Ned Seelye (ed.). *A Handbook on Latin America for Teachers: Methodology and Annotated Bibliography.* Springfield, IL: Office of Public Instruction, 1968, pp. 19-24.

Nostrand, Howard L. "Audiovisual Materials for Teaching the Social and Cultural Context of a Modern Foreign Language: Their Bearing Upon Pre-service Education." *The Department of Foreign Languages* (DFL) *Bulletin,* National Education Association, 5, iii (May 1966a):4-6.

Nostrand, Howard L. "Describing and Teaching the Sociocultural Context of a Foreign Language and Literature." In Albert Valdman (ed.). *Trends in Language Teaching.* New York: McGraw-Hill, 1966b, pp. 1-25.

Nostrand, Howard L. *Film Recital of French Poems: Cultural Commentary.* Seattle: University of Washington Press, 1964 (EDRS: ED 044 955).

Nostrand, Howard L. *The University and Human Understanding.* Seattle: University of Washington, Department of Romance Languages and Literature, 1963a.

Nostrand, Howard L. "Literature in the Describing of a Literate Culture." *French Review* 37 (Dec. 1963b):145-57.

Nostrand, Howard L. (ed.). *Background Data for the Teaching of French.* Seattle: University of Washington Press, 1967. *(Part A, La culture et la société Française au XXᵉ siècle; Part B, Exemples littéraires; Part C, Contemporary Culture and Society in the United States)* (EDRS: ED 031 964; ED 031 989; ED 031 990).

Nostrand, Howard L., et al. *Research on Language Teaching: An Annotated International Bibliography, 1945-64.* 2nd rev. ed. Seattle: University of Washington Press, 1965.

O'Brien, Gordon E., et al. *The Effects of Programmed Culture Training upon the Performance of Volunteer Medical Teams in Central America.* 1969 (EDRS: ED 039 807).

Oder, Marvin. *Culture and Social Psychiatry.* New York: Atherton Press, 1967.

Ogbu, John U. *Minority Education and Caste.* New York: Academic Press, 1978.

Oliver, Robert Tarbell. *Culture and Communication: The Problem of Penetrating National and Cultural Boundaries.* Springfield, IL: Thomas, 1962.

Oller, John W., Jr., "Transformational Theory and Pragmatics." *Modern Language Journal* 54 (1970):504-7.

Opler, Morris E. *Apache Odyssey: A Journey Between Two Worlds.* New York: Holt, Rinehart and Winston, 1969a.

Opler, Morris E. "Themes of Culture." In Wilhelm Bernsdorf and Friedrich Bülow (eds.), *Wörterbuch der Soziologie.* Stuttgart: Ferdinand Enke, 1969.

Opler, Morris E. "The Themal Approach in Cultural Anthropology and Its Application to North Indian Data." *Southwestern Journal of Anthropology* 24, iii (1968):215-27.

Opler, Morris E. "Cultural Anthropology and the Training of Teachers of Foreign Languages." In *Seminar in Language and Language Learning: Final Report.* Seattle: University of Washington, Department of Romance Languages and Literature, 1962, pp. 90-96.

Oppenheimer, Max, Jr. "Do Languages Seek Their Own Level of Abstraction?" *The Educational Forum* 32, iv (1967):478-90.

Ortali, Raymond J. *Entre nous.* New York: Macmillan, 1972.

Osgood, Charles E., William H. May, and Murray S. Miron. *Cross-Cultural Universals of Affective Meaning.* Urbana: University of Illinois Press, 1975.

Osgood, Charles E., and G. J. Suci. "Factor Analysis of Meaning," *Journal of Experimental Psychology* 50 (1955):325-38.

Osterloh, Karl-Heinz. "Intercultural Differences and Communicative Approaches to Foreign Language Teaching in the Third World." *Studies in Second Language Acquisition,* 3, i (Fall 1981):64-70.

Overholt, Kenneth D. *Voces de Puerto Rico: Contemporary Puerto Rico as Seen through Actual Interviews.* Lincolnwood, IL: National Textbook Co., 1982.

Padilla, Amado M., and K. Kilby Long. *Evidence for Bilingual A of Academic Success in a Group of Spanish-American College Students.* Mimeographed. Bellingham, WA: Western Washington State College, 1970.

Padilla, Amado M., and René A Ruiz. *Latino Mental Health: A Review of Literature.* Washington, DC: Superintendent of Documents, U.S. Government Printing Office (# 1724-00317), 1973.

Palomares, Uvaldo H., and Geraldine Ball. *Magic Circle: An Overview of the Human Development Program.* La Mesa, CA: Human Development Training Institute, 1974.

Paoletti, Michel. *Civilisation Française contemporaine.* Paris: Hatier, 1969.

Paoletti, Michel, and Ross Steele. *Civilisation Française quotidienne.* New York: Hatier, 1981.

Park, Robert E., and Herbert A. Miller. *Old World Traits Transplanted.* Chicago: University of Chicago Press, 1925.

Parker, John R., et al. "Political Simulation: An Introduction." In H. Ned Seelye (ed.). *A Handbook on Latin America for Teachers: Methodology and*

Annotated Bibliography. Springfield, IL: Superintendent of Public Instruction, 1968, pp. 25-28.

Pasternak, Michael G. *Helping Kids Learn Multi-Cultural Concepts: A Handbook of Strategies.* Champaign, IL: Research Press, 1979.

Paulston, Christina Bratt. *Implications of Language Learning Theory for Language Planning: Concerns in Bilingual Education.* Arlington, VA: Center for Applied Linguistics, 1974.

Peckham, Morse. *Beyond the Tragic Vision: The Quest for Identity in the 19th Century.* New York: Brazillier, 1967.

Pedersen, Paul (ed.). *Readings in Intercultural Communication,* Vol. 4. Pittsburgh, PA: The Intercultural Communications Network (4401 Fifth Ave.), 1974.

Pemberton, John E. *How to Find Out about France: A Guide to Sources of Information.* Oxford: Pergamon Press, 1966.

Pfeiffer, J. Williams, W. Jones, and John E. Jones, (eds.). *A Handbook of Structured Experiences for Human Relations Training.* Volumes I-V. Iowa City, IA: University Associates Press, 1969-1975.

Philips, Susan U. "Access to Power and Maintenance of Ethnic Identity as Goals of Multicultural Education: Are They Compatible?" *Anthropology and Education Quarterly* 7, iv (Nov. 1976):30-32.

Pietrzyk, Alfred, et al. "Language and Culture." In *1960-67 Selected Bibliography of Arabic.* Washington, DC: Center of Applied Linguistics, 1968, pp. 46-50.

Pike, Kenneth L. *Language in Relation to a Unified Theory of the Structure of Human Behavior,* 2nd rev. ed. The Hague: Mouton, 1971.

Pindur, Nancy. *The German Teen-Ager in Profile.* Detroit: Advancement Press, 1973.

Pindur, Nancy. "They Dance Their Way through German." *American Foreign Language Teacher* 2, iii (1972):34-35.

Plog, Stanley C., and Robert B. Edgerton (eds.). *Changing Perspectives in Mental Illness.* New York: Holt, Rinehart and Winston, 1969.

Polcyn, Kenneth A. "The Joint United States-India Educational Broadcast Satellite Experiment." *Educational Technology* 12, vi (1972):14-17, 20-25.

Popham, W. James. *The Teacher Empiricist.* 2nd ed. Los Angeles: Tinnon-Brown, 1970.

Popham, W. James, and Eva L. Baker. *The Prentice-Hall Teacher Competency Development System.* Englewood Cliffs, NJ: Prentice-Hall, 1973.

Pospisil, Leopold. *The Kapauku Papuans of West New Guinea.* New York: Holt, 1963.

Povey, John F. "Literature in TESL Programs: The Language and the Culture." *TESOL Quarterly* 1, ii (1967):40-46.

Prejudice and Ethnocentrism: A Curriculum and Resource Manual for Elementary School Teachers. Chicago: Illinois-Chicago Project for Inter-Ethnic Dimensions in Education, Dept. of Policy Studies, University of Illinois at Chicago Circle, 1975.

Primus, Pearl E. *A Pilot Study Integrating Visual Form and Anthropological Content for Teaching Children Ages 6 to 10 about Cultures ... A Danced Presentation with Lecture Interpreting Some of the Cultural Values in West and Central African Communities.* 1968 (EDRS: ED 027 095).

Prosser, Michael H. *Intercommunication Among Nations and Peoples.* New York: Harper and Row, 1973.

Prosser, Michael H. (ed.). *USIA Intercultural Communication Course: 1977 Proceedings.* Washington, DC: International Communication Agency, 1978.

Pusch, Margaret D. (ed.). *Multicultural Education: A Cross-Cultural Training Approach.* Chicago: Intercultural Press, 1979.

Pusch, Margaret D., H. N. Seelye, and J. H. Wasilewski. "Training for Multicultural Education Competencies." In Margaret D. Pusch (ed.). *Multicultural Education: A Cross-Cultural Training Approach.* Chicago: Intercultural Press, 1979, pp. 85-103.

Pye, Lucian W. (ed.). *Conference on Communication and Political Development.* Princeton, NJ: Princeton University Press, 1963.

Rallo, John A. *The Newspaper: Based on Selections from Major Newspapers from Italy.* Lincolnwood, IL: National Textbook Co., 1976.

Ramírez, Manuel, III. "Cultural Democracy: A New Philosophy for Educating the Mexican American Child." *The National Elementary Principal* 50, ii (1970):45-46.

Ramírez, Manuel, III, and Alfredo Castañeda. *Cultural Democracy, Bicognitive Development and Education.* New York: Academic Press, 1974.

Randolph, Gary, Dan Landis, and Oliver C. S. Tzeng. "The Effects of Time and Practice upon Culture Assimilator Training." *International Journal of Intercultural Relations* 1, iv (1977):105-12.

Raths, Louis E., Mevil Hamin, and Sidney B. Simon. *Values and Teaching.* New York: Charles E. Merrill, 1966.

Ravisé, J. Suzanne. *Tableaux culturels de la France.* Lincolnwood, IL: National Textbook Co., 1974.

Reinert, Harry. "Student Attitudes Toward Foreign Language—No Sale!" *Modern Language Journal* 54 (1970):107-12.

Renoir, Alain. "The Treason of the Clerks: Parable for 1970." *Southern California Modern and Classical Language Association Forum* 8, iii (1970):4-10.

Renwick, George W. *Evaluation Handbook for Cross-Cultural Training and Multicultural Education.* Chicago: Intercultural Press, 1980.

Rich, Andrea L. *Interracial Communication.* New York: Harper and Row, 1974.

Rich, Andrea L., and Dennis M. Ogawa. "Intercultural and Interracial Communication: An Analytical Approach." In Larry A. Samovar and Richard E. Porter (eds.). *Intercultural Communication: A Reader.* Belmont, CA: Wadsworth Publishing Co., 1976, pp. 24-32.

Richardson, Elwyn S. *In the Early World.* New York: Pantheon, 1964.

Richardson, Miles. *San Pedro, Colombia: Small Town in a Developing Society.* New York: Holt, Rinehart and Winston, 1970.

Rideout, W. Lecture on "Ethnicity." University of Southern California's Washington Education Center, July 1977.

Río, Angel del. *The Clash and Attraction of Two Cultures: The Hispanic and Anglo-Saxon Worlds in America.* Baton Rouge: Louisiana State University Press, 1965.

Rivers, Wilga M. "Motivation in Bilingual Programs." In Rudolph C. Troike and Nancy Modiano (eds.). *Proceedings of The First Inter-American Conference on Bilingual Education.* Arlington, VA: Center for Applied Linguistics, Oct. 1975, pp. 114-22.

Rivers, Wilga M., et al. (eds.). *Changing Patterns in Foreign Language Programs.* Report of the Illinois Conference on Foreign Languages in Junior and Community Colleges. Rowley, MA: Newbury House, 1972.

Rivlin, Harry N. "Research and Development in Multicultural Education." In Frank H. Klassen and Donna M. Gollnick (eds.). *Pluralism and the American Teacher: Issues and Case Studies.* Washington, DC: American Association of Colleges for Teacher Education, 1977, pp. 81-113.

Roberts, J. M. *Three Navajo Households.* Cambridge, MA: Papers of the Peabody Museum of Archaeology and Ethnology, 1951.

Robinette, Ralph F., et al. *SCDC Spanish Curricula Units.* Trenton, NJ: Crane Publishing Co., 1973.

Rock, Ernest. *An Individualized Program for Cultural Understanding.* Dayton, OH: Educaids, 1973.

Roeming, Robert F. "Bilingualism and the National Interest." *Modern Language Journal* 55 (1971):73-81.

Rogers, Carl R. *The Interpersonal Relationship in the Facilitation of Learning.* Virgil E. Herrick Memorial Lecture Series. Columbus, OH: Merrill, 1968.

Rogus, Timothy. *Lettres de France: Impressions of Contemporary France for Beginning Students.* Lincolnwood, IL: National Textbook Co., 1981.

Rohlen, Thomas P. "The Education of a Japanese Banker," *Human Nature* 1, i (Jan. 1978):22-30.

Rohlen, Thomas P. "*Seishin Kyoikuin* a Japanese Bank: A Description of Methods and Consideration of Some Underlying Concepts." In George D. Spindler (ed.). *Education and Cultural Process: Toward an Anthropology of Education.* New York: Holt, Rinehart and Winston, 1974, pp. 219-29.

Romney, A. Kimball, and Roy Goodwin D'Andrade (eds.). *Transcultural Studies in Cognition.* Special publication of *American Anthropologist* 66, iii (June 1964), Part 2.

Rosen, Harold. *Language and Class: A Critical Look at the Theories of Basil Bernstein.* Bristol, Eng.: Falling Wall Press, 1974.

Rosenzweig, Mark R. "Environmental Complexity, Cerebral Chance, and Behavior." *American Psychologist* 21 (1966):321-32.

Rosselot, LaVelle, et al. *Je parle Français, nouvelle éd.* Chicago: Encyclopaedia Britannica Educational Corp., *premier degré*, 1973; *deuxième degré*, 1971.

Rubin, Joan. *National Bilingualism in Paraguay.* The Hague: Mouton, 1968.

Ruddle, Kenneth, and Donald Odermann (eds.). *Statistical Abstract of Latin America 1971.* Los Angeles: University of California, Latin American Center, 1972.

Runte, Roseann. "A Cultural Mini Alphabet." *American Foreign Language Teacher* 3, iii (1973):24-25.

Ruple, Joelyn. "Teaching Cultural Themes Using the Spanish Theatre." *Hispania* 48 (1965):511-16.

Saitz, Robert L., and Edward J. Cervenka. *Handbook of Gestures: Colombia and the United States.* The Hague: Mouton, 1972.

Samovar, Larry A., and Richard E. Porter (eds.). *Intercultural Communication: A Reader.* Belmont, CA: Wadsworth Publishing Co., 2nd ed., 1976.

Samples, Bob. "Mind Cycles and Learning." *Phi Delta Kappan* (May 1977):688-92.

Samples, Bob, Cheryl Charles, and Dick Barnhart. *The Whole School Book: Teaching and Learning in the Twentieth Century.* Reading, MA: Addison-Wesley, 1977.

Santoni, Georges V. "Un Cours de civilisation Française au niveau universitaire." *Le Français dans le Monde* 84 (1971):27-33.

Santoni, Georges V., and Jean Noël Rey. "Langue et civilisation: Ouviers et étudiants: Préparation à une simulation." *Le Français dans le Monde* 88 (1972):26-34.

Sapir, Edward. *Language: An Introduction to the Study of Speech.* New York: Harcourt, Brace & World, 1921.

Savaiano, Geraldine. "Some Indications of Changes in Customs and Attitudes Among Certain Latin American Young People of the Middle Class," *Hispania* 57 (May 1974):254-69.

Savaiano, Geraldine, and Luz María Archundia. *The Folk Arts of Mexico.* American Association of Teachers of Spanish and Portuguese (AATSP) Cultural Unit III, 1968a. (Consult issue of *Hispania* for ordering information.)

Savaiano, Geraldine, and Luz María Archundia. *The Life Cycle in Mexico.* American Association of Teachers of Spanish and Portuguese (AATSP) Cultural Unit II, 1968b. (Consult issue of *Hispania* for ordering information.)

Savignon, Sandra J. *Communicative Competence: An Experiment in Foreign-Language Testing.* Lincolnwood, IL: Rand McNally, 1972a.

Savignon, Sandra J. "A l'écoute de France-Inter: The Use of Radio in a Student-Centered Oral French Class." *French Review* 46 (1972b):342-49.

Saville-Troike, Muriel. *A Guide to Culture in the Classroom.* Rosslyn, VA: National Clearinghouse for Bilingual Education (1500 Wilson Blvd., Suite 802), 1978.

Saville-Troike, Muriel. *Bilingual Children: A Resource Document.* Arlington, VA: Center for Applied Linguistics, 1973.

Saunders, Malcolm. *Multicultural Teaching.* New York: McGraw-Hill, 1982.

Sayers, Raymond S. (ed.). *Portugal and Brazil in Transition.* Minneapolis: University of Minnesota Press, 1968.

Scherer, Klaus R., and Howard Giles (eds.). *Social Markers in Speech.* New York: Cambridge University Press, 1979.

Schrank, Jeffrey. *Snap, Crackle, and Popular Taste: The Illusion of Free Choice in America.* New York: Dell, 1977.

Schulz, Renate A. *The Newspaper: French Mini-Culture Unit.* Lincolnwood, IL: National Textbook Co., 1982.

Schutz, Alfred. *Collected Papers. Vol. II: Studies in Social Theory.* The Hague: Martinus Nijhoff, 1964, pp. 91-105.

Scott, Andrew M., William A., and Trudi M. Lucas. *Simulation and National Development.* New York: Wiley, 1966.

Scribner, Sylvia, and Michael Cole. *The Psychology of Literacy.* Cambridge, MA: Harvard University Press, 1981.

Sebeok, Thomas A., et al. (eds.). *Approaches to Semiotics.* Transactions of the Indiana University Conference on Paralinguistics and Kinesics. The Hague: Mouton, 1972.

Seelye, H. Ned. "Individualizing and Sequencing Training for Inter-Cultural Communication." In *Foreign Language Learning, Today and Tomorrow: Essays in Honor of Emma M. Birkmaier.* J. D. Arendt, D. L. Lange, and P. J. Myers (eds.). New York: Pergamon Press, 1979, pp. 146-57.

Seelye, H. Ned. "Self-Identity and the Bicultural Classroom," in *Bilingual Education.* H. La Fontain, B. Persky, and L. H. Golubchick (eds.). Wayne, NJ: Avery, 1978a, pp. 290-98.

Seelye, H. Ned. "Intercultural Training for the First Six Months of Residence Abroad." In *Bridges of Understanding Symposium.* Provo, UT: Brigham Young University, Language and Intercultural Research Center, 1978b, pp. 201-3.

Seelye, H. Ned. "Teaching the Cultural Context of Intercultural Communication." In Muriel Saville-Troike (ed.). *Report of the Twenty-Eighth Annual Round Table on Languages and Linguistics, 1977.* Washington, DC: Georgetown University Press, 1977a, pp. 249-55.

Seelye, H. Ned. "Sociology and Education." In *Bilingual Education: Current Perspectives. Vol. 1: Social Science.* Arlington, VA: Center for Applied Linguistics, 1977b, pp. 99-103.

Seelye, H. Ned. "'Like Us or Like You'—The Challenge of Continuing Bicultural Education." *Curriculum Review* 14, v (1975):271-75.

Seelye, H. Ned. "Teaching the Foreign Culture: A Context for Research." In Jerald R. Green (ed.). *Foreign-Language Education Research: A Book of Readings.* Skokie, IL: Rand McNally, 1973a, pp. 74-89.

Seelye, H. Ned. *Culture Tests for Spanish.* Level I, Level II, Level III, Level IV. Honolulu: Hawaii State Department of Education, 1973b.

Seelye, H. Ned. "Analysis and Teaching of the Cross-Cultural Context." In Emma M. Birkmaier (ed.). *Foreign Language Education: An Overview.* ACTFL Review of Foreign Language Education, Vol. 1. Lincolnwood, IL: National Textbook Co., 1969b, reissued in 1972a, pp. 37-81.

Seelye, H. Ned (ed.). *Teaching Cultural Concepts in Spanish Classes.* Springfield, IL: Illinois Office of Education, 1972b (EDRS: ED 108 454).

Seelye, H. Ned. "Using Cultural Content to Develop Cultural Skills." *Hawaii Language Teacher* 14, 3 (April 1972c):3-6.

Seelye, H. Ned. "A Hard Look at Hard Times: A Reaction to Superintendent Lawson's 'Is Language Teaching Foreign or Dead?'" *Modern Language Journal* 55, 6 (Oct. 1971):358-61.

Seelye, H. Ned. "Performance Objectives for Teaching Cultural Concepts." *Foreign Language Annals* 3 (1970a):566-78.

Seelye, H. Ned. "Spanish Culture." In *Spain: Comparative Culture and Government.* Lincolnwood, IL: National Textbook Co., 1970b, pp. 33-48.

Seelye, H. Ned (ed.). *Perspectives for Teachers of Latin American Culture.* Springfield, IL: Illinois Office of Education, 1970c (EDRS: ED 047 579).

Seelye, H. Ned. "The *Yanqui* in the Banana Trilogy of Miguel Angel Asturias." In H. Ned Seelye (ed.). *Perspectives for Teachers of Latin American Culture,* op cit, 1970d, pp. 95-103.

Seelye, H. Ned. "An Objective Measure of Biculturation: Americans in Guatemala, A Case Study." *Modern Language Journal* 53, 7 (Nov. 1969a):503-14.

Seelye, H. Ned. "Culture in the Foreign Language Classroom." *Illinois Journal of Education* 59, iii (March 1968a):22-26.

Seelye, H. Ned (ed.). *A Handbook on Latin America for Teachers: Methodology and Annotated Bibliography.* Springfield, IL: Illinois Office of Education, 1968b (EDRS: ED 027 797).

Seelye, H. Ned. "Measuring the Ability to Function Cross-Culturally." In H. Ned Seelye (ed.). *A Handbook on Latin America for Teachers,* op cit, 1968c, pp. 34-43.

Seelye, H. Ned. "Item Validation and Measurement Techniques in Culture Tests." In H. Ned Seelye (ed.). *A Handbook on Latin America for Teachers,* op cit, 1968d, pp. 29-33.

Seelye, H. Ned. "Field Notes on Cross-Cultural Testing." *Language Learning* 16, i-ii (1966a):77-85.

Seelye, H. Ned. "The Spanish Passive: A Study in the Relation between Linguistic Form and Worldview." *Hispania* 49, ii (May 1966b):290-92.

Seelye, H. Ned. "Social Behavior of Non-Human Primates in Captivity." *Science Education* 50, i (Feb. 1966c):69-75.

Seelye, H. Ned, and Jacqueline Howell Wasilewski. "Toward a Taxonomy of Coping Strategies Used in Multicultural Settings." Paper presented at the meetings of the Society for Intercultural Education, Training, and Research, Mexico City, March 1979.

Seelye, H. Ned, Edward C. P. Stewart, and Joyce A. Sween. "Japanese Quality Control Circles: Survey Results." *The Quality Circles Journal* 6, ii (June 1983):20-22.

Seelye, H. Ned, and Joyce A. Sween. "Critical Components of Successful U.S. Quality Circles: Survey Results." *The Quality Circles Journal* 6, i (Mar. 1983): 14-17.

Seelye, H. Ned, and J. Laurence Day. *The Newspaper: A Reflection of Life-Styles in the Spanish-Speaking World.* Lincolnwood, IL: National Textbook Co., 1974; Rev. ed., 1982a.

Seelye H. Ned, and Joyce A. Sween."Quality Circles in U.S. Industry: Survey Results." *The Quality Circles Journal* 5, iv (Nov. 1982b):26-29.

Seelye, H. Ned, Edward C. P. Stewart, and Joyce A. Sween. *Evaluating Quality Circles in U.S. Industry.* Arlington, VA: Office of Naval Research, 1982c (NTIS: AD A118 649).

Seelye, H. Ned, and Jacqueline Howell Wasilewski. *Social Competency Development in Multicultural Children, Aged 6-13: Final Report of Exploratory Research on Hispanic-Background Children.* 1981 (EDRS: ED 209 363).

Seelye, H. Ned, Martha González Calat, Margarita López Raquec, Julieta Sánchez Castillo, and Joyce A. Sween. *Informe final del estudio de base sobre la educación bilingüe rural de Guatemala.* Guatemala City: Ministerio de Educación (Socio Educativo Rural), 1979.

Seelye, H. Ned, and Jacqueline Howell Wasilewski. "Historical Development of Multicultural Education." In *Multicultural Education: A Cross-Cultural Training Approach.* M. D. Pusch (ed.). Chicago: Intercultural Press, 1979, pp. 39-61.

Seelye, H. Ned, and V. Lynn Tyler (eds.). *Intercultural Communicator Resources.* Provo, UT: Brigham Young University (Language and Intercultural Research Center), 1977.

Seelye, H. Ned, and Billie N. Navarro. *A Guide to the Selection of Bilingual Education Program Designs.* Arlington Heights, IL: Bilingual Education Service Center, 1977.

Seelye, H. Ned, and K. Balasubramonian. "Accountability in Educational Reform Programs through Instrumentation Analyses and Design Variation: Evaluating Cognitive Growth in Illinois Bilingual Programs, 1972-1973." 1974 (EDRS: ED 112 635).

Seelye, H. Ned, and J. Laurence Day. "Penetrating the Mass Media: A Unit to Develop Skill in Reading Spanish Newspaper Headlines." *Foreign Language Annals* 5, i (Oct. 1971):69-81.

Seelye, H. Ned, and Marilyn B. Brewer. "Ethnocentrism and Acculturation of North Americans in Guatemala." *Journal of Social Psychology* 80 (April 1970):147-55.

Seelye H. Ned, and Mariá Guadalupe Mirón. "Phenotype and Occupational Mobility in Guatemala City: A Preliminary Survey." *Science Education* 54, i (January-March 1970):13-16.

Segall, M. H., D. T. Campbell, and M. J. Herkovits. *The Influence of Culture on Visual Perception.* Indianapolis, IN: Bobbs-Merrill, 1966.

Sen, Sondra. *The Asian Indians in America.* New York: Ethnic Heritage Studies Project, 1978.

Seward, Jack. *Japanese in Action: An Unorthodox Approach to the Spoken Language and the People Who Speak It.* New York: Walker and Company, 1969.

Shaftel, Fannie. *Role Playing for Social Values.* Englewood Cliffs, NJ: Prentice-Hall, 1967.

Shaw, Lawrence, and Elisabeth Combes. *Lettres des provinces.* Lincolnwood, IL: National Textbook Co., 1968.

Shaw, Marvin E., and Jack M. Wright. *Scales for the Measurement of Attitudes.* New York: McGraw-Hill, 1967.

Shiman, David A. *The Prejudice Book: Activities for the Classroom.* New York: Anti-Defamation League of B'nai B'rith (823 United Nations p/222), 1979.

Shirer, Robert K. *Kulturelle Begegnungen: Cross-Cultural Mini-Dramas.* Lincolnwood, IL: National Textbook Co., 1981.

Shirts, R. Garry. *Bafá Bafá: A Cross Culture Simulation.* Del Mar, CA: Simile II (P.O. Box 1028), 1973.

Sikkema, Mildred, and Agnes M. Niyekawa-Howard. *Cross-Cultural Learning and Self-Growth: Getting to Know Ourselves and Others.* New York: International Association of Schools of Social Work, 1977.

Silberman, Bernard S. *Japan and Korea: A Critical Bibliography.* Tucson: University of Arizona Press, 1962.

Simon, Paul. *The Tongue-Tied American: Confronting the Foreign Language Crisis.* New York: Continuum, 1980.

Simon, Sidney B., Leland W. How, and Howard Kirschenbau. *Composition for Personal Growth: Values Clarification through Writing.* New York: Hart Publishing Co., 1973.

Sindell, Peter S. "Some Discontinuities in the Enculturation of Mistassini Cree Children." In George D. Spindler (ed.). *Education and Cultural Process: Toward an Anthropology of Education.* New York: Holt, Rinehart and Winston, 1974, pp. 333-41.

Singer, Marshall R. "Culture: A Perceptual Approach." In Larry A. Samovar and Richard E. Porter (eds.). *Intercultural Communications: A Reader.* Belmont, CA: Wadsworth Publishing Co., 1976, pp. 110-19.

Singer, Milton. "On Understanding Other Cultures and One's Own." *The Journal of General Education* 19 (1967):1-23.

Skinner, B. F. *Beyond Freedom and Dignity.* New York: Knopf, 1972.

Slavins, R. E. "Effects of Biracial Learning Teams on Cross-Racial Friendships." *Journal of Educational Psychology* 71 (1979):381-87.

Smith, Alfred G. (ed.). *Communication and Culture, Readings in the Codes of Human Interaction.* New York: Holt, Rinehart and Winston, 1966.

Smith, Elise C., and Louise Fiber Luce (eds.). *Toward Internationalism: Readings in Cross-Cultural Communication.* Rowley, MA: Newbury House, 1979.

Smith, William Flint. *Noticiario: Primer Nivel.* Rowley, MA: Newbury House, 1981.

Smithson, Rulon N. "French Culture and Civilization for American High School Students." In Charles Jay and Pat Castle (eds.). *French Language Education: The Teaching of Culture in the Classroom.* Springfield, IL: Superintendent of Public Instruction, 1971, pp.80-87.

Snyder, Barbara. *Encuentros Culturales: Cross-Cultural Mini-Dramas.* Lincolnwood, IL: National Textbook Co., 1975.

Solís, Juan D. (comp.). *Cartel: Annotated Bibliography of Bilingual Bicultural Materials No. 12, Cumulative Issue, 1973.* Austin, TX: Dissemination Center for Bilingual Bicultural Education, 1973.

Spindler, George D. "Schooling in Schonhausen: A Study of Cultural Transmission and Instrumental Adaptation in an Urbanizing German Village." In George D. Spindler (ed.). *Education and Cultural Process: Toward an Anthropology of Education.* New York: Holt, Rinehart and Winston, 1974, pp. 230-71.

Spindler, George D. (ed.). *Education and Cultural Process: Toward an Anthropology of Education.* New York: Holt, Rinehart and Winston, 1974a.

Spindler, George D. "Why Have Minority Groups in North America Been Disadvantaged by Their Schools?" In George D. Spindler (ed.). *Education and Cultural Process: Toward an Anthropology of Education.* New York: Holt, Rinehart and Winston, 1974b, pp. 69-82.

Spindler, George D. "The Transmission of American Culture." In Alfred Aarons et al. (eds.). *Linguistic-Cultural Differences and American Education. Florida FL Reporter* 7, i (1969):1-9.

Spolin, Viola. *Improvisation for the Theatre: A Handbook of Teaching and Directing Techniques.* Evanston, IL: Northwestern University Press, 1963.

Stadsklev, Ron. *Handbook of Simulation Gaming in Social Education: Part 2—Directory.* University, AL: University of Alabama (Institute of Higher Education Research and Services), 1975.

Stadsklev, Ron (ed.). *Handbook of Simulation Gaming in Social Education: Part 1—Textbook.* University, AL: University of Alabama (Institute of Higher Education Research and Services), 1974.

Steele, Ross, and Annie Deville Bourlon. *Elle.* Paris: Didier, 1980.

Steiner, Florence. *Performing with Objectives.* Rowley, MA: Newbury House, 1975.

Steiner, Florence. "Behavioral Objectives and Evaluation." In Dale L. Lange, (ed.). *Individualization of Instruction,* ACTFL Review of Foreign Language Education, Vol. 2. Lincolnwood, IL: National Textbook Co., 1972, pp. 35-78.

Steiner, Florence. "Culture: A Motivating Factor in the French Classroom." In Charles Jay and Pat Castle (eds.). *French Language Education: The Teaching of Culture in the Classroom.* Springfield, IL: State Superintendent of Public Instruction, 1971, pp. 28-35.

Stening, Bruce W. "Problems in Cross-Cultural Contact: A Literature Review." *International Journal of Intercultural Relations* 3, iii (1979):269-78.

Stewart, Edward C. "The Survival Stage of Intercultural Communication." *International Communications Yearbook,* 1978.

Stewart, Edward C. Lecture on "Brain Function." University of Southern California's Washington Education Center, July 1977.

Stewart, Edward C. *American Cultural Patterns: A Cross-Cultural Perspective.* Chicago: Intercultural Press, 1972.

Stone, James C., and Donald P. DeNevi (eds.). *Teaching Multi-Cultural Populations: Five Heritages.* New York: D. Van Nostrand Co., 1971.

Storr, Anthony. *Human Destructiveness.* New York: Basic Books, 1972.

Strasheim, Lorraine A. "A Rationale for the Individualization and Personalization of Foreign-Language Instruction." In Dale L. Lange (ed.). *Individualization of Instruction,* ACTFL Review of Foreign Language Education, Vol. 2. Lincolnwood, IL: National Textbook Co., 1972.

Strasheim, Lorraine A. "The Anvil or the Hammer: A Guest Editorial." *Foreign Language Annals* 4 (1970):48-56.

Sumner, W. G. *Folkways.* New York: Ginn, 1906.

Sutman, Francis K. *Educating Personnel for Bilingual Settings, Present and Future.* Washington, DC: American Association of Colleges for Teacher Education, 1979.

Svobodny, Dolly D. "Information Sources for the Foreign-Language Teacher-Researcher." In Jerald R. Green (ed.). *Foreign-Language Education Research: A Book of Readings.* Chicago: Rand McNally, 1973, pp. 37-50.

Symonds, John, Gordon O'Brien, Marvi Vidmar, and John Hornik. *Honduras Culture Assimilator.* Urbana: University of Illinois, Department of Psychology, 1967.

Szalay, Lorand B., and James Deese. *Subjective Meaning and Culture: An Assessment through Word Association.* Hillsdale, NJ: Erlbaum, Wiley and Sons, 1978.

Szalay, Lorand B., and Jack E. Brent. "The Analysis of Cultural Meanings through Free Verbal Associations." *The Journal of Social Psychology* 72 (1967):161-87.

Szalay, Lorand B., et al. *The Hispanic American Cultural Frame of Reference: A Communication Guide for Use in Mental Health, Education, and Training.* Washington, D.C.: Institute of Comparative Social Studies, 1978.

Tanner, Daniel, and Laurel Tanner. *Curriculum Development: Theory Into Practice.* New York: Macmillan, 1975.

Taylor, Archer. "Folklore and the Student of Literature." In Alan Dundes (ed.). *The Study of Folklore.* New York: Prentice-Hall, 1965.

Taylor, Barbara Howland. *Mexico: Her Daily and Festive Breads.* Claremont, CA: Creative Press, 1969.

Taylor, H. "Toward a World University." *Saturday Review,* 1969:24-52.

Taylor, H. Darrel, and John L. Sorenson. "Culture Capsules." *Modern Language Journal* 45 (Dec. 1961):350-54.

Taylor, Harold. *Students without Teachers: The Crisis in the University.* New York: McGraw-Hill, 1969.

Taylor, James S. "Direct Classroom Teaching of Cultural Concepts." In H. Ned Seelye (ed.). *Perspectives for Teachers of Latin American Culture.* Springfield, IL: State Superintendent of Public Instruction, 1970, pp. 42-50.

Taylor, James S. *The World and the American Teacher: The Preparation of Teachers in the Field of World Affairs.* Washington, DC: American Association for Teacher Education, 1968.

Taylor, Lee, et al. *Internationalizing Rural Sociology: Training-Practice-Recruitment.* Ithaca, NY: State University of New York College of Agriculture, 1970 (EDRS: ED 053 838).

Taylor, Robert B. *Cultural Ways: Compact Introduction to Cultural Anthropology.* Boston: Allyn and Bacon, 1969.

Teichert, Herman U. "An Experimental Study Using Learning Packages in Beginning College German." *Modern Language Journal* 56 (1972):488-90.

Teitelbaum, Herbert, and Richard J. Hiller. "Bilingual Education: The Legal Mandate." *Harvard Educational Review* 47, ii (May 1977):138-70.

Theroux, Paul. *The Great Railway Bazaar: By Train through Asia: New York:* Houghton Mifflin, 1975.

Therrien, Melvin G. *"Learning French via Short Wave Radio and Popular Periodicals." French Review* 46 (1973):1178-83.

Thiagarajan, Sivasailam (ed.). *Current Trends in Simulation/Gaming.* Bloomington: Indiana University (School of Education), 1973. (Special edition of *Viewpoints* 49, VI.)

Thompson, Marion E. "A Study of International Television Programming within the Structure of Global Communications." *Dissertation Abstracts International* 32 (1971):3469A (University of Wisconsin).

Tidhar, Hava. *Using Television for Teaching a Second Language through Dramatized Everyday Situations* (EDRS: ED 053 578).

Tiedt, Pamela L., and Iris M. Tiedt. *Multicultural Teaching.* Boston: Allyn and Bacon, 1979.

Tinsley, Royal L., Jr. "Study Abroad." *Arizona Foreign Language Teachers' Forum* 18, iii (1971):2-3.

Toffler, Alvin. *Future Shock.* New York: Random House, 1970.

Torrey, Jane W. "Motivation in Foreign Language Learning." In Joseph A.Tursi (ed.). *Foreign Language and the "New" Student.* Reports of the Working Committees, Northeast Conference on the Teaching of Foreign Languages. New York: MLA Materials Center, 1970.

Travaux pratiques de civilisation, Rennes. Saint Paul: College of Saint Catherine, 1963-68 (annually).

Treue, Wolfgang. *Deutschland seit 1848.* Verlag, Wiesbaden: Franx Steiner, 1968.

Triandis, Harry C. *Interpersonal Behavior.* Belmont, CA: Wadsworth Publishing Co., 1977.

Triandis, Harry C. et al. *The Analysis of Subjective Culture.* New York: Wiley-Interscience, 1972.

Troyanovich, John. "American Meets German: Culture Shock in the Classroom." *Die Unterrichtspraxis* 5, ii (1972):67-79.

Tsoutsos, Theodora M. *A Tentative Gesture Inventory for the Teaching of French.* Master's thesis. Brooklyn: Queens College, 1970.

Turbowitz, Julius. *Changing the Racial Attitudes of Children.* New York: Praeger, 1969.

Tursi, Joseph A. (ed.). *Foreign Languages and the "New" Student.* Reports of the Working Committees, Northeast Conference on the Teaching of Foreign Languages. New York: MLA Materials Center, 1970.

Troike, Rudolph C. *Research Evidence for the Effectiveness of Bilingual Education. Rosslyn, VA: National Clearinghouse for Bilingual Education, 1978.*

Trueba, Henry T., Grace Pung Guthrie, and Kathryn Hu-Pei Au (eds.). *Culture and the Bilingual Classroom.* Rowley, MA: Newbury House, 1981.

Tyler, V. Lynn, and James S. Taylor. *Reading Between the Lines.* Provo, UT: Eyring Research Institute, 1978.

UNESCO. *Anthropology and Language Science in Educational Development.* Paris: UNESCO, 1973.

UNESCO. *Study Abroad.* New York: UNESCO Publications Center, latest edition.

United States Bureau of the Census. *Statistical Abstract of the United States.* Washington, DC: United States Government Printing Office, latest available edition.

University of Birmingham Centre for Contemporary Cultural Studies. *Sixth Report, 1969-71.* Edgbaston, Birmingham: University of Birmingham, 1971.

Upshur, John A. "Cross-Cultural Testing: What to Test." *Language Learning* 16, iii, iv (1966):183-96.

Valette, Rebecca M. *Modern Language Testing: A Handbook.* New York: Harcourt, Brace, Jovanovich, 2nd ed., 1977.

Valette, Rebecca M., and Jean-Paul Valette. *France: A Cultural Review Grammar.* New York: Harcourt, Brace, Jovanovich, 1973.

Valette, Rebecca M., and Renée S. Disick. *Modern Language Performance Objectives and Individualization: A Handbook.* New York: Harcourt, Brace, Jovanovich, 1972, Chapter 12.

Vallejo, Bernardo. "La Enseñanza del Quechua Como Segunda Lengua." In Rudolph C. Troike and Nancy Modiano (eds.), *Proceedings of the First Inter-American Conference on Bilingual Education.* Arlington, VA: Center for Applied Linguistics, 1975, pp. 96-111.

Vander Zanden, James W. *American Minority Relations.* 4th ed. New York: Knopf, 1983.

vanLoon, J. F. Glastra. "Language and the Epistemological Foundations of the Social Sciences. Report of the Fifteenth Annual (First International) Round Table Meeting on Linguistics and Language Studies." In C. I. J. M. Stuart (ed.). *Monograph Series in Languages and Linguistics,* No.17. Washington, DC: Georgetown University Press, 1964, pp. 171-85.

van Willigen, Daam M. "International Cooperation in Foreign Language Teaching." *Contact* 9 (Dec. 1966):18-27. (Available from ERIC.)

Vassiliou, Vasso. *Attitudes after Reading an Ethnographic Essay: An Exploratory Study.* Springfield, VA: Clearinghouse for Federal Scientific and Technical Information, 1968 (EDRS: ED 031 119).

vonHofe, Harold. *Kultur und attag.* New York: Charles Scribner's Sons, 1973.

Vonnegut, Kurt, Jr. "Afterword." In Francine Klagsbrun (ed.). *Free To Be . . . You and Me.* New York: McGraw-Hill, 1974.

Wachner, Clarence. *General Language: English and Its Foreign Relations.* New York: Holt, Rinehart and Winston, 1968.

Wagley, Charles (ed.). *Social Science Research on Latin America.* New York: Columbia University Press, 1964.

Waitschies, Heidi, and Eduard Mayr. *So macht man's in Deutschland.* Mimeographed. Minneapolis: Minneapolis Public Schools, 1971.

Wallace, Anthony F. C. *Culture and Personality.* New York: Random House, 1963.

Wallach, Martha Kaarsberg. "Cross-Cultural Education and Motivational Aspects of Foreign Language Study." *Foreign Language Annals* 6 (1973):465-68.

Walsh, John E. *Humanistic Culture Learning.* Honolulu: East-West Center, University Press of Hawaii, 1979.

Warren, Richard L. *Education in Rebhausen: A German Village.* Case Studies in Education and Culture Series. New York: Holt, Rinehart and Winston, 1967.

Wasilewski, Jacqueline Howell. *Effective Coping and Adaptation in Multiple Cultural Environments in the United States by Native, Hispanic, Black, and Asian Americans.* Doctoral dissertation, University of Southern California, 1982.

Wasilewski, Jacqueline Howell, and H. Ned Seelye. "Curriculum in Multicultural Education." In *Multicultural Education: A Cross-Cultural Training Approach.* M. D. Pusch (ed.). Chicago: Intercultural Press, 1979, pp. 62-84.

Watts, Alan W. *Psychotherapy East and West.* New York: Ballantine, 1969.

Wax, Rosalie H. "Oglala Sioux Dropouts and Their Problems with Educators." In Joan I. Roberts and Sherrie K. Akinsanya (eds.), *Schooling in the Cultural Context.* New York: David McKay, 1976, pp. 216-26.

Wedge, Bryant. *Visitors to the United States and How They See Us.* Princeton, NJ: Van Nostrand, 1965.

Weeks, William H., Paul B. Pedersen, and Richard W. Brislin (eds.). *A Manual of Structured Experiences for Cross-Cultural Learning.* Chicago: Intercultural Press, 1977.

Weiss, Bernard J. *American Education and the European Immigrant, 1840-1940.* Urbana, IL: University of Illinois Press, 1981.

Weitz, Shirley. *Nonverbal Communication: Readings with Commentary.* New York: Oxford University Press, 1979.

Wells, Alan. *Picture-Tube Imperialism?: The Impact of U.S. Television on Latin America.* Maryknoll, NY: Orbis Books, 1972.

White, Leslie A. "On the Concept of Culture." In Robert A. Manners and David Kaplan (eds.). *Theory in Anthropology.* Chicago: Aldine, 1968, pp. 15-20.

Whitehead, Alfred North. *The Aims of Education, and Other Essays.* NY: MacMillan, 1929.

Wight, Albert R., et al. *Guidelines for Peace Corps Cross-Cultural Training, Part III. Supplementary Readings.* Washington, DC: Peace Corps, Department of State, 1970a (EDRS: ED 059 939).

Wight, Albert R., and Mary Anne Hammons. *Guidelines for Peace Corps Cross-Cultural Training, Part II. Specific Methods and Techniques.* Washington, DC: Peace Corps, Department of State, 1970b (EDRS: ED 059 938).

Wilgus, Karna, S. (comp.). *Latin America Books: An Annotated Bibliography for High Schools and Colleges.* New York: Center for Inter-American Relations (680 Park Ave.), 1974.

Williams, Robin M. *American Culture: A Sociological Interpretation,* 3rd rev. ed. New York: Knopf, 1970.

Williamson, Kay. "The Rivers Reader Project in Nigeria." In Ayo Bamgbose (ed.). *Mother Tongue Education: The West African Experience.* London: Hodder and Stoughton, 1976a.

Williamson, Kay. "Small Languages in Primary Education: The Rivers Reader Project as a Case History." Paper presented to the International African Institute's Fourteenth International African Conference on African Languages in Education, Kinshasa, Zaire, Dec. 13-15, 1976b.

Williford, Miriam (ed.). *It's the Image that Counts: Cartoon Masters for Latin American Study.* Albuquerque: University of New Mexico, Latin American Studies Association, 1976.

Wilson, Charles E. "The Case for Black Studies." *Educational Leadership* 27 (1969):218-21.

Witkin, H. A., C. A. Moore, D. R. Goodenough, and P. W. Cox. "Field-Dependent and Field-Independent Cognitive Styles and Their Educational Implications." *Review of Educational Research* 47, i (Winter 1977):1-64.

Witucki, Jeannette Renner. "Personal References and Personal Security: An Experiment in Language and Culture Research." *Dissertation Abstracts* 27 (1966), 1707B. Los Angeles: University of California.

Wolcott, Harry F. "The Teacher as Enemy." In George D. Spindler (ed.). *Education and Cultural Process: Toward an Anthropology of Education.* New York: Holt, Rinehart and Winston, 1974, pp. 411-25.

Wolfenstein, Martha, and Nathan Leites. *Movies, A Psychological Study.* Glencoe, IL: Free Press, 1950.

Wood, Richard E. "Shortwave Radio as a Teaching Aid for German." *Die Unterrichtspraxis* 5, i (1972):36-40.

Wright, Elizabeth A. *Educating for Diversity.* New York: John Day, 1965.

Wylie, Lawrence. "A Treasury of Facts about France." *French Review* 33 (1960):281-85.

Yousef, Fathi S. "Cross Cultural Testing: An Aspect of the Resistance Reaction." *Language Learning* 18, iii, iv (Dec. 1968):227-34.

Zaidi, S. M. Hafeez. "Students' Attitude toward Living with Different Ethnic Groups." *The Journal of Social Psychology* 72 (1967):99-106.

Zijderveld, Anton C. *The Abstract Society: A Cultural Analysis of Our Time.* Middlesex, Eng.: Pelican Books, 1974.

Zuckerman, David W., and Robert E. Horn. *The Guide to Simulations/Games for Education and Training.* Cambridge, MA: Information Resources, 1973.

Index